THE REFUGEE AND THE WORLD COMMUNITY

THE REFUGEE

and the

WORLD COMMUNITY

John George Stoessinger

THE UNIVERSITY OF MINNESOTA PRESS
Minneapolis

PRINTED AT THE NORTH CENTRAL PUBLISHING COMPANY, ST. PAUL

Library of Congress Catalog Card Number: 56-12464

PUBLISHED IN GREAT BRITAIN, INDIA, AND PAKISTAN BY THE OXFORD UNIVERSITY PRESS, LONDON, BOMBAY, AND KARACHI

Preface

The birth of a book, like the choice of a profession, is seldom a completely rational process. The present volume is no exception. My youth as a refugee in Europe and the challenging years of my work for the International Refugee Organization in China after World War II generated a lasting interest in the refugee problem.

The present volume is no polemic nor, on the other hand, does it treat the refugee problem as a stagnant pool of statistics. I have attempted to use the tools of political and social science to analyze the problem and the response of the world community to it. My hope is that this study may make a modest contribution to the understanding of a significant issue in international relations and provide insight into the character and activities of the international organizations created to deal with it.

My debts are many. Mrs. Claudia E. Machol of the International Refugee Organization's China office was instrumental in expediting my emigration to the United States. Without her, I would have remained a refugee. The generosity of the B'nai B'rith Hillel Foundation made possible the continuation of my studies in the United States. Professor Joseph Dunner, chairman, Department of Political Science, Grinnell College, gave me a basis of scholarship and through his idealism provided much of the inspiration for this work.

A great debt is due to Professors Inis L. Claude, Jr., and Daniel S. Cheever of Harvard University, who with clear-sighted objectivity and a virtually inexhaustible fund of patience steered this analysis away from many fallacies. Professors Harry T. Moore and John D. Montgomery of Babson Institute read parts of the manuscript with a critical eye for its stylistic vagaries. Dr. Dorothy Hellman of Harvard University and Jeanne Sinnen of the University of Minnesota Press have contributed many valuable editorial suggestions. Eva Jane Neumann deserves a special acknowledgment for infinite patience with the author during the process of publication. The ultimate responsibility for the final product is, of course, mine alone.

J. G. S.

Babson Park, Massachusetts
July 1956

Contents

THE REFUGEE AND THE WORLD COMMUNITY

1

The Refugee and the Rights of Man

"A man consists of a body, a soul, and a passport." RUSSIAN PROVERB [1]

SINCE antiquity the refugee has been the barometer of intolerance. Throughout recorded history the custodians of truth, whether spiritual or temporal, have seldom excelled in tolerance. Movements of the uprooted have reflected the rigidity of prevailing orthodoxies ever since the Jewish Exodus in search of the Promised Land.

Religious or secular authorities, in their efforts to enforce conformity, traditionally offered two choices to the dissident. Flight in quest of asylum was always a channel of refuge because of the absence of strictures against migration. Socrates, the most renowned heretic of ancient times, was offered the opportunity to seek asylum by members of the very jury which had condemned him to death. Conversion, the other means of rescue, was possible even during periods of the most intense ideological crusades in history. Even the extreme dogmatism that prevailed during the Spanish Inquisition left apostasy as a possible road to safety.

The twentieth century introduced new social forces that critically narrowed these two historical avenues of escape in the course of a single generation: a new racism made conversion almost impossible and a universal network of immigration restrictions rendered physical flight extremely difficult. Hence, complete control of the globe by sovereign nation-states has made possible the expulsion of men from civilization. In this sense, the refugee of the twentieth century faces a situation without precedent in history. To gain perspective, we may find it useful to place the refugee phenomenon in the context of a brief evolutionary account of political doctrines pertaining to the rights of man.

In man's unceasing struggle to free himself from savagery, a major and as yet undecided battle against his own inhumanity has raged throughout history. Since ancient times, the problem of government has been, for the most part, the problem of tyranny; this has been reflected in political thought ever since Plato in the *Republic* made his eloquent distinction between tyrant and philosopher king. The great thinkers of the Athenian polis formulated their distinction between tyranny and true monarchy on the basis of superior wisdom and unselfish service to the citizenry; but their assumption of the inherent inequality of men excluded the large majority of the population from the responsibilities as well as the rights of citizenship in the body politic. This parochial aspect of Greek political thought contributed largely to the eventual dissolution of the city-state and its reintegration on a more inclusive basis.

Foreigners, tradesmen, slaves, and other disfranchised elements of the polis, after a period of withdrawal from political thought and life, came to produce intellectual giants from their own midst. These men, in formulating the egalitarian philosophy of Stoicism, hoped to bring all mankind under the aegis of one authority common to all men — the law of nature. This law was conceived by the Stoic philosophers as the embodiment of right reason, a universal and unchangeable standard of what is just and right, binding upon all human beings, whether rulers or subjects. One of its finest expressions is Cicero's affirmation: "Out of all the material of the philosophers' discussions, surely there comes nothing more valuable than the full realization that we are born for Justice, and that right is based, not upon man's opinion, but upon Nature." [2] Another expression of this principle is St. Augustine's redefinition of the law of nature as the law of God: "There will be one law, eternal and unchangeable, binding at all times upon all peoples; and there will be one common master and ruler of man, namely God, who is the author of this law, its interpreter and its sponsor." [3]

Cicero's formulation of the law of nature, by subjecting both the ruler and the governed to one common higher standard, was essentially an attempt to protect the individual against arbitrary action. If both king and subject were bound by the same law of reason, or, as amended by the Church Fathers, the law of God, any act contravening that norm would place the transgressor outside the pale of civilized humanity.

The philosophers of the Enlightenment eagerly seized upon the law of nature and transformed it into a law of the natural rights of man. The American Declaration of Independence expressed this new theory: "We hold these truths to be self-evident, that all men are created equal, that *they are endowed by their Creator with certain unalienable Rights* . . ."[4] The doctrine that man, by virtue of the fact that he is a human being as distinguished from a beast, has natural rights was eloquently stated by Thomas Paine: "Men are all of one degree and consequently all men are born equal, and with equal Natural Rights . . . *Natural Rights are those which appertain to man in right of his existence.*"[5]

A crucial difficulty inherent in the natural rights doctrine became apparent for the first time to the authors of the French Declaration of the Rights of Man and the Constitution of the First Republic. Critics of the new theory voiced their objections by contending that, ultimately, "natural rights" would be subject to the will of the state and could be removed or circumscribed by legislation or even pure fiat. The authors of the Constitution were aware of the Achilles' heel of the new theory and this led them to decree that the Constitution should be *preceded* by the Declaration of the Rights of Man. "The intention, apparently, was to endow the latter with an authority superior even to that of the Constitution. The Declaration had acquired, in a sense, a sacred and religious character. It was, in the minds of its authors, the 'fundamental law of the laws of our own and of other nations which ought to last as long as time itself.'"[6] This device was actually a tacit admission of the fact that "natural and unalienable rights" depended for their ultimate sanction upon the will of the sovereign state. It was a harbinger of the intense emphasis upon nationalism and sovereignty characteristic of the nineteenth century as well as of our own generation.

It is no accident that the natural rights theory, as formulated by the children of the Enlightenment, defined rights as essentially defensive instruments to protect those areas of individual freedom upon which the state should not encroach. Before the consolidation of the national state system, when major areas of the globe were still outside civilization, the great colonial powers of the eighteenth and nineteenth centuries thought in terms of acquiring human material. The growth and extension of colonial empires, with their many features of abuse and exploitation, lent strength to the natural rights theory as an ideology of protest. It was no coincidence that Thomas Paine, the most articulate proponent of the theory of natural rights, was also a partisan of those peoples who were struggling against colonial dependency. As long as the nation-state was striving to bring ever greater numbers of human beings under its sovereignty, the sole emphasis of the theory of natural rights was upon the inviolability and integrity of the individual human being *vis-à-vis* the state.

As the course of empire absorbed the remaining areas of the earth and built a global, universally interrelated civilization, and as the lines of sovereignty became more sharply drawn, an exclusive, rather than inclusive, attitude toward human raw material became characteristic of the nation-state. The value placed upon national and racial homogeneity inspired networks of immigration restrictions and visa requirements in areas where freedom of movement had been unimpeded for centuries, and finally led to attempted expulsions of minority groups, reaching a climax with the Nazi extermination policy toward the Jewish people. The twentieth century, which spread civilization across the globe, brought a civilization of sovereign nation-states striving for homogeneity. Hence, the stage was set for the development of a new mass phenomenon — the political refugee.

The characteristic of the refugee, loss of home, has ample precedent. What distinguishes the refugee of the twentieth century is the immense difficulty, and often impossibility, of finding a new home. If the heretic of the ancient Greek polis found the all-absorbing democracy of Athens intolerable, he could take up residence elsewhere. While excommunication was the dread penalty for heresy in the Middle Ages, that sanction was not usually identical with civil death, provided the heretic sought refuge in another more friendly environment. It is only in the twentieth century with its world war and aftermath of intense nationalism and exclusiveness that we find the new concept of statelessness as the characteristic attribute of the political refugee.

As mass expulsions of various ethnic groups and attempts to annihilate others became more and more typical of the international scene, political thinkers perceived a new difficulty in the natural rights theory. The prime concern of a Thomas Paine had been the protection of individual rights *against* a national state system spreading across the globe; but once that system was firmly entrenched throughout the civilized world, protection of natural rights could only be effectively guaranteed *by* the national state.

This observation lent a bitter significance to the pragmatic contentions with which Edmund Burke had attacked the French Declaration of the Rights of Man. His assertion that the Declaration was but a "digest of anarchy," and his criticism that natural rights were mere abstractions, gather renewed strength in the light of the refugee phenomenon. Burke's claim that it was "far better to possess the rights of an Englishman rather than the inalienable rights of man" [7] seems sound since, in the case of hundreds of thousands of human beings within the last three decades, the loss of national rights became identical with the loss of human rights. The new "inalienable" rights to nationality and asylum, like the traditional rights of individual liberty and property, were inalienable only if each sovereign state thus defined them. The vast stream of homeless people originating after World War I, and gathering increased force and momentum as it rushed through our century, showed that most states chose otherwise.

After World War I the expelled minorities had already realized that there was no inherent sanctity in the fact that they were human. Since it had become increasingly clear to Russian and Armenian refugees that even a remaining shred of nationality would make them the aristocracy of the homeless wanderers of the 1920s, they had steadfastly insisted upon their Russian or Armenian nationality and had refused to be lumped together indiscriminately with other stateless people.[8]

As intolerance increased during the 1930s, the long-standing tradition of political asylum broke down completely. First, because of unprecedented numbers of refugees, the mechanisms of immigration and naturalization which had been adjusted to relatively small numbers of people ground to a standstill. It became evident that sovereignty reached its most absolute form in matters of immigration. Second, asylum traditionally granted to people because of a heretical thought or deed which was not outlawed in the country of asylum was not available to the great mass of Jewish refugees under Hitler, who had been denationalized because of what they unalterably *were*.

The breakdown of the new natural rights theory became obvious when neither the several European nation-states nor the international authority of the League of Nations was able to prevent the grossest abuse of the most basic human rights, and when, moreover, it became possible for the persecuting governments to impose their standard of values even upon their opponents. "Those whom the persecutor had singled out as scum of the earth — Jews — actually were received as scum of the earth everywhere. The incredible plight of an ever-growing group of innocent people was a practical demonstration that no such thing as inalienable human rights existed and that the affirmations of the democracies to the contrary were mere prejudice, hypocrisy, and cowardice in the face of the cruel majesty of a new world. The very phrase 'human rights' became for all concerned — victims, persecutors, and onlookers alike — the evidence of hopeless idealism or fumbling, feeble-minded hypocrisy." [9]

Burke's definition of human rights as "entailed inheritances" probably never seemed truer than during the interwar period and World War II, when human rights declined to a new nadir in history. Hundreds of thousands of human beings became an anomaly on the international scene. Their treatment in countries of temporary refuge depended upon charity and chance. It depended upon law and right only if they committed a crime, but otherwise "privileges in some cases, injustices in most, blessings and doom were meted out to them according to accident and without any relation whatsoever to what they did." [10]

The feeble and groping efforts on behalf of refugees made by the League of Nations strikingly illustrated the breakdown of the natural rights theory. Fridtjof Nansen, appointed by the League as High Commissioner for Refugees, demonstrated extraordinary zeal in his efforts to bring the refugees under the protection of the international community. But he met concerted opposition from the sovereign members of that community. The spark which Nansen ignited inflamed the conscience of the world only after the utter destruction of human rights had taken place during the Jewish massacre by Hitler's Germany. It took the near annihilation of a whole people to salvage the natural rights doctrine from the oblivion into which it had fallen.

After World War II, a part of the international community, through an international organization, tried to give some measure of protection to the remaining refugees. The International Refugee Organization was unable to substitute the international community for the sovereign nation-state as the guarantor of human rights. But its efforts implied, at least, a recognition of the natural rights of man, denuded though he was of his national rights. Also, the Organization, by adopting a quasi-sovereignty of its own, did break down some of the most rigid restrictions on the part of its members. And, although it was prematurely terminated, the IRO provided a pattern for the world community to follow in the future – if it would.

It is a judgment on our times that the age of the Atlantic Charter and of the Universal Declaration of Human Rights should also be the Century of the Homeless Man.[11] Never before have so many human beings been abandoned in the interstices of the world community. Today, the community of exiles confronts the community of nations.

The primary task of this book will be to examine the role of international organization as a new technique which our generation has, for the first time in history, brought to bear upon the refugee problem. Conversely, the effects of the administration of a common task upon the character of international organization itself will be examined. Finally, a study of the refugee in our time may shed additional light upon the fate of human rights in general, for the refugee in his extremity, perhaps more than any other man, stands naked in his humanity.

PART I · THE LEAGUE OF NATIONS ERA AND WORLD WAR II

2

The Diaspora

> "Man has not sunk so low as we feared because he has never risen so high as we believed."
> FREUD [1]

THE RUSSIAN REFUGEES AND THE LEAGUE

THE heart of the Russian refugee question, the first such problem to set international machinery into motion, lay in the Soviet Revolution of 1917. During the post-revolutionary struggles of the Soviet government and the abortive counterrevolutionary attempts of Generals Kornilov, Denikin, Yudenitch, and Wrangel, one and a half million enemies of the new regime had been forced into exile.[2] Scattered throughout France, Germany, the borderlands of the Soviet Union, and parts of the Far East, these exiles hoped that the Soviet experiment would fail and thus enable them to return to their homes.

As the world incredulously watched the entrenchment of the new social forces in Russia, aid to the refugees in most countries was based on the assumption that the counterrevolution would be successful. Large sums were spent by governments and private charitable organizations within the host countries as temporary emergency expenditures. The Yugoslav and Czechoslovak governments alone spent twenty million gold francs on the refugees,[3] and sizable contributions were made by the various Red Cross organizations and the Save the Children Fund. The work done by these charitable organizations was significant, but it was mostly in the nature of relief. No effort was made to integrate refugees permanently into their countries of refuge nor was there any attempt to move the Russian refugees to areas where they might have resettled under more favorable circumstances.

As it became increasingly obvious that the new Soviet regime was firmly entrenched in Russia, the various countries harboring the White Russian refugees indicated their eagerness to rid themselves of this new, unwelcome, and apparently permanent burden. All during 1920, bilateral negotiations took place among European countries attempting to transfer refugees from their own territories to those of other states. These efforts for the most part ended in failure, for two main reasons. First, the legal position of the new refugees as prospective immigrants was immensely complicated because, while some held on to documents which had been issued by the Tsarist government, most of them possessed no identity papers of any kind. This new legal and political phenomenon of statelessness constituted one of the severest handicaps under which the refugees labored. Although some of the host countries, such as Poland and Czechoslovakia, issued papers of their own to refugees on their soil, these commanded no international recognition and the refugees were immoblized in the countries in which they found themselves.[4] Second, no country, whether European or overseas, was willing to admit unidentified people, mostly destitute, who might add to the economic strain of postwar reconstruction.

The need for a comprehensive and coordinated plan was evident as time went on and governments became more and more dissatisfied with the *status quo*. Emergency relief measures by private organizations could not be sustained on a permanent basis; funds that might have been used for resettlement purposes instead of stopgap measures were running low, and those countries which sheltered the highest percentage of refugees were precisely those whose economic structures had been most seriously affected by the war.

It was natural under the circumstances that the states in which the refugees found themselves should look for guidance to an international organization, the League of Nations. They assumed that a problem of such vast proportions, repercussions of which had been felt throughout the world, could be successfully tackled only by internationally coordinated action. Thus, in February 1921, with the approval of the member states of the League, "the Joint Committee of the International Committee of the Red Cross and the League of Red Cross Societies . . . decided to invite the [League] Council to appoint a High Commissioner to define the status of refugees . . . and to coordinate measures for their assistance."[5] The Council of the League accepted this responsibility and on 1 September 1921 appointed the first international civil servant to deal with the refugee problem — High Commissioner Fridtjof Nansen of Norway.

Sixty years of age when appointed to the post of High Commissioner, Nansen had behind him a life rich in experience and adventure. Widely known as a daring explorer of the frozen polar zones, he brought to his new post a name which had stirred imaginations throughout the world. Much of his early life had consisted of lonely adventure — for three years he had wandered the frozen North, his fate unknown — but in his maturity the tireless spirit of this man, as if by compensation, turned to his fellow men. Having wandered so long voluntarily in regions where others had feared to enter, he now set about helping those whose fate it was to wander because they had no home. Nansen also brought to the new High Commission the prestige which he, as an individual mediator, had gained by the important part he played in the exchange of prisoners between Russia and the Central Powers after the war. A measure of his reputation may be seen in the fact that the new Soviet government refused to negotiate with either the Central Powers or the League of Nations, but readily cooperated with Dr. Nansen, whose unwavering course through the greatest of difficulties finally resulted in the exchange of 427,886 prisoners of war.[6] During this trying period, Nansen's integrity gained the confidence of the member states of the League as well as of the Soviet Union; he also managed to mobilize behind him the potential of many charitable organizations, national and international. It was generally agreed in 1921 that "no other man would have had the same influence and authority with governments and charitable organizations, or would have brought to the problems before him a more comprehensive outlook."[7]

Although no direct stipulation with regard to refugees was contained in the League Covenant,[8] the High Commissioner's Office was made responsible directly to the League Council. The High Commission was to be assisted by an advisory committee composed of the representatives of the various philanthropic organizations participating in refugee work, and was to function for a period of ten years.

The responsibilities of the new High Commissioner and his Office, as defined by the League Assembly, were "to coordinate the action of governments and private organizations for the relief of Russian refugees, to regulate the legal status of a large class of persons who had been rendered stateless, and to assist them to find permanent homes and work."[9] For this huge task, the League Assembly allocated an annual administrative budget of £4000.[10] With this sum, Dr. Nansen was able to employ three administrative assistants. The High Commissioner himself declined any remuneration.

The broad problem facing the High Commissioner was the reintegration of the Russian refugees into society as productive human beings. Dr. Nansen's attitude toward a solution may be summed up in the words "Repatriation if possible, resettlement in countries of refuge or other areas, if necessary." Since the Russian refugees, dispersed in over a dozen countries, were practically rightless and at the mercy of their host nations because of the lack of identity papers, Nansen saw that his first step would have to be the legal rehabilitation of the refugees. Lacking the necessary funds himself, Nansen approached Albert Thomas, director-general of the International Labour Organization, with a request that the ILO conduct a census of refugees wherever their presence constituted a problem of public importance. Nansen won not only the support of the ILO but the friendship of its director-general, himself a man of great heart and fiery imagination. This liaison became a source of enrichment for the two men involved and stimulated a lifelong interest in the refugee question on the part of Albert Thomas.

The ILO census upon completion showed that over one and a half million Russian refugees were scattered throughout twenty countries, and that their treatment by the authorities differed widely from one area to another.[11] Most of the host countries had issued temporary residence certificates to their homeless wards and a few had granted them the right to work. In most cases, when the allotted time of residence had expired, the refugee was expelled and forbidden to return under penalty of imprisonment. The practice of *refoulement*, the expulsion of refugees from one country before they had obtained formal admission to another, was brought by border officials to a high level of sophistication. The result was the shadowy kind of existence between borders described by Erich Maria Remarque in his novel *Flotsam.*

Not only did the existing situation bring untold misery to the refugees, it also contributed to friction among the member states of the League, since states frequently resorted to violation of the territorial sovereignty of others. A country could rarely rid itself of stateless persons unless it violated the laws of another, and the receiving country, in order to expel its refugees, would have to infringe upon the rights of a third nation.

The refugees themselves usually were forced to violate the laws of the countries where they were residing or else the laws of those to which they were expelled.

As a result of the ILO census, Nansen knew the rough extent and dimensions of the problem. He perceived clearly that, in order to make the refugees "respectable" before the world, he would have to equip them with some sort of identity document. Accordingly, this was the task he now set himself.

Since Dr. Nansen had to spend the meager funds at his disposal on administrative salaries, supplies, and the like, he had to find elsewhere the money necessary for even such a modest scheme as equipping the refugees with identity documents. The High Commissioner therefore issued an appeal to the League Assembly for a small additional appropriation, but his request was turned down. Most member states agreed with the Swiss delegate to the Assembly who contended that "it was not the business of the High Commissariat to finance Russian refugees."[12] After this initial failure, Nansen appealed for contributions directly to the member states of the League; he also requested the host countries to continue to provide a minimum standard of subsistence for their refugee wards until they could be removed from their territories. He pointed out to the governments that any funds they might be willing to contribute would be used systematically and constructively to bring about a solution to the refugee problem, and that in view of the large expenditures in the past few years for mere relief purposes, a small additional outlay which would enable the High Commissioner to tackle the problem at its roots might be a sound investment.[13]

The responses to Dr. Nansen's appeal were largely disappointing. Although all governments concerned stated their intention not to let the refugees starve provided they would be able to divest themselves of their unwelcome presence soon, only Great Britain, at the insistence of Sir Samuel Hoare, its representative on the League Council, offered to make a special grant of £20,000 to the High Commissioner.[14] This one contribution was enough to give the sinews of the High Commission, almost threatened with paralysis, new strength, and the first task, the provision of refugees with identity papers, could begin.

Since Nansen realized that any identity certificate which the High Commission might issue would be dependent for its validity upon the approval of the governments concerned, he called an intergovernmental conference at Geneva in July 1922 to consider his proposals.[15] Protracted negotiations resulted in the acceptance of most of the essential attributes which, in the eyes of the High Commissioner, an identity document for refugees should have. The certificate, which subsequently became widely known as the "Nansen Passport," was approved in its final form by the League Council, but the actual issuing of it was to be the responsibility of individual governments. The Nansen Certificate was essentially a substitute for a national passport, but it was inferior in the sense that it did not confer the right to return to the country of issue unless such a right was expressly stipulated by that country. Moreover, the validity of the document was restricted to a period of one year and renewal was at the discretion of the country in which the refugee found himself. Nansen was not able to eliminate these two weaknesses, but in its final form the Nansen Passport went a long way toward re-establishing a measure of uniformity in the legal status of the refugees. The document was "accepted in principle" by fifty-three states[16] and most countries adhered to the provisions as proposed by the High Commissioner. In its original form, the certificate was available only to Russian refugees, however, and some countries, notably Germany, instituted arbitrary cut-off dates beyond which new arrivals would not be eligible for identity documents.[17]

Despite its shortcomings, the Nansen Passport at least returned to the Russian refugees their identity and made them somewhat less vulnerable to arbitrary action. While the refugee without an identity certificate was a prey for the police, the holder of a Nansen Passport could turn to the representatives of the High Commission who filled a quasi-consular role in the European capitals. The High Commissioner's Office intervened on behalf of refugees in the appropriate ministries, and concerned themselves with seeing that no government deviated too sharply from the agreed norm.

The Nansen Passport, then, gave the refugee some measure of advantage. A refugee could never be sure whether he could obtain a visa from a given consulate by means of the Nansen Certificate, but he could be sure that without the Certificate he would never get one. After having thus returned to the refugees a measure of their legal identity, Nansen was able to turn to the difficult task of reintegrating the homeless into the international body politic.

Dr. Nansen visualized two possible solutions for the Russian refugee problem: one through repatriation to the Soviet Union and the other through gradual dispersal by resettlement in new environments. The former alternative was considered repeatedly as a preferable solution by both the League Council and the Assembly and most member states shared the view that repatriation, provided it was voluntary, constituted the advisable mode of settlement. On the other hand, many private organizations which had been responsible for the maintenance of refugees in host countries expressed the fear that returning Russians might find themselves the victims of political persecution. The High Commissioner, who inclined toward this view, finally persuaded the League Council that the principle of repatriation should remain a voluntary one and that full guarantees of good treatment would have to be supplied by the Soviet government.[18]

When the League approached the Soviet Union on the repatriation question, its members were surprised by the thoroughly negative attitude of the new Soviet regime. It had been widely believed that industrial and agricultural planning programs in the Soviet Union would call for a large supply of workers, both manual and intellectual, and that, therefore, the return of the émigrés would be welcomed. It now became obvious, however, that these considerations were outweighed by the Soviet government's suspicion that returning refugees would engage in counterrevolutionary activities and thus threaten the stability of the regime.

While the Soviet government refused to negotiate with the League itself, it declared its intention to accept the mediation of the High Commissioner's Office. Dr. Nansen knew from the ILO census that only a small percentage of Russian refugees would be willing to return and he realized that repatriation, even if successfully accomplished, would remove only a small part of the problem. Nevertheless, the High Commissioner carried on negotiations with the Soviet government throughout 1922, and finally was able to obtain the promise of an amnesty and a guarantee of good treatment for all those who should choose to return.[19] The matter of Russian repatriation was placed in the hands of the Russian Red Cross committees and a small number of refugees decided to re-enter the Soviet Union from Greece and Bulgaria. Even a few thousand of Wrangel's counterrevolutionary forces ventured to return and were settled in the Don district where the High Commissioner visited them on an inspection tour. As the League eagerly watched to see whether the Soviet government would keep its promise, Nansen reported from the Soviet Union that "I have worked with the Soviet Government now for more than a year in connection with repatriation . . . and I must say that, in spite of numerous difficulties, the Soviet Government has actually kept all its obligations and all its agreements and promises it has made to me and to my organization." [20]

Unable to find a general solution through repatriation, Nansen's organization had to turn to the task of moving the refugees from congested and inhospitable areas to countries where a brighter future for the uprooted would be possible. The job of relocating over one million refugees was first attacked in a pragmatic, piecemeal fashion when France admitted a few thousand of them. Dr. Nansen found that the identity certificate stood the refugees in good stead, but just at the moment when France declared herself ready to admit three hundred thousand more, the High Commission was confronted by its persistent enemy – lack of funds.

Once again the High Commissioner appealed to the League for a grant of £30,000, not for relief, but solely to finance the transport of refugees from Constantinople to their new homes.[21] There was little support for the appeal in the international organization; the League reaffirmed the principle it had originally adopted: that League funds must be applied solely to administrative expenses and could not be used for relief or resettlement of refugees. Sir Samuel Hoare of Great Britain, a stanch supporter of Dr. Nansen and the same man who had managed to persuade his government to contribute funds to Nansen's passport scheme, again pointed out to the League the plight of the High Commission:

> I am aware that the League has never undertaken any financial obligation regarding the refugees. Nonetheless I say that, a year ago, when the High Commissariat for Russian refugees was officially formed, the League undertook some kind of obligation. And I am quite certain that the League's conduct of the refugee problem will be mainly judged by its succcess or failure in dealing with Constantinople. Without money it cannot hope to deal with the problem. With a limited sum it cannot only hope to deal with it, but it can actually hope to solve it. It is on this account that I press the Council as strongly as I can to provide this small sum . . . and by this means to gain for the League the credit, not only in Constantinople, but throughout the world, of having solved an administrative problem that for its urgency and human interest is second to none in importance . . .[22]

Although Hoare's appeal elicited little enthusiasm in official League circles, a determined fund drive conducted by private organizations, under the leadership of the International Red Cross, was initiated. Generous contributions to these private societies, especially from American sources, placed at the indirect disposal of the High Commission a sum of $250,000 with which to begin resettlement on a larger scale.[23]

The tireless efforts of the High Commission in seeking resettlement opportunities for its wards did not go unrewarded. In early 1924, France declared herself willing to accept "all Russians who were fit and anxious to work, either as industrial or agricultural laborers, or as day laborers." [24] By the end of the year over 400,000 refugees had been absorbed into the French economy. A somewhat more painful process was the reintegration of an approximately equal number of Russians into the German economy which, as the result of the stabilization of the mark, was undergoing a severe unemployment crisis. Hence, the relief activities of private charitable agencies were probably more necessary and helpful in Germany than anywhere else in Europe.

France and Germany were the only two countries which absorbed large numbers of the Russian refugees. The remainder were dispersed in forty-five countries,[25] through painstaking and sometimes sacrificial efforts on the part of representatives of the High Commissioner. A small beginning was made with overseas settlement in 1924 when several thousand families were sent from Germany to Brazil and a similar number migrated to the United States under its quota system of immigration.

The great majority of the refugees found resettlement only as manual laborers, a condition which created much hardship for many intellectuals among the Russians. Dr. Nansen was very much concerned with this aspect of the problem and persistently warned recipient governments against an "embargo on brains." His pleas went unheeded, with a few exceptions, the most notable one being the case of Czechoslovakia which maintained at government expense a Russian university for the émigrés.[26] Although all countries placed a heavy premium upon young male refugees, the High Commission by and large succeeded in maintaining the unity of families and in placing the sick and otherwise infirm refugees in the care of charitable organizations.

An almost insoluble problem faced the High Commission in the Far East, particularly in the Manchurian city of Harbin, where over 100,000 Russian refugees, mostly White Army personnel, had found refuge.

Chaos reigned in that area when the High Commission first was able to give some attention to it. An eye witness reported:

In an atmosphere of perpetual insecurity, of civil wars and bandit raids, of threatened foreign invasion, of spying and intrigue, of private guards and armed civilians, of kidnapping and robbery with violence, of conflict between honor and necessity, of prostitution and drug trafficking, of economic desperation and of shrill and hysterical gaiety, the life of the city flamed and hissed like an *auto da fé* . . .[27]

Because of the great geographic distances, the High Commission was unable to transport the Harbin refugees to European countries for resettlement, but was compelled to encourage integration of the émigrés into the Manchurian economy. Only with the greatest difficulty and with the aid of sizable contributions by private relief organizations did Nansen and his staff succeed in restoring some measure of order in the Far Eastern refugee situation. About one third of the refugees filtered into the Chinese coastal city of Shanghai while most of the remainder eked out a meager existence in Harbin and a few other of the larger Manchurian and Chinese cities. Nansen toured Manchuria and China and did what he could to improve the lot of the refugees, but was compelled to report that

the conditions under which the refugees are existing are pitiable in the extreme. Their inability to speak the Chinese language and the rigorous winters of Manchuria, where most of them are, make their lot an exceedingly hard one. It is noteworthy that comparatively few acts of violence have occurred. Their stoical endurance is amazing. The fact that nearly all the men have had military training and have served in the army partly explains it. Nevertheless it is remarkable.[28]

The difficulties of the Far Eastern refugees were increased by the fact that China had not recognized the Nansen Certificate. The émigrés were thus almost wholly unable to find productive employment nor could they leave the country. Their lot was probably more difficult than that of the refugees in Europe, who at least enjoyed a minimum of mobility and had been able to make a somewhat more favorable cultural adjustment.

As the Russian refugee problem was nearing solution, Dr. Nansen, who had always looked at his work with refugees as a task of temporary character, began to hope that the job could be completed within the ten-year life span of the High Commission. In the last request for funds from the League, Nansen had specified that "the credit should be regarded as temporary. The Commission hopes that it will be possible for the item to disappear from the League budget at the earliest possible moment."[29] Renewed outbursts of intolerance and inhumanity, however, proved that the hopes of the High Commissioner were premature. As one aspect of his work was drawing to a close with the gradual dispersal of the Russian refugees, a stark new challenge and responsibility confronted him—the Armenian, Greek, and Bulgarian refugee problems.

THE BALKAN REFUGEES AND THE LEAGUE

The origin of the Armenian problem is a particularly tragic one. The Armenians had behind them forty years of intermittent massacres under Ottoman rule before the outbreak of World War I. During the war itself, Armenia fought on the side of the Entente Powers in exchange for a promise of independence from Turkish rule after successful conclusion of hostilities. About 200,000 Armenians had served in the Russian Army during the war, thus bringing down the wrath of the Turkish authorities upon the Armenian communities living in Smyrna and Constantinople.[30] After the Armistice, in early 1919, Constantinople was occupied by French forces, while Smyrna came under Greek control. Most of the two million Armenians in Turkish territory were then temporarily free from Turkish rule.

In 1920, the victorious powers had recognized *de facto* an independent Armenian government; it was a co-signatory to the Treaty of Sèvres under which Turkey recognized an independent Armenia within frontiers to be stipulated by President Wilson of the United States. But Turkey, despite its obligations toward Armenian minorities within its territory, repudiated the Treaty of Sèvres in 1922 and invaded Armenia, indulging in frightful massacres as the Turkish armies advanced. When Armenia appealed desperately to the First Assembly of the League, "the Belgian delegate urged the formation of a single front of all the armies and navies of the World under an International General Staff of the League while the Rumanian delegate suggested the dispatch of an international expeditionary force."[31] The result of heated debates in the Assembly was the passage of a resolution expressing the concern of the League and its desire that "some Power should intervene to stop hostilities."[32] Three powers paid heed to this resolution: "President Wilson offered his good offices and mediation, Spain her moral and diplomatic cooperation and Brazil was ready to assist either alone or in conjunction with other Powers in putting an end to Armenia's desperate plight."[33]

To complicate the situation further, the Bolshevik Revolution, which had spread to Armenia, resulted in further confused fighting and finally the establishment of the Soviet Republic of Armenia, renamed Erivan by the new Soviet government. This new Soviet Republic, which constituted roughly one tenth of the prewar Armenian territory, was enjoying relatively stable conditions by 1922; but the rapid advance of the Turks into Armenian territory prompted the French authorities to attempt the appeasement of Turkey by the restoration of a large sector of Armenia to Turkish sovereignty. The Franklin-Bouillon Agreement incorporating this compromise also included Turkish pledges of amnesty and recognition of minority rights, although neither of these promises was supported by any guarantees.

Despite strenuous efforts on the part of the French authorities to persuade the Armenians to remain in their communities, the Turkish promises were not able to erase the memories of all too recent massacres. Armenian refugees began to leave their homes in the wake of the retreating French occupation forces. When the League Council in February 1924 authorized its High Commission for Refugees to extend the benefits of its service to the Armenian refugees, the number of Dr. Nansen's new wards had grown to 320,000. They were scattered throughout Syria, Iraq, Cyprus, Palestine, Greece, Bulgaria, and many other European countries.[34]

Once more the charitable organizations stepped into the breach to give the new refugees initial comfort. The British Lord Mayor's Fund of £100,000 narrowly averted the threat of famine and the contribution of private organizations in the United States reached the figure of $11,000,000.[35]

Although Nansen was still occupied with the Russian refugee question, his energies were immediately directed to the new catastrophe. Since his experience had taught him that legal identification of refugees greatly enhanced their opportunities for successful settlement and integration, the High Commissioner summoned another intergovernmental conference with the purpose of extending the Nansen Passport to Armenian refugees. On 31 May 1924, thirty-five states acceded to the new arrangement.[36] With remarkable efficiency, Armenian refugees were provided with identity documents by the offices of the High Commission.

When the work was threatened again with bankruptcy, the High Commissioner hit upon an ingenious scheme which made the passport system an almost self-supporting enterprise. Every refugee who, in the opinion of the governmental authority issuing the certificate, was capable of paying the sum of five gold francs as a fee was required to pay this tax. A receipt, the "Nansen Stamp," was then attached to his identity document and the money paid into a revolving fund under the control of three trustees: one nominated by the League Council, one by the ILO, which had contributed 300,000 francs for the relief of Armenian refugees, and the third was Dr. Nansen himself. The Nansen Stamp became in fact a tax exacted from the richer refugees for the benefit of the poorer. The money paid into the revolving fund not only met the expenses of providing the refugees with identity certificates, but also served as an emergency fund for transport purposes. The stamp system was used effectively in most countries and "apart from the material benefits it provided, the system embodied a very useful principle of organized self-help, and was a symbol of the solidarity existing in the refugee community."[37]

In October 1924, the League Assembly voted 50,000 Swiss francs to establish a Commission of Enquiry which would conduct a census of Armenian refugees and establish their preferences with regard to migration.[38] The completed statistics showed that the overwhelming majority of the refugees desired to migrate to the new Armenian Soviet Republic, Erivan. Nansen took advantage of his cordial relations with the Soviet government and managed to reach an agreement whereby that government offered to receive all Armenians desiring to come to Erivan. The new Armenian Republic also promised the High Commissioner that land for settlement purposes would be supplied to the refugees free of charge and that they would be excused from payment of taxes for the first three years.[39] However, the Soviet government declared itself unable to provide any funds for the transport and initial settlement expenses of the refugees.

Agreement in principle having been reached, the High Commissioner appointed a special subcommission which was to study the cost of resettlement. The subcommission consisted of financial experts, technicians, engineers, and people well versed in matters of migration. The report it produced, after thorough study of conditions in the Armenian Republic, estimated a total cost of £300,000 for the initial settlement of 25,000 refugees in Erivan.[40]

The High Commissioner, immediately upon receipt of the subcommission's report, issued an urgent appeal to all member states of the League for "any assistance your Government is able to give." Only nine governments answered Dr. Nansen at all and, of these, five refused to make any contribution whatsoever while the other four were neutral toward the scheme. Nansen then issued a further and stronger appeal to the four noncommittal governments, but only one affirmative reply was received: Albania offered to contribute the sum of 1000 francs.[41]

Dr. Nansen finally tried to raise a loan through the League of Nations under the guarantee of the Armenian government, the Soviet government, and the Russian State Bank in Moscow. The subcommission on the Erivan settlement question expressed the opinion that, in its judgment, the engineering and financial aspects of the scheme were sound. The High Commissioner, in a moving address to the League Assembly, pleaded his case, stating that

> repeated pledges have been given to the Armenians and nothing has been done, nothing of any kind to carry them out. I want to use this platform to make an appeal to the Members of the League and to the people of Europe and of the world, that they should come forward and by their contributions help to wipe out the stain which must remain on the honor of Europe so long as nothing is done to redeem the pledges which have been made.[42]

But only a few member states were willing to risk small sums in the Armenian venture and the whole scheme broke down when the Conservative Ministry in Great Britain assumed a hostile attitude, refusing all financial support. At this crucial juncture, the High Commissioner was advised that wealthy private sources in Erivan were willing to contribute £100,000 to the cause of their fellow Armenians provided that member states of the League would contribute the rest.[43] Without a guarantee of the remaining £200,000, however, these sponsors would not be willing to make any contribution. The High Commissioner once more went before the members of the League with an urgent appeal, but to no avail. Not even a small fraction of the required sum could be raised.

For the first time since Dr. Nansen had assumed his duties as High

Commissioner, the strains of his office visibly weighed him down. The patience of this tireless man was near the breaking point, and in bitter disappointment he mounted the rostrum of the Assembly of the League, asking the assembled delegates:

Was it [the Armenian scheme] in reality nothing but a gesture? It was assumed that the League of Nations would not espouse a cause of this nature without being able to deal with it satisfactorily – especially after all the pledges given by the Powers. Does the League consider that it has done its duty? And does it imagine that it can let the matter drop without undermining its prestige? [44]

The plea was a cry in the wilderness. The League Assembly contented itself with allocating 15,000 Swiss francs to the High Commissioner for "publicity purposes." [45]

It is of lasting credit to Dr. Nansen that he did not abandon his work with refugees after this fiasco. With the support of numerous private organizations, the High Commission attacked the Armenian refugee problem in a practical piecemeal fashion with considerable results. Armenians were dispersed throughout forty countries in a manner similar to that of their Russian predecessors, but mostly under conditions of minimum subsistence. The greatest single group, 100,000, was resettled in Syria at the initiative of the French government, but as reports by the High Commissioner's representative indicated, conditions were appalling. Nansen himself observed in 1928 that "the history of the succeeding years is that of a long struggle against appalling physical conditions, of over-crowding in insanitary quarters, semi-starvation and disease." [46]

The interest of the ILO's Albert Thomas in the refugee problem prompted him, in 1925, to suggest to the High Commissioner the possibility of large-scale overseas migration, a solution to which Nansen had previously not given much thought. Thomas was of the opinion that Europe was too congested already and that any fruitful migration would have to be directed overseas. The essence of Thomas's plan was the settlement of self-sufficient agricultural refugee communities in the Americas.[47] Nansen appointed a subcommission to visit South America in order to report on resettlement opportunities. The findings of this body were extremely optimistic, but an intergovernmental conference called by the High Commissioner to explore the reactions of Latin American states to refugee immigration ended largely in failure because of the unwillingness of these countries to relax stringent immigration restrictions.

While the Russian and Armenian problems continued to occupy the High Commission, old wounds — thought to be healed years before — opened once more and began to fester. The sacking of Smyrna by Turkish troops in September 1922 and the succeeding massacre of much of the city's Greek population had prompted Dr. Nansen to evacuate Greeks from Asia Minor to various Greek ports. The problem had been considered solved by the exchange of Turkish nationals of Greek orthodox religion for Greek nationals of Moslem religion under the Treaty of Lausanne, and by moderately successful settlement schemes for the Greek refugees in western Thrace. In 1925, a severe famine in those parts of Greece where most of the refugees had been settled drew the renewed attention of the High Commission to the Greek problem.

The Refugee Settlement Commission, a body independent of Dr. Nansen's organization and accountable directly to the League Council, was the only organization responsible for refugee work in Greece. It had been financed by an international loan, but its funds were nearly exhausted. With the means at its command, the Refugee Settlement Commission, administered by Greek experts, had aided in the settlement of 170,000 families,[48] but it was unable to cope with the new threats of famine and epidemic confronting it in late 1925. The High Commissioner did not have sufficient funds to prevent famine, but he immediately placed £5000 at the disposal of the Epidemics Commission of the League. Although greater assistance was not in Dr. Nansen's power, "he enabled the Epidemics Commission of the League to carry out a most valuable anti-epidemic campaign, which had remarkable results; the half-starving, over-crowded and exhausted refugees in Greece were kept relatively immune from the epidemics which would else unfailingly have decimated them."[49]

In addition to the new Greek problem, the High Commission was harassed in 1926 with a critical situation in Bulgaria. This country, which had suffered great losses of territory by the Treaty of Neuilly, was flooded with Bulgarian nationals from the areas which had been ceded. When by early 1926 the number of unsettled refugees had reached 125,084,[50] the Bulgarian government appealed for help to the League. Great hostility to any international aid for Bulgaria's refugees was shown by all her neighbors, who feared that any money which the

League might contribute would be used for military aggression.[51] However, when the Bulgarian government fell in June 1926, and a new, more conservative cabinet proclaimed an amnesty for all its political refugees in neighboring countries, tempers were assuaged and a loan of £2,400,000 was floated by the League in December 1926 for settlement purposes.[52] M. René Charron, Dr. Nansen's representative in Bulgaria, was commissioned to organize urban and rural settlement plans for the refugees.

Dr. Nansen, pleased with this auspicious beginning, toured Bulgaria, but found many of his expectations overly optimistic. The lands provided for refugees by the Bulgarian government were already largely occupied by native peasants, some areas were uninhabitable because of marshes, and disease stalked the countryside. Finally, a violent earthquake in 1928 made the difficulties of the Commission almost insuperable. Yet, in the face of these obstacles, land reclamation projects and small community settlement schemes were carried out. Slow yet noticeable progress was made by the Commission in its Bulgarian venture and wise investment of the available funds brought a solution nearer. Early in 1930, the High Commissioner was able to report notable improvements in the condition of most of the Bulgarian refugees.[53]

In May 1930, refugees throughout the world were grieved and alarmed to learn that Dr. Nansen had died. His death was considered by most friends of the refugees as an irreparable loss. Everything that had been done for the homeless in the decade since 1920 had been instigated and influenced by him. His personality had had a determining influence in the League; his zeal had repeatedly been able to overcome international apathy and hostility and to mobilize public opinion behind his work. In 1920 he had assumed his duties with high earnestness and the hope that a solution to the refugee problem might be attained within his lifetime. At the time of his death, his energy and zeal had not diminished, but he harbored no further illusions about his work. By 1929, the aging man saw clearly that the ten-year status of the High Commission was far too brief a span; he realized that no single man in one lifetime, no matter how devoted, could attain a solution. His last recommendations before his death were to the effect that all refugee work should be made a permanent part of League operations by integrating it into the Secretariat.[54] But he was not able to see the fulfillment of his last wish on behalf of refugees, nor, on the other hand, did he have to see the disaster to come.

The death of Dr. Nansen preceded by only three years the ascent to power of Adolf Hitler.

THE NANSEN OFFICE

The loss of Dr. Nansen was followed by extensive reorganization in refugee work in the League of Nations. The personality of the High Commissioner had so dominated every phase of his work and his reputation as humanitarian, administrator, and scholar had been so widely established that no single man was deemed qualified by the League Council to assume his mantle. Instead, the League Assembly decided to establish a plural body to be named the Nansen International Office for Refugees. The post of High Commissioner was abolished and administrative authority over the affairs of the Nansen Office was vested in a Governing Body with a president acting as *primus inter pares*, to be nominated by the Assembly.[55] As in the case of the High Commission, only funds for administrative expenses were allotted to the new Nansen Office and it was scheduled for liquidation by the end of 1938. Although the Nansen Office was described as an "autonomous organization," the League Council reserved for itself final policy-making authority. Nansen's wish to institutionalize refugee work permanently in the League was not completely ignored by his successors. A new division between humanitarian work, on the one hand, and legal and political protection activities, on the other, was created. While the former was considered temporary and was made the responsibility of the Nansen Office, the latter were integrated into the League Secretariat. However, this artificial distinction was soon discarded and
the Nansen Office undertook all phases of the work. The Secretariat had no general scheme of local representation and had to depend upon the local representatives of the Nansen Office who were invested annually by the Secretary-General with power to undertake certain quasi-consular functions for refugees arising from the Arrangement of 1928.[56]

A generally deteriorating situation confronted the new Nansen Office at the beginning of its operations in 1931. The world depression and unemployment throughout most countries resulted in a tightening up of labor legislation and a refusal to grant refugees the right to work. Many countries ignored the pledges given when they had signed the Nansen Certificate agreements, and most others refused to extend the validity of the certificates held by refugees in their territories. Naturalization protected only a very small percentage of the refugees; the great majority were ordered to leave their countries of refuge as soon as their Nansen Passports expired. The almost forgotten practice of *refoulement* reached unprecedented proportions during the early 1930s and it is estimated that the annual cost to France alone of maintaining thousands of refugees in prison for violating her border laws was 12,000,000 francs.[57] The Nansen Office in 1933 called an intergovernmental conference in order to ameliorate some of the worst features of current discriminatory measures against refugees, but to little avail.

An acute problem faced the Nansen Office in the form of a renewed massacre in 1932. Iraq, which had just been granted membership in the League, celebrated its new independence with the slaughter of much of its Assyrian population. Twenty-five thousand desperate Assyrian refugees managed to flee and subsequently scattered throughout most of the Middle East. The Nansen Office, with the limited means at its command, established a refugee camp for them in Syria, but the condition of these refugees was even more intolerable than that of their Armenian brethren in misfortune who had previously found asylum in Syria. Repeated and urgent appeals by the Nansen Office to the League for a minimum of funds were greeted with even greater indifference than the efforts of Dr. Nansen had been.

As the shadow of rising dictatorship lengthened across Europe, intolerance created further hundreds of thousands of refugees. The rise of Fascism in Italy resulted in the expulsion of almost one million opponents of Mussolini's regime, most of whom found a temporary haven in France. Although the Italian refugees did not become technically stateless, but retained their Italian nationality, their lot was nevertheless a miserable one. The burden on France was further increased by the influx of roughly 500,000 Spanish Loyalist refugees fleeing the newly established government of General Franco. Although approximately half of the Spanish refugees subsequently returned to Spain, the responsibility of the French government for almost one and a half million new émigrés from the neighboring countries was almost beyond its capacity. Only the generosity of numerous French relief organizations and a humane policy adopted by the government averted a catastrophe.

The Nansen Office could do but little. The League Council decided that no funds should be allotted for the benefit of either Italian or Spanish refugees.[58] It was deemed unwise by most member states of the

Council to provoke the Italian and Spanish governments by supporting the enemies of their regimes, and repeated appeals by the representatives of the Nansen Office in France to the head office in Geneva proved fruitless. Bitter discussion on the refugee problem became almost daily routine in the League Assembly of the 1930s, but next to nothing was actually accomplished.

CONCLUSIONS

In an evaluation of the League's work on behalf of refugees during the 1920s and early 1930s, one striking factor emerges. The League was an organization of nation-states aiming for universality, and thus protection of refugees from a given state was bound to arouse the hostility of an actual or potential member of the League of Nations. Refugees were *ipso facto* enemies of some nation-state which was already a member of the League or which, it was hoped, would become a member. Hence, all political refugees were a source of political embarrassment to the League and the organization, in its work on behalf of the uprooted, was actually divided against itself. This largely explains the extreme reluctance of the League to allot any funds for operational responsibilities to the High Commission and the Nansen Office. That the organization made some effort to come to the rescue of the Russian refugees may be explained by the fact that the Soviet Union was not then a member of the League and was regarded with hostility by most of its members. Characteristically, after the admission of the Soviet Union to League membership, the activities of the organization on behalf of the Russian and Armenian refugees were severely curtailed. In sum, it may be said that the outstanding work done by High Commissioner Nansen was accomplished not with the aid of the League of Nations, but with its reluctant toleration.

As a corollary it followed that the organization, in its dealings with the refugee issue, refused to go beyond the mere symptoms of the problem. Never did the League of Nations attempt to strike at the roots of the matter by negotiating with the country producing the refugees, whether it was the Soviet Union, Turkey, Spain, Italy, or Germany. The organization dealt very superficially with some of the symptoms of the malaise of the international body politic, but not with the basic cause, the persistent abuse of basic human rights by some member states.

A final misconception of the League was its treatment of the refugee problem as temporary. The organizational structure to deal with the question was testimony to the fact that the League considered the problem of uprooted people an emergency to be handled by stopgap emergency measures. A consistent reluctance on the part of the League to commit itself to long-range planning prevailed in both organs of the international organization. The fallacy of this assumption was clearly seen by Dr. Nansen shortly before the end of his life, but his recommendations to institutionalize refugee work in the League on a permanent basis were never fully accepted.

Although the broad picture of the League's work for refugees is gloomy, the image of Dr. Nansen, pervading all the manifold aspects of this work until 1930, lends a somewhat brighter hue to the overall impression. The determined leadership of this man brought the uprooted under the protection of a nascent international community for the first time in human history. Dr. Nansen's identity document, although hardly a substitute for a national passport and ultimately largely ineffective, established a precedent for later years. The undramatic, unsensational, yet indispensable salvage work done for refugees by the High Commission under Dr. Nansen in the face of great obstacles constitutes a bright page in the annals of international organization. The rapid decline of the Nansen Office after the death of the High Commissioner is probably not solely attributable to the deteriorating political climate, but in some measure to the lack of inspired leadership.

But the greatest catastrophe was yet to come. Neither Nansen nor Albert Thomas foresaw the accession of the National Socialist regime to power in Germany in 1933. No determined spokesman represented the increasing numbers of Jews fleeing from anti-Semitic persecutions in Germany. When the severest refugee crisis in history began to confront the League in 1934, the Nansen Office stood robbed of prestige, funds, and determined leadership. Refugee work by international organization had reached its lowest ebb at a time when authority, inspiration, and humanity were needed as never before.

3

Amok

"Refugees have their own way of counting time: Pre-Hitler and post-Hitler."[1]

THE JEWISH REFUGEES AND THE LEAGUE

In 1834, one hundred years before the ascent to power of Adolf Hitler, one of Germany's foremost poets registered an ominous prognosis: "The insane fury of those who run amok, will come into its own again. And when it comes, this German thunder, the eagles will drop dead from the skies, and the lions will slink into their caves . . ."[2] The vision of the apostate Heinrich Heine foreshadowed one of the most horrible social phenomena of the twentieth century – genocide.

Throughout recorded history the religious or ideological heretic had been able to avert the extreme penalty at the hands of an oppressive majority. If death had been the price of heresy, recantation had remained the price of life. The advent of the National Socialist system added a new dimension: for the first time in history conversion no longer provided an escape. "The aristocrat of the French Revolution could save himself by becoming a *citoyen*. The Russian bourgeois could save himself by becoming a *tovaritch*. The German Jew could never become an Aryan."[3] It was blood itself which was now polluted – hence nothing within the control of the victim could prevent permanent ejection from his society.

According to the 1933 census, the Jewish population in Germany numbered 502,799.[4] It was considered one of the best assimilated branches of European Jewry and had contributed to German culture in all fields of endeavor out of proportion to its numbers. Of the forty-four Germans to whom the Nobel Prize had been awarded, no fewer than eight were of Jewish origin.[5] As a thorough student of the Jewish people in Germany concludes: "It is indeed one of the greatest ironies of history that a country that owed so much of its greatness to its Jewish citizens should have become their most relentless enemy, seeking actually their complete physical extermination."[6]

Hitler's intention to annihilate all Jews under his jurisdiction had been announced repeatedly throughout *Mein Kampf*, but the Nazi regime preferred to adopt a gradual method to attain its final goal. The process may roughly be divided into two major stages: The first, commencing with Hitler's accession to power, concentrated on economic, social, and political strangulation. The second, beginning in 1938, aimed at utter physical annihilation.

Between 1933 and 1938, all Jewish businesses were "Aryanized," a procedure which was tantamount to outright theft. The notorious Nuremberg racial laws, promulgated in 1935, proscribed marriage between Jews and Aryans and defined as "hybrid," that is, polluted with Jewish blood, any person with one Jewish grandparent. All Jews were expelled from government and other official positions and a different legal code was applied in cases involving Jewish litigants. The prelude to the fate in store for Jewry under the Nazis was an act passed by the government depriving all Jews of German citizenship. Five years after the collapse of the Weimar *Rechtsstaat* the German Jew was stripped of civil rights.

For centuries the Jews in Germany had been Germans first and Jews second. Germany was their *Vaterland*, and they simply would not believe the avowed intentions of the Nazi government. At first, therefore, only a trickle of refugees left the country, settling mostly in neighboring European states since they believed the Nazi phenomenon to be a passing phase. In 1935, however, after the passage of the Nuremberg laws, larger numbers of refugees attempted to leave German soil. The policy of the government was, by and large, to rob the Jews of most of their belongings and then to let them go. However, most of the Jews who decided to leave Germany before 1938 settled in countries which were subsequently annexed by Hitler. Some, who attempted to flee to France, Belgium, Holland, or Switzerland, had to wander endlessly from border to border; as stateless persons, they were not entitled to permanent residence in their countries of refuge. Only a small minority sought resettlement overseas, thus permanently breaking all bonds with their homeland.

The response of the international community to the first phase of the

Nazi campaign reflected an evident refusal of the member governments of the League of Nations to take the avowed intentions of the Nazi regime at face value. The problem of the increasing exodus of Jews from Germany was brought to the attention of the League in September 1933 by the Dutch delegation.[7] Significantly, the emphasis of the Dutch representative was less upon the reprehensible character of Nazi policy than on the serious problem of the imbalances in labor markets resulting from an influx of refugees. A statement to similar effect, endorsed by the representatives of the Netherlands, France, and Belgium, was brought to the attention of the International Labour Office.

While the International Labour Office referred the document for "further study," some action was taken in the League of Nations. Over the strenuous objection of the German delegation, a "High Commission for Refugees Coming from Germany" was established, with James G. McDonald as High Commissioner. However, in view of German opposition and the lukewarm attitude of most of the member governments, it was provided that all funds for the High Commission, both administrative and operational, would have to come from private sources.[8] Furthermore, it was provided that the High Commission should operate as a quasi-autonomous organ, responsible to its own Governing Body, rather than to the League Council.[9] This provision implied a further weakening of the powers of the High Commission. It would not have the support of the League of Nations as did the Nansen Office.

High Commissioner McDonald repeatedly petitioned the League for funds in view of the lack of sufficient private contributions. He was not granted any, nor was he successful in his frequent requests that the jurisdictional mandate of the League be extended to cover his own wards. The Assembly discussions show that it was deemed unwise by most governments to provoke Hitler by such a step. It is significant, however, that when a nation came forward decisively on behalf of a group of refugees, positive results could be attained. For example, immediately following the return of the Saar to Germany, the French delegation requested the League to place all Saar refugees under the protection of the Nansen Office. The French resolution was adopted, Nansen Certificates were issued to Saar refugees, and a special grant was made by the Assembly to the Nansen Office for the resettlement of Saar refugees in Paraguay.[10] But the Jewish refugees lacked a determined spokesman to plead their case in the international forum, with the notable exception of Mr. McDonald, who finally resigned in protest in December 1935.

McDonald's letter of resignation is a significant document. After stating his reasons for leaving the post of High Commissioner, he expressed his conviction that the Nazi phenomenon portended greater disaster for the Jewish people than most member governments of the League seemed to realize, since "the attitude of the German government was based not only on the theory of 'Nordic race' supremacy and the desire to eliminate 'foreign racial' elements from the life of the country; it rested also on the conception of the absolute subordination of the individual to the state." [11]

Taking heed of this warning, the Norwegian government, in the tradition of its long-time spokesman for the homeless, proposed that a central organ for all refugees be created under the direct authority of the League.[12] But the Norwegian proposal was not accepted by the League Assembly and the division of refugee organs continued. Sir Neill Malcolm succeeded Mr. McDonald as High Commissioner for Refugees from Germany. His impotence was almost as frustrating as that of his predecessor. One improvement was the League's authorization to the High Commissioner to issue a limited number of Nansen Certificates to refugees from Germany.

Thus, at the time of Germany's annexation of Austria in March 1938, three separate international organizations dealing with refugees were in existence. First, the Nansen Office, under the aegis of the League, cared for Russian, Saar, and Armenian refugees. Its appropriation was small, but since most of its task had by this time been completed, the situation was not desperate. Its most significant function by 1938 was the issuance of Nansen Certificates to its stateless wards. Second, the High Commission for Refugees from Germany, although facing an ever-increasing load, lacked adequate funds and authority to cope with it satisfactorily. Finally, the International Labour Office confined its activities regarding refugees during the 1930s mostly to studies of the effects of such movements upon the European labor market.

Despite rather clearly defined spheres of action, much duplication of activities as well as a general lack of coordination characterized the relationships of these three organs. The Nansen Office refused to come to the assistance of the High Commissioner for Refugees from Germany with the issuance of identity documents and the International Labour

Office, in turn, repeatedly rejected requests by the Nansen Office for statistical services.[13] All attempts to amalgamate the three organs, or even to achieve a higher degree of coordination, ended in failure.

The full fury of the Nazi onslaught began in 1938 after the Austrian *Anschluss.* The last façades were now stripped from the extermination camps and the crematoria of the new Reich. Within a few months half of Austria's 200,000 Jews were herded into concentration camps. A similar fate overtook most of the Jewish population of Czechoslovakia after its annexation a year later. By now almost a million Jews were under the Nazi sway, most of them desperately attempting to escape from imminent disaster. In most cases, after having been rendered penniless, they were free to leave their native soil. In view of the openly embraced policy of extermination, most of the Jews of "Greater Germany" cast around for immigration opportunities in countries overseas. These now seemed to provide the safest havens of refuge from the Nazi holocaust.

The victims of Nazism met with resistance almost everywhere. Many countries stiffened their immigration requirements in order to prevent the entry of these doomed people into the Western hemisphere.

Argentina ordered its consuls in Europe to delay, under every possible pretext, issuing visas even to those Jews who met all the requirements for obtaining entry. Brazil instructed its representatives in Europe to require baptismal certificates of all prospective immigrants, which meant the automatic exclusion of Jews unless they apostatized. Bolivia declared any person with "Jewish blood" ineligible for entry.[14]

Tortuous legal interpretations were resorted to in some instances. For example, "at one time the Australian law forbidding entry to Asiatics was taken to mean that, since Palestine was in Asia, all Jews were to be refused admission to Australia." [15] Tens of thousands of refugees within sight of freedom were turned back to their death because of legal technicalities. An instance among many was the case of 907 refugees fleeing from Germany to Cuba on the *SS St. Louis* on May 15, 1939, who were shipped back to certain destruction because of expired visas.[16] Also, the persistent refusal of Great Britain to admit Jewish refugees to the British Mandate of Palestine forced many thousands into the maws of the Nazi crematoria.

The American response to the plight of the Hitler victims was also lacking in generosity. Immigration into the United States since 1924 had been regulated by the "quota system" of national origins. A figure based on census statistics was allocated to each country for immigration purposes. For example, since the largest number of Americans were of Anglo-Saxon descent, Great Britain was given the largest quota number. But the figures allocated to Germany, Austria, Czechoslovakia, and other areas heavily populated with Jews, such as Poland, were only small fractions of those desperately attempting to flee. Despite some pressure, the United States Congress refused either to enlarge the quota figures for the threatened nations or to transfer some of the unused quotas, such as the British one, to those of the heavily oversubscribed countries.

In the meantime, the Nazis continued to murder hundreds of thousands of Jews in Buchenwald, Auschwitz, Bergen-Belsen, and scores of similar extermination centers. The tragic inadequacy of American immigration laws prompted Senator Herbert H. Lehman to cry out bitterly:

While from 90,000 to 110,000 quota numbers were being forfeited year after year, thousands of visa applicants were refused admission because they were born in the "wrong" countries. Many of these unfortunate people died in Hitler's concentration camps a few years later. Our immigration laws were written with utter disregard for the impact of such legislation on the international scene . . .[17]

In September 1938 the League Assembly finally decided to amalgamate the Nansen Office with the High Commission for Refugees from Germany into a single High Commission for Refugees under the authority of the League.[18] However, Sir Herbert Emerson, who was appointed High Commissioner, continued to labor under great difficulties. Owing largely to the insistence of Nazi Germany and Soviet Russia, the new High Commission had to rely mostly on private contributions with which to come to the aid of the ever-increasing number of refugees fleeing the Nazis.

THE EVIAN CONFERENCE AND THE INTERGOVERNMENTAL COMMITTEE

While the League of Nations was losing ground rapidly, President Franklin D. Roosevelt of the United States took a determined step to bring international action to the aid of the Nazi victims. Aghast at the Nazi atrocities, which he called "hard to believe in our twentieth century civilization," he sent an urgent message to thirty nations requesting them to send representatives to an international conference in order to discuss resettlement opportunities for the Jews under German jurisdiction.[19] The delegates met at Evian, France, amidst a flood of reports of new atrocities perpetrated by the Nazis against the Jewish populations, but the reaction of most of the representatives remained a lukewarm one.

The attitudes Great Britain and France adopted at the outset of the conference struck the keynote for the whole session. Lord Winterton, the British delegate, immediately ruled out the possibility of Jewish resettlement in Palestine and, with regard to Great Britain herself, explained that "the United Kingdom is not a country of immigration. It is highly industrialized, fully populated, and is still faced with the problem of unemployment. For economic and social reasons, the traditional policy of granting asylum can only be applied within narrow limits." [20] Similarly, the delegate of France regretted the fact that although his government was in "fullest agreement in principle with the task [of aiding refugees], France has almost exhausted her resources which unfortunately are not so boundless as her zeal to serve the cause of humanity." [21] Most of the other European delegations, including the Scandinavian countries as well as Belgium and Switzerland, followed suit. They stated their objections to the relaxation of immigration restriction in terms of fear of undue economic competition which might result from a large influx of refugees.

The responses of most of the South American delegations were also discouraging. Regardless of the existence of vast, still underdeveloped areas for which the possibility of colonization projects might have been explored, only one country in Latin America came forward with an offer to revise its immigration laws in order to take in 100,000 Jewish refugees for colonization – the Dominican Republic.[22] All other South American states explained their inability to absorb refugees by stating that "they were grappling with low wages and unemployment." [23] Also, all of them "had large German populations and extensive trade agreements with Germany; their actions were hesitant because of the fear of German disapproval." [24]

The United States Congress failed to revise American immigration laws despite constant prodding by President Roosevelt and the Department of State. In view of the fact that the United States government had initiated the conference, the American failure to assume a role of leadership at Evian proved particularly harmful.

After prolonged, mostly fruitless conversations, the representatives at the Evian Conference decided to establish an Intergovernmental Committee for Refugees whose membership would comprise the states represented at Evian.[25] The main function of the IGCR would be the exploration of resettlement opportunities and "the substitution of an orderly system of departure from countries whence there is involuntary emigration for the existing disorderly exodus of men, women, and children who have no definite place to go." [26] The achievements of the Intergovernmental Committee were, however, minimal. The reasons for failure were similar to those of the High Commission under the League of Nations.

First, most governments still adhered to the illusion that the Nazi phenomenon in Germany was a passing phase. At least, so most representatives contended, the aspect of virulent anti-Semitism would not be a permanent one. Second, most members of the IGCR were reluctant to admit refugees for economic reasons. It was felt quite generally that serious economic competition resulting in depression might follow the lifting of immigration barriers, particularly because most Jewish refugees, upon leaving the Nazi-occupied areas, were practically paupers. Third, it was felt by most delegates that concerted international action with regard to the Jewish refugees might unduly provoke the German government. This position was held particularly by the South American delegations. Fourth, the situation was made even more difficult by the fact that the German government steadfastly refused to recognize the existence and authority of the Intergovernmental Committee. The point was stressed with great force by the delegate of France, who contended that

> the nations which expel have towards the masses expelled more duties than the nations which receive them. So long as those duties are not recognized, defined and put into practice by an understanding between the Governments which expel and the Governments which receive, the end of this disorder cannot really be expected. The Government which expels should leave the expelled their properties which are their only means of livelihood . . .[27]

Finally, a general international apathy concerning refugees prevailed among most of the member governments of the League and the IGCR. Vital questions of security with regard to Germany, Italy, and the Soviet Union consistently occupied the attention of the international community and took precedence over the refugee problem.

The German invasion of Poland in 1939 pronounced the death sentence over most of European Jewry. Poland and the Balkan countries, subsequently overrun by the Nazi war machine, were the domicile of over five million Jews who were now faced with annihilation. Greater and greater became the number of Jews who failed to procure immigration visas and who were subsequently swallowed by the insatiable ovens of the Nazi death factories. After 1940, the German government exhibited increasing reluctance to allow its Jewish victims to leave German-controlled territory. Nothing short of physical extirpation was able to satisfy the Nazi leaders.

In view of the new German policy, little could now be accomplished by international organization. The two hitherto separate refugee organs, the League High Commission for Refugees and the Intergovernmental Committee, were amalgamated (although the committee retained its title) under the leadership of Sir Herbert Emerson of Great Britain.[28] However, the impotence of the two previous organs was now simply "writ large." The complete repudiation of the pleas repeatedly voiced to the German government by the new High Commissioner and a continuing reluctance on the part of the democracies to lower their immigration barriers made the new amalgamation of refugee organs little more than a gesture.

A last futile effort was made by President Roosevelt who in 1943 called another conference of the IGCR in Bermuda. On this occasion, ten new states adhered to the Intergovernmental Committee, including the Soviet Union.[29] The legal competence of the committee was broadened to include "all persons wherever they may be, who as a result of events in Europe, have had to leave or may have to leave, their countries of residence because of the danger of their lives or liberties on account of their race, religion, or political beliefs."[30]

Notwithstanding this broad definition of refugees eligible for IGCR assistance, the actual result was extremely disheartening. No major policy change was adopted either by the German government or by the countries of refuge.

One bright spot in that bleak epoch is found in the persistent and often sacrificial efforts of voluntary organizations, national and international, to come to the rescue of the Jewish people during their great trial. The records of these organizations include significant accomplishments: "Tens of thousands were rescued from the Nazis by clandestine means. 8,000 orphaned Jewish children were kept alive in France by means of American funds sent from Switzerland. These children were hidden in convents, schools, and private homes by compassionate Christian families."[31] The numbers saved were relatively small, but the efforts put into saving them were great. It seemed almost as if the world were offering penance for its apathy during the years when rescue might have been accomplished more easily.

There is hardly a major religious, nationality, or welfare group that has not come to the aid of the victims of Hitlerism. Outstanding among the agencies that have helped the refugees . . . are the American Jewish Joint Distribution Committee, the World Jewish Congress, the American Friends Service Committee, the Unitarian Service Committee, the War Relief Services of the National Catholic Welfare Conference, the International Rescue and Relief Committee, the Hebrew Sheltering and Immigrant Aid Society, Hadassah, the Jewish Labor Committee, the National Refugee Service, and other refugee service committees.[32]

By executive order of President Roosevelt, on 22 January 1944, the War Refugee Board of the United States was established. The task of the board was to be the taking of "all measures within its power to rescue the victims of enemy oppression who are in imminent danger of death, and otherwise to afford such victims all possible relief and assistance consistent with the successful prosecution of the war."[33] The board was able to rescue about 50,000 Jewish concentration camp inmates by buying their lives from the Nazis for American funds through the mediation of Switzerland.[34] Also, it was able to assist the refugees once they had arrived in their countries of refuge. However, by 1944 "the main obstacle which faced the Board was the adamant attitude of the enemy. The Nazis were determined to wipe out innocent minority groups and did not regard them as being protected by any law, national or international."[35]

In summary, the policy of appeasement followed toward Germany during the 1930s was transferred to the Jewish refugee problem at a cost of six million lives. No firm stand was adopted by the democracies when such a stand might still have done some good. The responses of governments to pleas by representatives of international refugee organs were conspicuously lacking in generosity. The extermination policy of the Nazi government was tacitly tolerated by most of the democracies until the time when an awakening to the price of procrastination and vacillation came too late for effective action. In that sense, if the crime of the Nazi government was one of commission, then the apathy of the free world was indeed a crime of omission. When, finally, the last mask had dropped from the face of Nazi Germany, awakening the world from its slumbers, it was already too late.

4

The Aftermath

> "I will even gather and assemble ye out of the countries where ye have been scattered."
> EZEKIEL [1]

DISLOCATIONS DURING WORLD WAR II

THE outbreak of World War II merged the tragedy of the Jewish people into the greater tragedy of world conflagration. The bitter struggle scattered millions of people throughout the world as a crazed giant would scatter the seeds of future unrest. The mass movements set in motion by the expansionist policies of the Axis eclipsed all previous human floods in history.

While the star of Hitler Germany was in its ascendancy, millions of refugees fled before the advancing Nazi armies. The German conquest of Poland in September 1939 made 300,000 Poles seek sanctuary within the frontiers of the Soviet Union.[2] As the blitzkrieg continued throughout 1940, and the Netherlands, Luxembourg, Belgium, and northern France were overrun, an avalanche of over five million desperate refugees swept into southern France, only to be overtaken by the Germans in November 1942.[3] The Balkan campaign launched in April 1941 resulted in a further 300,000 refugees who preferred homelessness to the Nazi yoke.[4] Finally, when Hitler's quest for *Lebensraum* precipitated his attack upon the Soviet Union in June 1941, a seemingly endless stream of fugitives from the Nazi onslaught sought refuge in the vast spaces of inner Russia. It has been estimated that over twelve million people were made homeless by the advancing Nazi armies.[5]

Throughout her conquered territories, Germany attempted to fill the vacuum left by the fleeing civilian populations by more or less ambitious colonization programs. Her armies were followed by German *Gauleiters*, workers, and settlers who intended to exploit the conquered territories for the Reich. At the zenith of its power in 1942, approximately two and a half million such colonists were attempting to weld the economies of the subjected countries to the economy of Germany.[6] Shortly before the Nazi retreat began, a prominent German newspaper clearly implied that, while the perennial problem of *Lebensraum* seemed now to be solved, a shortage of administrators was beginning to make itself felt. "The proportion between space and people has been reversed," the paper stated; "the problem of how to feed a great people in a narrow space has changed into that of the best way of exploiting the conquered spaces with the limited number of people available." [7]

While Germans were fighting – and "colonizing" – throughout Europe under the swastika, the domestic German economy supplying the basis for her armies could not be allowed to relax. A steady stream of workers from conquered territories were shipped to Germany where, under slave labor conditions, they had to take the place of German workers, farmers, and technicians. Thus, "like a gigantic pump, the German Reich sucked in Europe's resources and working population. The total number of foreign workers in Germany . . . exceeded six million in 1943. In 1944, the high mark of eight million was reached." [8]

While the Nazi victories were accompanied by mass movements of slave laborers set in motion to support the German economy, the Jews from all occupied areas were herded into concentration camps in Poland. The forced labor deportations took place for economic reasons, but the aim of Jewish mass movements toward camps in the east was physical annihilation. The Nazi concentration camp system contributed neither to the economy nor to the war effort of Nazi Germany. Six million people were uprooted from all parts of Europe for largely sadistic reasons, since

> any work that was performed [in the concentration camps] could have been done much better and more cheaply under different conditions. The incredibility of the horrors was closely bound up with their economic uselessness. The Nazis carried this uselessness to the point of open anti-utility when in the midst of the war, despite the shortage of building material and rolling stock, they set up enormous, costly extermination factories and transported millions of people back and forth.[9]

Most leading authorities emphasize sadism as the reason for and extermination as the goal of the Jewish deportation movements. "A large part of the work exacted in the concentration camps was useless or it was so miserably planned that it had to be done over two or three times,"[10] one analyst reported. "Prisoners were forced to perform nonsensical tasks . . . and preferred even harder work when it produced something useful," said another.[11] The extermination camps were simply a dragged-out process of dying. "Hell in the most literal sense was embodied by those types of camp perfected by the Nazis, in which the whole of life was thoroughly and systematically organized with a view to the greatest possible torment."[12]

Three major population movements resulting from the policies of the German government may be discerned during the period of Nazi triumphs up to 1943. First, over fifteen million people throughout Europe became homeless when they fled from the advancing *Wehrmacht.* Second, more than eight million Europeans from all parts of the continent were deported to the Reich as forced laborers. Finally, six million Jews were deported from all parts of Europe under the Nazi sway and concentrated in camps in Poland. While most of the uprooted in the first two categories became refugees and displaced persons in the immediate postwar period, the Jews were almost all destroyed by the Nazi crematoria.

Mass refugee movements were not limited to the European continent. Germany's Asian partner, Japan, embarked upon her own aggressive course and in the process of establishing the hegemony of her "Co-Prosperity Sphere," drove over thirty million Chinese from their native soil.[13] When the Japanese conquest spread to Burma, the Malay States, the Philippines, and Indochina, new masses of homeless wanderers fled from the approaching armies. Thus, in 1943 when the Axis forces had attained their greatest territorial expansion, approximately sixty million human beings had been displaced from their homes.[14]

When the fortunes of war turned in 1943 and the Soviet armies began to push back the German invaders, the twelve million displaced Russians who had sought sanctuary in the inner recesses of the Soviet Union followed in the wake of the Red soldiers. Simultaneously, as the German flood receded from the European continent, the *Reichsdeutsche*[15] colonizers, settlers, and exploiters, panic-stricken, attempted to evade retribution by fleeing toward the Reich. In the east, the ethnic German minority groups long resident in Russia, Poland, Hungary, Czechoslovakia, and the Balkans began to fear the wrath of the approaching

Soviet armies. These *Volksdeutsche*,[16] about four million of whom fled in the direction of Germany prior to the end of hostilities, had been "the foremost exponents of the German policy of oppression and exploitation of non-Germans and were the privileged representatives of the 'master race'";[17] in large numbers they now accompanied the German armies on their retreat, or were simply abducted by the *Wehrmacht* in order to fill the badly decimated labor supply at home. In addition to the German minority populations, a sizable group of native "collaborationists," fearing reprisals, followed the retreating Nazis. The evacuation of this conglomeration of *Reichsdeutsche, Volksdeutsche*, and native quislings at first proceeded in an orderly manner, but when the Allied armies accelerated their advance, became "a cargo of wailing and terrified humanity, moving in deep snow and cold, enduring the fate which the German armies had in previous years imposed upon millions of innocents." [18]

In addition to these groups, a new and separate stream of refugees began to swell. As it became more and more evident that another form of totalitarianism, as intolerant of dissent as the Nazi variety, was spreading westward in the wake of the Soviet armies, over a million people from eastern areas joined the stream of refugees to escape the specter of Communist domination which threatened their native countries. Russians, Ukrainians, Byelorussians, Poles, Latvians, Lithuanians, and Estonians mingled with the Germans fleeing from the Soviet advance.

As the sun of the Axis continued its downward course, the Asian populations dislocated by Japanese expansion in the Far East began to return to their former homes. Unlike their brethren in misfortune on the Continent, the Chinese displaced persons had not moved over long distances, but for the most part had hidden in the neighboring hills of the Chinese countryside, and they found it easier to return to their homes as the Japanese retreated. Out of thirty million displaced Chinese, it has been estimated that only about three to five million actually emigrated to Free China, and many of these returned home after the end of hostilities.[19] They returned to a gutted land and a broken economy, however, and faced as difficult a time as the European refugees.

At the end of the war, then, a ravaged Europe and Asia confronted the victorious Allies. Not only did poverty and hunger stalk the two continents, but the misery and confusion were accentuated by major dislocations. Only a determined effort by the Allied powers would now be able to restore some measure of equilibrium.

THE WORK OF UNRRA

Soon after the first Allied soldiers set foot upon liberated soil it was realized that a major international reconstruction and rehabilitation program would have to be initiated to prevent the war catastrophe from having permanent effects. Early in 1943, the British Foreign Office suggested an Allied Post-War Requirements Bureau.[20] The proposal was vigorously supported by President Roosevelt of the United States, who was interested in an international relief organization to be established as soon as possible while the sense of cooperation and urgency was still strong among the Allies. Negotiations led to a conference of forty-four nations in Washington, D.C. On 9 November 1943 all participating states signed the charter of a new international organization, the United Nations Relief and Rehabilitation Administration.[21] Although it was determined at the Washington Conference that the main task of the new organization should be the reconstruction of devastated areas and the provision of relief food, clothing, and medical supplies to needy United Nations nationals, the repatriation of uprooted people was also considered an important function.[22]

The first major problem confronting the governing body of UNRRA, the General Council,[23] was the question of eligibility. Several attempts were made to divide the uprooted into separate classes, finally resulting in three major categories. First to be classed were "refugees," who were defined as persons who had left their native countries of their own free will to escape persecution or the ravages of war.[24] Most persons who had fled from the advancing Axis forces fell into this group. "Displaced persons" were considered people who had been removed by official or para-official action.[25] Slave workers who had been shipped to the Reich and the small remnant of Jews surviving the extermination camps were in this group. It was soon discovered by the delegates that it was practically impossible to distinguish meaningfully between "refugees" and "displaced persons." The distinction became sterile since many who left "of their own free will" had escaped just in time to avoid official expulsion. The pressures exerted upon the people concerned, although they might not have been official, had been so severe that little choice remained but to flee if flight was still possible. These two groups were therefore amalgamated by UNRRA for all practical purposes; "refugees" and "displaced persons" were deemed eligible for material assistance and repatriation after screening for collaborators by Allied military authorities.

The second major category comprised the *Volksdeutsche*, or ethnic German minority groups in the eastern areas who had fled in the wake of the German retreat. Unanimous agreement reigned among the delegates that these fugitives should not be eligible for UNRRA assistance because of their obvious connection with the Nazis. The problem was complicated, however, with the conclusion of the Potsdam Agreement which placed international sanction behind the expulsion of German minority groups from beyond the Oder-Neisse line. Article XIII of the agreement stipulated that "the transfer to Germany of German populations, or elements thereof, remaining in Poland, Czechoslovakia, and Hungary, will have to be undertaken." [26] When the agreement went into operation on 20 November 1945 and monthly quotas of destitute German expellees [27] began to arrive in Germany, the question was raised whether the 9.7 million "Potsdam Transfers" [28] should be eligible for UNRRA assistance. After some discussion, it was unanimously agreed that UNRRA, being essentially a United Nations organization, would exceed its competence if it gave material assistance to refugees who were not United Nations nationals.[29]

This decision, which was reached very quickly, reflected a punitive attitude on the part of the Allies toward the Germans at large. It may be contended with some strength that this attitude was misplaced. Those German elements who were involved in the Nazi conquest, and participated in it through exploitative tactics, were the first to flee before the Allies, while the very fact that the "Potsdam Transfers" had voluntarily remained behind may be cited as proof that they were least afraid of political retribution and thus least involved in the Nazi cause. At any rate, a valid establishment of the various nuances of guilt, all the way from active participation down to ideological association, would have been impossible to determine by either the Allied authorities or UNRRA itself; and no justifiable distinction could be made in theory which might have been applied with equal justice in practice. The UNRRA decision extended the principle of "collective guilt" to the "Potsdam Transfers," whose ancestors had been living in non-German areas for centuries. The net results were additional drains upon the already chaotic German economy, severe unemployment crises, overcrowded housing conditions, disease, and much downright starvation.

Shortly after the *Volksdeutsche* had summarily been declared ineligible for UNRRA assistance, a third category of persons began to crystallize within the group classed as "refugees and displaced persons." They were those who prior to and shortly after the end of hostilities had fled from Communist-dominated areas and now refused to be repatriated. Over one million Russians, Poles, Jews, and Balts confronted UNRRA with a deeply significant problem. Since the avowed purpose of the organization was only the "assistance in caring for persons found in any area of any of the United Nations who, by reason of war, were displaced from their homes, and in agreement with the appropriate governments, military authorities, or other agencies *in securing their repatriation or return*," [30] UNRRA care and assistance to refugees explicitly refusing to return became a highly debatable issue.

It was on this point of "unrepatriable refugees" that a strong cleavage became apparent in the UNRRA General Council. At first, when the quantity of "unrepatriables" was still quite negligible, a temporary compromise was reached by stipulating that UNRRA would continue "to assist, for a reasonable period, in the care of refugees as cannot be repatriated, until the Inter-Governmental Committee for Refugees is prepared to remove them to new places of settlement." [31] However, when "within a reasonable time" the number of "unrepatriables" grew to over one million, a serious clash occurred in the UNRRA General Council between the Western and the Eastern powers. The Soviet Union and her adherents in the UNRRA plenary body contended that only "collaborationists" would refuse to be repatriated — bona fide refugees would have no objections to returning.[32] Moreover, the Eastern countries held that, as contributors to UNRRA, they could not be expected to supply people with material assistance for an indefinite period of time.[33] The Western powers, on the other hand, under the leadership of the United States, argued that the "unrepatriables," being United Nations nationals, should certainly be considered eligible. Since the United States shouldered 72 per cent of the operational budget of UNRRA and most of the cost of the "unrepatriables" would thus devolve upon her, the Western states were able to reach a compromise agreement with the Soviet Union.[34] It was unanimously decided that it should be within the competence of UNRRA to render material assistance to the non-repatriable refugees. However, in order to meet as far as possible the desires of the Eastern countries, it was also stipulated that such assistance should not exceed a period of six months.[35] Simultaneously, the UNRRA General Council recommended that the Executive Committee "make every effort to consult and cooperate with the local military authorities and the Governments concerned with regard to steps encouraging repatriation." [36]

In order to implement this policy decision, the Executive Committee on 1 October 1946 decided on the Sixty Day Ration Plan, whereby, effective from that date, all displaced persons willing to be repatriated were to be issued food rations for a period of two months at the frontiers of their home countries.[37] Since, by late 1946, about fifteen million uprooted people had already returned with the aid of the Allied military authorities, and another eight million had been repatriated by UNRRA without an extra food incentive, the Sixty Day Ration Plan was aimed mainly at the "last million" refugees classified as "unrepatriable" as well as at the small remnant of Jews who had survived the Nazi holocaust. A study of repatriation statistics before and after the ration plan went into effect shows that no significant increase in repatriation resulted from the extra food incentive.[38] It became increasingly clear to most delegates that a lasting solution for this group of refugees could be attained only by a concerted attempt to resettle them in new environments.

While UNRRA was casting about for a solution to the problem of unrepatriables, the Inter-Governmental Committee on Refugees, which had been in a somewhat dormant state since the fiasco of the Evian Conference, began to take an interest in the problem. Since the *raison d'être* of the IGCR was the exploration of resettlement opportunities, it was only logical that it should concern itself with the "last million." When the forty member states of the committee met for consultation in early 1946, it became painfully apparent immediately that its inveterate twin enemies, lack of funds and lack of cooperation, were again conspicuously present at the conference table. Only the United States, the United Kingdom, France, Norway, and Belgium offered to make small token contributions to the organization, and the offers were made only on the condition that other nations would follow suit. The sum total of pledged contributions represented a negligible amount, inadequate to resettle even a small fraction of the people concerned.

Apart from financial difficulties, the powers were unable to agree upon policy, particularly upon the classes of eligible refugees. Although the constitution of the IGCR provided that its Executive Committee might make decisions by simple majority vote of the delegates present and voting, in practice the policy organ was extremely reluctant to make important decisions by anything less than a unanimous vote. The Soviet

Union, which had joined the IGCR at the Bermuda Conference in 1943, steadfastly refused to grant resettlement assistance to refugees from Soviet-dominated areas. The result was that the representatives on the IGCR Executive Committee could agree upon only very limited categories of refugees, and unanimous agreement was reached only on assistance to Spanish Loyalist refugees from Franco Spain and the small remnant of Jewish concentration camp survivors. The IGCR, although it managed to conclude a few minor immigration agreements with three Latin American states, again succumbed to the apathy and even active opposition of many of its member states.

UNRRA had not been called into existence to carry out resettlement and hence was not able under its Articles of Agreement to solve the problem of the remaining "last million" non-repatriables. In an evaluation of UNRRA's job for refugees and displaced persons the emphasis should therefore be placed upon success, not failure. For the achievements of the organization within a short space of time were remarkable. An essentially international staff of over seven thousand civil servants accomplished the repatriation of more than eight million refugees within less than a year. Despite numerous shortcomings of the staff, most of which were due to hasty recruitment practices under wartime conditions, a strong sense of *esprit de corps* as well as a goodly amount of practical zeal on the job was characteristic of most UNRRA employees. Although most of the actual conveyances used for repatriation purposes were Allied Army vehicles, UNRRA officials performed invaluable supplementary services. Strict health measures were instituted to keep threatening epidemics from developing, and the distribution of food rations, clothing, and medical supplies to millions of recipients was carried on under very difficult conditions. When most of the occupants of UNRRA camps had been repatriated and the hard core of unrepatriables remained, the UNRRA staff attempted to organize vocational training services, educational institutions, and community services. UNRRA itself also provided employment opportunities to thousands of displaced persons during the period of their stay in the camps.

One of the most significant inventions of the UNRRA staff was the creation of a Central Tracing Bureau to locate relatives and friends of refugees whose families had been scattered by the Nazis. A special service for "unaccompanied children," mostly Jewish orphans whose parents had been gassed to death in Nazi extermination camps, was instituted. Its job became the placement of children in foster homes and the search for remaining relatives. By and large, the staff was imbued with a sense of urgency; as one staff member put it, "Here is a job to be done that can be seen and felt." For the most part, the balance sheet of the UNRRA staff shows that it successfully met the task for which it had been recruited from forty-four different lands.

Generally the same observations hold for the UNRRA service in the Far East. There the job of repatriation was facilitated by the fact that most escapees from Japanese aggression had not fled far and could return without much difficulty. Also, the problem of non-repatriable refugees did not plague the Far Eastern Office of UNRRA, except for a small group of 5000 European refugees in Shanghai. The UNRRA China Office acted mostly in a supervisory capacity, leaving the actual operational responsibilities largely to the Chinese National Relief and Rehabilitation Administration (CNRRA). The quality of the CNRRA staff was decidedly lower than that of UNRRA and the poison of corruption at one time had corroded its ranks to such an extent that UNRRA Director Fiorello La Guardia halted all further relief shipments to China.[39] A somewhat easier job was accomplished by a somewhat inferior staff in the Far East with generally satisfactory results.

A tracing of UNRRA policy during its operation reflects a persistent quest for political conciliation of the Soviet bloc by the Western powers. When the decision to exclude all *Volksdeutsche* from UNRRA assistance was made at the instigation of the Eastern powers, there was little opposition to it in the General Council. In part the Western nations adhered to the principle of "collective guilt" when they agreed to the Soviet demands, but perhaps the main reason for Western agreement was a desire for compromise with the Soviet Union on political grounds. When the question of non-repatriable refugees emerged, the Soviet Union reaffirmed its negative position of non-assistance while the Western powers attempted to meet Soviet demands as far as possible without sacrificing the principle of voluntary repatriation. Western efforts at conciliation were evident in the adoption of such provisions as the Sixty Day Ration Plan and the six-month time limit of UNRRA assistance to non-repatriables.

The fact that neither the ration incentive nor the threat to withdraw assistance resulted in any significant increase in repatriation probably illustrates the profound sense of divorce which these people felt toward countries where totalitarian governments had come to power. Nothing short of physical force would compel most of them to be repatriated to their countries of origin.

Hence UNRRA, though successfully concluding its task of voluntary repatriation, faced an entirely new situation two years after its birth, a situation which the organization was constitutionally unable to tackle. The Inter-Governmental Committee on Refugees, on the other hand, while constitutionally competent to deal with the "last million," was largely ineffective because of political and financial considerations. Moreover, it had become more and more evident by late 1945 that the refugee problem revolved around the unrepatriables scattered throughout Europe, and that the existing division of responsibility for them among the Allied military authorities, UNRRA, and the IGCR had resulted in much duplication, inefficiency, and sheer wasted effort. It was becoming increasingly apparent that a new unified organization dealing with the refugee problem in totality would have to be created if this challenge was to be met successfully.

THE "LAST MILLION" REFUGEES

As their fate was being debated by UNRRA, the IGCR, and the Allied military authorities, the non-repatriable refugees – of fifty-two nationalities [40] – were lingering in 920 camps throughout Germany, Austria, and Italy.[41] While the group included people of practically every ethnic origin, all had one factor in common: they had fled intolerance in some form, and refused to expose themselves to it once more through repatriation. Buddhists, Jews, Moslems, Christians, and atheists, Kalmucks, Spaniards, Latvians, and Poles, though vastly different in their religious convictions or cultural perspectives, all shared the common quest of freedom from political oppression.

The largest group among the "last million" were the Polish refugees who numbered 275,000. About half of these were scattered throughout UNRRA and military camps in the American zones of Germany and Austria, while the remainder had found their way into the British zones.[42] The Polish group was partly the remainder of the resistance forces which had fought on the side of the British against the Nazi invaders. While approximately 100,000 Polish troops had been granted settlement throughout the British Commonwealth, the rest had voluntarily returned to Poland, where many became disillusioned with the new Communist regime in power. Roughly 125,000 Poles left Poland for the West, hoping to be granted asylum, preferably by Great Britain where many of them had lived for a prolonged period during the war.[43] About 175,000 of the Polish refugee group had been German slave laborers, but refused to go home because of the change of government in Poland since the end of the war. They, too, were hoping for resettlement, preferably overseas.

The Polish government, vigorously supported by the Soviet Union, adamantly insisted in the UNRRA General Council that the Polish refugees be repatriated without delay, forcibly if necessary. UNRRA camps frequently received visits from representatives of the Polish government, exhorting the remaining refugees to return, but with little success.

A second large and cohesive refugee group was formed by the Jewish survivors of the Third Reich. These were the poorest of the poor, most of them dying skeletons who, upon seeing the liberating Allied armies, had begun to live again. This remnant, about 200,000[44] – all that had remained of the six million Jews under Hitler's domination – was largely concentrated in the American zones of Germany and Austria. About half of the group were German and Austrian Jews while the remainder were largely of Polish origin.[45] The group as a whole was violently opposed to any thought of repatriation to the places of their sufferings, particularly since new pogroms had broken out in Poland shortly after the end of hostilities. They were practically united upon a single aim: emigration to Palestine. A resurgence of Zionism expressing itself in the hope for the realization of a national Jewish home was characteristic of most of these people. The Polish government, although it welcomed repatriation of its Jewish nationals, respected their desire to resettle elsewhere, and neither it nor the Soviet government pressed for their repatriation with any great force.

A third group of comparable strength consisted of 200,000 Spanish Loyalists, most of whom were assembled in camps maintained by voluntary agencies throughout France.[46] They were unique among the unrepatriables in the sense that they did not reject the alternative of repatriation outright, but merely requested French asylum "temporarily until the Falangist regime would be succeeded by a democratic regime."[47] Most of them were not interested in permanent resettlement, but hoped eventually to return to Spain. The request of the Spanish Loyalists was endorsed unanimously by the UNRRA General Council. Harmony reigned on this issue between the West and the East, while France declared herself willing to shoulder the burden of asylum until the time when the refugees should desire to return.[48]

A considerable segment of the refugee population consisted of 190,400 Lithuanians, Latvians, and Estonians, the majority of whom had congregated in the British zone of Germany.[49] These Balts represented a particularly tough bone of contention between the Eastern and Western powers in the UNRRA General Council. UNRRA screening had shown that the group could be subdivided into three main categories. Over one half of the Baltic refugees had been victims of Nazi forced labor deportations, and, like their Polish brethren, now refused to return to their Communist-dominated homelands. Approximately 70,000 had followed the retreating German armies toward the end of hostilities and had thus taken the opportunity to escape. They too were bitterly and unalterably opposed to repatriation. A small percentage of the Baltic refugees in Germany had collaborated in varying degrees with the Nazis. During the actual process of screening by UNRRA and the Allied military authorities it was found to be extremely difficult, if not impossible, to establish categorical standards for the definition of "collaborators," since many of the accused had been forced to work for the Germans under threat of violence. After protracted and repeated investigations, only a small number of proven "collaborators" were excluded from UNRRA eligibility. The large majority, as United Nations nationals, a status which ironically enough the Balts had gained through Soviet annexation, were eligible.

The Soviet government steadfastly demanded the unconditional repatriation of all Baltic refugees. In both UNRRA and the IGCR the Soviet delegations maintained that most of the Balts in Germany had been "quislings and traitors" during the war and that justice demanded their speedy repatriation. Those who had not collaborated with the Germans would have nothing to fear upon their return. The Western powers, in view of the UNRRA principle of voluntary repatriation, refused the Soviet demands, and a deadlock resulted.

A similar problem existed in the form of about 150,000 Yugoslav refugees, most of whom were dispersed in UNRRA and military camps throughout Italy.[50] The group was a colorful combination of Serbs, Croatians, former partisans, and monarchists, all of whom had in common their opposition to the Tito regime in Yugoslavia. Many of them had fled their homeland during the period of civil strife while others had smuggled across the frontier after Tito's accession to power. While the Yugoslav government violently demanded their forcible repatriation, the refugees were just as adamant in their refusal.

Soviet representatives in UNRRA and the IGCR were very much concerned about the return of approximately 100,000 Ukrainians from various UNRRA camps of Germany and Austria.[51] The large majority of this refugee group had followed the Soviet armies across the frontier and now refused to be repatriated. Some of the Ukrainians presented extremely complicated screening problems to the Allied and UNRRA authorities because of varying states of collaboration with the Germans. As in the case of the Balts, standards of eligibility were not too rigidly enforced and almost all became eligible for UNRRA assistance.

A particularly serious problem was posed by the presence of 10,800 Soviet citizens in the Western zones of Germany and Austria.[52] Over a million Soviet soldiers had already been repatriated by the military authorities in agreement with the stipulation of the Yalta Conference that all Soviet prisoners and deportees would be returned without delay. The large majority were willing to leave the West, but the Allies had to resort to forcible means in order to repatriate some of the Russians. Frequent cases of tragic suicides, as well as reports that some of the repatriates immediately upon their return had been shot by the Soviet authorities, prompted the decision to halt the repatriation of the small number of remaining Soviet citizens. Needless to say, the Soviet Union was particularly firm in its demands for the return of its subjects.

In addition to the major groups outlined above, refugees of many other nationalities populated the assembly centers which dotted the map of Europe. Small groups of non-repatriables were spread as far as the El Shatt UNRRA camp in the Sinai desert near the Suez Canal. Another small enclave of European refugees had formed a little community in faraway Shanghai. Thousands of White Russian refugees who had fled their homeland at the time of the Bolshevik Revolution were now scattered across the earth from Paris to Harbin. A particularly cruel fate could be seen behind the UNRRA figure of seven thousand "unaccompanied children" most of whom had been abducted by the Nazis for "Germanization" purposes, and whose parentage or nationality could not be determined.

This hard core of non-repatriable refugees were now awaiting the decision that would determine their future lives — or deaths. For, scattered across the globe though they were, a unifying bond held them together. Whether anti-Fascist, as were the Spanish Loyalists, or anti-Communist, like the Baltic, Polish, Yugoslav, Russian, and Ukrainian refugees, all these uprooted people were as one in their refusal to return to countries where a dictatorship was in power. The utter degradation of the human being, of which totalitarian governments were capable, was symbolized to these refugees by the Jews in their midst who had survived the most ruthless scheme of genocide yet devised by man.

UNRRA's job of repatriating eight million people, though a major achievement, was actually a quantitative triumph only. Its wards had not really been refugees in the true meaning of the term, as defined by Sir John Hope Simpson in his classic treatise on refugees:

> The essential quality of a refugee is that he has sought refuge in a territory other than that in which he was formerly resident as a result of political events which render his continued residence in his former territory impossible or intolerable. He must have left his former territory, either in the sense of having departed or in the sense of being, when already outside it, unable or *unwilling to return to it, as a direct consequence of the political conditions existing there.*[53]

UNRRA, in its capacity as a temporary housing, supply, and transport agency, had been successful. But a real challenge to the new United Nations Organization about to be born was the problem of those of the uprooted who would *not* be repatriated. The IGCR, whose concern the "last million" refugees was supposed to be, was without funds or prestige. Besides, its name was associated with the stigma of the failure of the League of Nations. Hence, it was not surprising that, among the delegates to the newly created United Nations Organization, a desire to include the refugee problem in the forum of the world organization gathered momentum. By the time the General Assembly of the United Nations prepared to convene for its first session most of the delegates were prepared to place the prestige of the United Nations behind a concerted effort to solve the refugee problem. But on the question of *what* constituted a solution, the positions of governments differed widely. In view of the serious disagreements on the issue among the powers most concerned, it seemed to many observers that a new and dramatic struggle could hardly be avoided.

5

The Great Debate

"There are human values which transcend states and governments." BELGIAN DELEGATE TO THE UNITED NATIONS GENERAL ASSEMBLY, JANUARY 1946 [1]

"The highest value to which a human being can aspire is to have a homeland, to be part of a sovereign state." UKRAINIAN DELEGATE TO THE UNITED NATIONS GENERAL ASSEMBLY, JANUARY 1946 [2]

A GUARDED optimism prevailed at the opening of the First Session of the United Nations General Assembly in London in January 1946. Delegates from fifty-one member states converged on the British capital from all parts of the globe, and were welcomed by King George VI in a terse, earnest address reminding the delegates of their collective responsibility for the peace. The King emphasized the importance of collaboration, not only in political affairs but in economic and social matters as well.[3] The San Francisco Conference on International Organization in April 1945 had already stressed the importance of universal respect for human rights and fundamental freedoms. The *London Times* echoed this sentiment when it commended the institutionalization of economic and social activities in the United Nations system.[4]

"The League is dead; long live the United Nations," was the obituary pronounced over the funeral pyre of the League of Nations as it formally went out of existence in January 1946. The two organs of its successor that were entrusted, among other things, with the solution of social problems international in character—the General Assembly and the Economic and Social Council—were widely acclaimed as new and encouraging developments in the evolution of international organization. The preservation of the peace was visualized in broader terms than merely the police function of the Security Council whose job would be "to save succeeding generations from the scourge of war."[5] Searching analyses had shown that peace did not signify merely the absence of strife and physical combat. "Conditions of stability and well-being . . . were necessary for peaceful and friendly relations among nations" and "solutions to international . . . social . . . problems"[6] would therefore have to be sought. The problem was not only "how to keep nations peacefully apart, but how to bring them actively together."[7] It was hoped by many that, through cooperation in relatively noncontroversial activities, nations would build habits of cooperation which ultimately might be transferred to matters of significant political consequence.[8]

THE INTERNATIONAL CHARACTER OF THE REFUGEE PROBLEM

The question of refugees and displaced persons appeared as Item 17 on the agenda of the First Session of the General Assembly. There is little evidence to suggest that the United States, France, and the United Kingdom, in drawing the attention of that body to the remaining uprooted people, regarded the matter as one of major political import. Most of the debate in the General Assembly focused on the problem of finding a permanent home for the new world organization, while the Security Council was already occupied with the Iranian dispute.[9] Item 17 seemed innocuous enough and was quietly referred to the Third Committee of the General Assembly, concerned with social, humanitarian, and cultural questions. At the same time, the matter was placed on the agenda of the First Session of the Economic and Social Council.

An analysis of the discussions leading to the final adoption on 20 December 1946 of the Constitution for the International Refugee Organization might be divided into two phases. The debate in the Third Committee of the General Assembly[10] dealt mostly with the broad contours of the problem; the positions of the member governments toward the refugee question as a whole were explored and crystallized in the course of the session. During the two weeks from 28 January through 12 February 1946, the conversations ranged in tone from dogmatic rigidity to flexible compromise as the delegates in the Third Committee considered the two important issues confronting them: first, whether the refugee problem was a concern of the international community, and, second, whether repatriation to the refugee's country of origin was a desirable solution. The second phase of the debate turned on less philosophical and ideological but more technical matters. It continued during the discussions of the Special Committee on Refugees and Displaced Persons which was established by the Economic and Social Council at the recommendation of the General Assembly on 12 February 1946.[11] The twenty member governments[12] of this *ad hoc* committee sat from 8 April to 1 June 1946. Positions by then had become rigid and since the participants could not agree on basic premises, there was little agreement on the form and operational sphere of the projected organization.

A scrutiny of the proceedings in the Third Committee of the General Assembly affords insight into the international attitudes on the subject of refugees and displaced persons immediately after the inception of the United Nations system. It was during these conversations that the general positions of the member governments were initially outlined. Perhaps most important, through their attitudes toward the political refugee the member governments indicated quite clearly their conceptions of individual freedom *vis-à-vis* the state, and, by implication, *vis-à-vis* an international organization.

The first issue which confronted the delegates was the dimension of the refugee problem. At an informal meeting in New York City in September 1945, the delegates of the United States, United Kingdom, and France had agreed that some kind of an international organization would be necessary to liquidate the problem of the "last million" refugees.[13] It was agreed that, since repatriation had dwindled to a trickle, it could no longer be regarded as a solution; the primary task of the projected organization would have to be the permanent reestablishment of these unrepatriables. Some international authority would be best equipped for such a task.

In accordance with this view, P. J. Noel-Baker, delegate of the United Kingdom, proposed at the first meeting of the committee that "there might be created, under the United Nations, under the direct authority of the Assembly, an organ of the United Nations which would take over the responsibilities of the existing bodies."[14] Mrs. Eleanor Roosevelt, delegate of the United States, after agreeing with Mr. Noel-Baker, emphasized the necessity of establishing an international organization to come to the aid of the refugees in order to restore social equilibrium throughout the world. The Yugoslav delegate, Dr. T. R. Bebler, challenged this contention and denied the international character of the problem, asserting that "if in nine months' time, out of twelve million, eleven million have returned to their countries . . . the problem of displaced persons is likely to cease altogether in a relatively short time."[15] The source of the refugee problem, Dr. Bebler contended, had disappeared when Hitler and Mussolini fell. A. A. Arutiunian, the Soviet delegate, drew the logical corollary to the Yugoslav position when he proposed that "the most practical way to solve this problem of Displaced Persons is by bilateral agreement between the two countries concerned – the country of origin and the country of refuge."[16] The Soviet position on the character of the problem already suggested Russian preference as to its solution. The possibility of resettlement was not mentioned; implicit in the suggestion of bilateral negotiation between the country of refuge and that of origin was the liquidation of the refugee problem through repatriation.

A scrutiny of the declarations of the remaining delegations shows a clear division between East and West. By and large, the Western delegates were united in their diagnosis of the international implications of the refugee question, while the five delegates from eastern Europe defended the opposite view. The discussions threatened to reach a stalemate. The delegate of France cited the League experience as an example of the necessity for international treatment of the problem, only to be challenged by Dr. Bebler of Yugoslavia, who exclaimed: "I think we are wrong if we blindly follow the policies of the League of Nations. It was not able to prevent a second world war; the League of Nations has not been able to solve the problem of refugees which still exists."[17] Mr. Arutiunian of the Soviet Union added laconically that "The League of Nations practically preserved the institution of refugees."[18]

At this juncture, the press began to pay attention to the proceedings in the Third Committee. The lack of agreement was described as an "ominous portent" by the *London Times*. The *New York Times* in an editorial sharply reminded the delegates that "this involves the fate and status of hundreds of thousands of human beings who are clearly an international responsibility. Unless UNO develops this human side of cooperation . . . it will labor in vain to lay the foundations for peace."[19] It was M. R. Knowles, the delegate from Canada, who brought some incisive logic to bear on the apparent deadlock. "If there is a problem," he asserted,

> the proposal put forward by the United Kingdom will make it possible to find out what the problem is and to decide what should be done about it. On the other hand, if the United Kingdom proposal is adopted and it is discovered that the Yugoslav contention is correct, that there is no problem, no harm will have been done . . . if the Yugoslav proposal is adopted, it seems to me that, in effect, it closes the door.[20]

It was apparently the strength of this argument which prevailed upon the minority and resulted in the unanimous acceptance by the committee of the international character of the problem.[21] Of course, the minority acquiescence on this issue did not to any degree weaken the position of the Eastern countries with regard to the main job the projected international organization was to perform. In this respect, as will become more evident in a further analysis of the debates, the concession by the countries of origin was largely a tactical one.

THE "PRIORITY RESOLUTION"

The issue now confronting the delegates was how the refugee problem could most equitably and speedily be settled. Mr. Arutiunian from the Soviet Union struck the keynote when he asked, "What does every refugee expect from the organization of the United Nations? . . . He expects help to be able to return to his native country." [22] V. N. Sassen, delegate of the Netherlands, while agreeing with the Soviet statement in part, took issue with the inclusiveness of the generalization:

> A desire of an uprooted person not to return to his country of origin, should be respected by the authorities of his country of origin as well as by those of the country where he has found refuge, unless it is proved that—according to existing international agreements—such a person is liable to be extradited to his country of origin . . . in order to be brought to justice.[23]

S. R. Stanczyk of Poland challenged the premise of the Dutch statement when he defended the view that the "basic reasons which prevented the return of these persons to their countries have disappeared." [24] His view was supported by Dr. Bebler of Yugoslavia, who declared in effect that the only Yugoslavs outside the borders of his country refusing to be repatriated must by definition be war criminals, quislings, and traitors.[25] He pointed to the examples of the Ustashis,

Zborachis, and the Chetniks as pro-Fascist elements who should be made to face justice at home without delay. His conclusions from these observations were logical enough:

Has it ever been known in the history of international relations that a Government contributed to the cost of maintaining its political enemies who have fled abroad or — a forteriori — emigrants who have in fact committed crimes against the people? No, nothing of the sort has ever been known.[26]

The assumption implicit in the Yugoslav rhetorical question was challenged by A. M. Egeland, delegate from the Union of South Africa, who stated that "the problem would be simple if the forced repatriation, actual or implied, which seems to me — I hope wrongly — implicit in the Yugoslav proposals were resorted to." [27] The point was stated positively by Mr. Sassen: "A person who has expressed his desire not to return to his country of origin is entitled to resettlement elsewhere." [28]

Thus, the outlines of the two positions began to assume form and substance. The majority and the minority were in agreement on the international character of the refugee problem, but a sharp cleavage emerged regarding the scope of operations to be assigned to the new organization. The Western countries felt that political dissidence was a legitimate phenomenon; refugees were not necessarily composed only of war criminals, quislings, and traitors, as the minority contended; in view of the fact that voluntary repatriation to the countries of origin had practically reached a standstill, the logical task of the new organ would be the resettlement and permanent re-establishment of the remaining refugees. The position of the countries of origin did not admit the existence of bona fide refugees not wishing to return. Such persons were *ipso facto* traitorous and reprehensible. The only just course would therefore be speedy repatriation and retribution. As for genuine refugees, none would hesitate to return home, where they would be received with open arms.

In its broad implications, the Western position defended the right of the individual to differ politically from his government. The minority denied that right and considered it a punishable offense. The majority visualized the new organization to be primarily a service organ for the re-establishment of the political dissident in a more friendly environment while, in the minds of the delegates from the countries of origin, the punitive element in the character of the projected refugee organ assumed top priority. The Western powers insisted that the alternative of repatriation must remain a voluntary one, while the Eastern governments repeatedly stated and continuously implied the principle of enforced repatriation of all their dissident nationals. The West's conception of international organization in this instance was a service organ for the benefit of *individuals* whereas that of the East was a service organ for the attainment of the political aims of *states.*

The debates on this controversial issue are masterpieces of parliamentary strategy hardly surpassed elsewhere in the annals of international organization. Much patient search, some evidence of willingness to compromise, as well as some flares of temper and impassioned oratory were characteristic of both sides. This painful process yielded a temporary solution but, finally, it too proved impracticable.

Thus, the United Nations Organization, in its infancy, was already beginning to realize that social problems could not be divorced from politics. The Security Council was grappling with the Iranian and Syria-Lebanon disputes with little evidence of workable solutions. This had, in fact, been anticipated. But the discouraging trend in the Third Committee of the General Assembly was too much even for the sober *New York Times.* "UNO organs deadlocked," it reported, adding a reference to "sharp clashes in evidence everywhere in the UNO."[29] The opinion was shared by most of the press and the public throughout the western hemisphere. *Pravda*'s comments were terse and brief; no attention at all was paid by that paper to the proceedings being carried on in the Third Committee.

It must be stated here that this general censure was somewhat too harsh. Disagreement in the Third Committee did not, on any occasion, automatically lead to a vote. Always present was the quest for unanimity by most members. Only as a last resort was a formal vote taken, and then admittedly a decision by majority vote was considered by all delegates as an inferior substitute for unanimous consent.[30] Whereas a parallel situation in the Security Council might easily have led to the casting of a veto, the delegates of the Third Committee continued to pursue the search for agreement.

The debates in the committee deserve close attention. Mr. Arutiunian of the Soviet Union reaffirmed the position of the Eastern delegations when he asserted that "only traitors, quislings, and war criminals would refuse to return to the countries of origin since liberation."[31] Hector

McNeil, the British delegate, after again taking issue with the Soviet statement, introduced a barbed dart into the debate:

We have had a refugee of whom we are very proud . . . Using our libraries and his brains, he laid down a series of principles which were directed dramatically and basically against the kind of society in which he was sheltering . . . Let none of us be so vain as to imagine that all the prophets are dead; there are still some among traitors, and it may be that some are among refugee traitors.[32]

After that allusion was dismissed as pure rhetoric by the Byelorussian delegate, Fernand Dehousse of Belgium commented that a refugee, for very legitimate political reasons, might not wish to return home. The element of treason would not have to enter into the decision at all; such a person might simply disagree with the nature of the regime in his native country.[33] This drew a sharp rejoinder from P. N. Bajan, the Ukrainian delegate: "Such so-called refugees are not refugees at all; they are simply traitors who jeopardize world law and who must be dealt with accordingly."[34] Mr. Egeland of the Union of South Africa protested heatedly that such a blanket definition would signify treason to the United Nations Charter and would betray the principles for which the United Nations had fought. He was supported by the delegates of France, the United States, and the Netherlands.

The debate then degenerated into repetitive accusations and finally the delegates were admonished by Sir George Rendel, speaking for the United Kingdom:

The United Nations must show a spirit of tolerance and generosity rather than a desire for vengeance. It is not the business of the Committee to institute a kind of glorified witch-hunt, but to bring help to people who have a reasonable claim to international assistance; its task is to bring peace, not the gallows.[35]

Oil was poured on troubled waters by P. R. Bělehradek, delegate from Czechoslovakia, who suggested that, after all, no hard and fast delineation between repatriation and re-establishment would be necessary. The committee, he proposed, should arrive at a compromise solution by voicing its collective preference in terms of a priority.[36] This suggestion was welcomed by the harassed committee. The Soviet delegate admitted that two exceptions to his general principle certainly were in order: The Polish Jews could not be expected to remain in Germany and Austria nor should they be compelled to return to Poland where a renewed wave of anti-Semitic sentiment was on the upgrade. Similarly, the Spanish Loyalist refugees in France should not be compelled to return to Franco's Spain. Other solutions would have to be found for those two groups.[37] Most of the delegates agreed with this assertion. H. E. Yussef Vey Salem of Lebanon cautioned the committee, however, that "it must be made clear that the problem of Jewish refugees is quite distinct from the Palestine problem."[38] A. N. Abbras from Iraq added that he "did not see any legitimate connection between Jewish migration to Palestine and the problem of refugees."[39] Nevertheless, the proposal of the Czechoslovak delegation found general support in the committee and was unanimously adopted. The desire of many delegates was probably reflected in the statement by Mr. Knowles of Canada: "We should think of ourselves not as delegates of governments thinking in political terms, but people who sit here on behalf of the peoples of all the United Nations – and indeed, on behalf of the peoples of the world."[40]

Surprisingly, the committee did not deliberate long on the nature of the priority. It was agreed by all delegates that repatriation would be preferable to a renewed establishment for a refugee in a foreign country. Such a solution, as long as it remained a voluntary one, would eliminate the inevitable difficulties a refugee would have to face in a new environment, and also would involve much less expense for the new organization. The wording of the committee's resolution was left vague enough to be a general statement of policy only: "the [new refugee organization's] main task concerning displaced persons [is] to encourage and assist in every way possible their early return to their countries of origin."[41] The Soviet delegation insisted on the inclusion in the resolution of the statement that "no action taken as a result of this Resolution shall be of such a character as to interfere in any way with the surrender and punishment of war criminals, quislings and traitors . . ."[42]

With the general form and outline of the proposed international organ thus cast, it remained for the delegates to devise techniques of implementation. In the course of the ensuing debates, however, it became abundantly clear that this initial compromise formula was destined to be short-lived.

THE "RATION BRIBE"

Once the committee had unanimously agreed that repatriation of a voluntary nature was preferable to re-establishment, ways of effectuating that decision had to be explored. It was noted that most of the refugees were concentrated in camps scattered throughout Germany, Austria, and Italy, making it comparatively easy to adopt a unified policy for the operation of all these camps. It was at this point that a report from UNRRA reached the committee revealing that repatriation of refugees to their countries of origin had been diminishing steadily to a negligible monthly total.[43] Various reasons were given in the report to explain this trend, the most important being the repugnance the average refugee felt toward his homeland as a result of his sufferings there, as well as his increasing disinclination to return to countries where regimes feared by the refugee had come to power.

This news could not have come as a surprise to the delegates of the Third Committee. The delegate from Australia nevertheless attempted to reopen on the basis of new evidence the debate on the function of the new refugee organization; but this move was ruled out of order on the ground that general agreement had already been reached on the issue. The report evidently had a somewhat disturbing effect on the delegates from the countries of origin, who now attempted to follow up and consolidate their position.

The French delegate had already mentioned the poverty of most of the refugee population and the resulting necessity to render some material assistance to all bona fide refugees and displaced persons. The committee had agreed with the principle of the suggestion, but no agreement could be reached on exactly what should be done. It was now that the Soviet delegation came forth with the proposal that all repatriates should be supplied with food rations to cover a period of about three months.[44] The French delegate suggested that such assistance should not be reserved to repatriates, but should be made equally available to refugees seeking re-establishment elsewhere.[45] Mr. Arutiunian countered that, in view of the destruction evident in the countries of origin, repatriates certainly should be given preferential treatment. He was supported in this opinion by Sir George Rendel of the United Kingdom.[46] Mrs. Roosevelt, United States delegate, disagreed: "No premium should be given to anyone to return to his country of origin. Six and a half million have returned without such a premium."[47]

Mrs. Roosevelt's implication that the food ration was a form of bribery was undoubtedly justified. The Eastern powers found themselves desperately short of manpower needed to rebuild their devastated areas.

An inducement of a three months' ration supply might well make up a refugee's mind to decide in favor of repatriation. The Soviet proposal, advanced under the guise of a purely humanitarian suggestion, was certainly motivated at least in part by political considerations. The delegates of France and the United States asserted that re-establishment would, in effect, mean a much more difficult process of initial adjustment for the refugee and would therefore be deserving of at least equal material assistance.[48] The Damocles Sword of bankruptcy was raised over the proposed organization by the delegate of the United Kingdom who reminded the committee that it would be a financial impossibility to supply every refugee with pecuniary aid. Only the most desperate cases could be considered.[49] Immediately, the Ukrainian delegate contended that, since the main task of the organization, as had been resolved, would be "to assist and encourage in every possible way the early repatriation of refugees to their countries of origin," obviously such material assistance would fall within the framework of the adopted resolution. Since the means at the disposal of the projected organ would be extremely limited, he continued, only repatriates should be supplied with rations.[50]

The logic of this strategy was unassailable and the implications of the "Priority Resolution" became increasingly clear to the dismayed delegates defending assistance to resettlers. The budgetary limitation was absolute. A choice had to be made, since none of the delegates proposed the huge additional expense implied in the French suggestion. On the other hand, there was no move in favor of reducing the three months' supply of rations per capita in order to increase the coverage. The delegates agreed reluctantly that a three months' ration supply should be given to all refugees and displaced persons choosing to be repatriated.[51]

The seriousness of this decision was not at first apparent. Although the Eastern delegates had not succeeded in pushing through a resolution embracing the principle of enforced repatriation, the new provision constituted in fact a form of bribery offering an inducement to repatriation. It denied, in effect, a form of international assistance to one group of refugees while granting it to another, thus imposing a penalty upon freedom of choice. Considered in perspective, the decision constituted a tactical victory for the minority. It was the last issue on which a precarious sort of unanimity prevailed. The attitude of the Western delegates began to harden perceptibly and the next subject for discussion brought into sharp focus the ever-widening chasm between two divergent conceptions of the measure of liberty accruing to the individual human being in relation to a corporate authority.

END OF COMPROMISE: THE ISSUE OF INDIVIDUAL FREEDOM

At the opening of the ninth session of the committee on 8 February 1946, Dr. Bebler of Yugoslavia submitted the following resolution for adoption by the committee: "No propaganda should be permitted in refugee camps against the interests of the Organization of the United Nations or her members, nor propaganda against returning to their native countries." [52] The proposal was accompanied by a vitriolic attack on the UNRRA administration of several dozen refugee camps in Germany, Austria, and Italy. Dr. Bebler contended that "camp personnel indulge in physical pressure to prevent refugees from choosing repatriation. Blows and beatings are freely resorted to to dissuade those who wish to return to their former homes." [53]

On the next day, a communication was received by Peter Fraser, delegate from New Zealand and chairman of the committee. It was from UNRRA headquarters and was signed by Herbert H. Lehman, director-general.[54] In it Mr. Lehman stated that to his knowledge, twenty-two of the thirty camps cited by Dr. Bebler did not exist at all. As for the others, the director-general continued, it was the administration's policy to exert no pressure on camp inmates, but rather to encourage an independent and intelligent decision based on information regarding the conditions of life in the refugees' countries of origin. Such information was being regularly distributed by UNRRA authorities. He concluded with an emphatic denial of all the accusations leveled at the administration by the Yugoslav delegation.

The Yugoslav statement, even though supported by Mr. Arutiunian of the Soviet Union, was thus discredited before the committee. The minority, however, insisted on a consideration of the proposal by the assembled delegates since it rested squarely upon the premise of the "Priority Resolution." "Repatriation should be encouraged and assisted in every way possible," the Soviet delegate reiterated. Consequently, propaganda discouraging refugees from returning should not be tolerated in any refugee assembly center.

The implications of the proposal were set forth clearly by Sir George Rendel of the United Kingdom when he asserted:

Wherever individuals gather, they will inevitably discuss politics, they will have their little newspapers and films and discussion meetings. If we should now introduce such a rigid prohibition, we might easily find that we have gone farther than it is advisable for us to go.[55]

Mrs. Roosevelt succinctly showed the committee the full impact of the proposed resolution: "Who is to decide what is propaganda? We are here to encourage as much individual freedom as possible. We shall do nothing to restrict individual liberty."[56]

Mr. Arutiunian countered sarcastically that it was not the business of the committee to encourage war criminals, quislings, and traitors (his favorite phrase) to disseminate their propaganda in refugee camps. "We are being entirely too tolerant," he exclaimed. "But such tolerance is the tolerance of Munich. It is in fact, appeasement which must lead, in the final analysis to serious international repercussions."[57]

Mrs. Roosevelt then posed the following question to the assembled delegates: "Are we of the United Nations so feeble that we have to forbid human beings to voice their thoughts; are we so weak that we have to fear their discussion with their friends?"[58] The spirit of her husband pervaded the chamber when she added, "We should not exaggerate our fears and begin to be afraid of fear itself."[59]

The press took up her cry on the following day. "Mrs. Roosevelt leads the fight for free speech in the Refugee Committee," the *New York Times* reported.[60] "Soviet bloc frightened of refugee gossip," taunted the *Christian Science Monitor*.[61] It was evident that the meaning of the "Priority Resolution" could not be stretched to cover this point. Here neither retreat nor compromise was possible. Mr. MacNeil and Mr. Fraser continued to clarify the position of the West. Both delegates contended that the majority was not defending an unlimited liberty which in fact would lead to anarchy, but rather the maximum amount of liberty possible within the framework of a democracy.

The Dutch delegate challenged the Soviet position by pointing out that such a resolution would in fact prevent Zionist propaganda from being disseminated in refugee assembly centers. Since the minority had admitted the "unrepatriability" of most Jewish refugees, he continued, the proposed Soviet resolution was in fact inconsistent.[62]

As a result of this concerted pressure, Mr. Bajan, delegate of the

Ukraine, proposed an alternative resolution to the effect that the countries of origin should have complete freedom to disseminate information in the refugee camps.[63] Sir George Rendel stated in his reply that such freedom should exist for countries of refuge and potential areas of resettlement as well.[64] It would not be equitable to guarantee such privileges only to the countries of origin and not to others, he said. The issue seemed deadlocked in the committee.

At this crucial moment, Mme. N. M. Lefoucheux, delegate of France, stepped into the breach, offering the following resolution for adoption by the committee:

> No refugees or displaced persons who have finally and definitely, in complete freedom, and after receiving full knowledge of the facts including adequate information from the governments of their countries of origin, expressed valid objections to returning to their countries of origin, and who do not fall in the category of war criminals, quislings, and traitors, shall be compelled to return to their country of origin.[65]

The principle of voluntary repatriation was implicit in the French proposal. Since this was already incorporated in the "Priority Resolution" that particular aspect was not discussed. The ensuing discussions turned on the two points involving the dissemination of information in the refugee assembly centers. The debates focused on the two phrases "adequate information" and "valid objections." Mrs. Roosevelt, strongly supporting the French resolution, insisted on the broadest possible definition of "adequate information." Only a painstaking and conscientious observance of the principle of freedom of speech would ensure freedom of choice for the refugee – the only desirable solution. As for "valid objections," such objections might legitimately include political dissidence from the governments in power in the countries of origin.[66]

Mr. Arutiunian of the Soviet Union countered in reply that, since most of the refugees were nationals of Eastern nations, it was only fair to give the Eastern governments precedence in the matter of information. The French and American definition of "valid objections," he continued, "would invite the protection and escape from punishment of elements hostile to the United Nations."[67] He then suggested that the committee should constitute itself as a Commission of Enquiry in order to determine the eligibility of refugees expressing "valid objections" to their return.

The delegate of Panama defended the majority. "The refugee must be allowed to make up his own mind and must be given the tools to do so," he exclaimed.[68] He was supported by the delegation of Belgium whose representative took issue with the Soviet contention by asserting that "this Committee has neither the competence nor the time to constitute itself as a sort of High Tribunal. Let the organization come into being and let it include a quasi-judicial authority to pass on matters of eligibility, rather than waste our time now."[69] All delegates of the majority, although admitting that some reprehensible elements could no doubt be found among the refugees, agreed that such persons would certainly be in the minority. It was not the wish of the majority to help undesirables escape from justice. But because of these few, the large majority of refugees should not be allowed to suffer.

The Soviet position remained adamant; a similar rigidity was by now characteristic of the majority. Further debate seemed fruitless and Mr. Fraser called for a vote. It showed a clear division between East and West on the issue of free speech in refugee camps. The French resolution was passed by the committee by a vote of 13 to 5 with three abstentions.[70]

The vote was the first instance of a majority decision in the committee. This was noted with regret by the chairman. The *New York Times* greeted the event somewhat more joyfully in an editorial entitled "Free Speech Wins Out in UNO Refugee Committee."[71] *Pravda*, on the other hand, decried bitterly the "betrayal of United Nations principles and protection of quislings, war criminals, and traitors by the capitalist Powers." Furthermore, the Soviet organ continued,

> One is tempted to believe that those nations who defend so ardently the right of refugees to emigrate to new countries of resettlement want to profit from the occasion through the acquisition of cheap labor. Recently, American papers have expressed the opinion that it would be advisable to take in 20,000 refugee women as domestics.[72]

The rigidity of the Soviet stand was not surprising. Neither the Soviet Union nor the other countries of origin could well afford the loss of manpower implied in refugee resettlement. Similarly, the nations of origin certainly would not look benignly upon hundreds of thousands of political dissidents scattered throughout Central Europe. On the other hand, the Western tradition of freedom of speech and the right of political asylum were too deeply entrenched to be lightly dismissed. No international organization comprising the major Western powers could be expected to operate on any other principle. The ultimate cleavage was thus a reflection of the tensions and competing ideologies emerging on the international scene.

The minority now attempted a different approach to attain a measure of control over the international organization to be established to deal with the refugee problem. A new resolution was proposed by Mr. Arutiunian. It stipulated that "the personnel of refugee camps should be comprised mainly of representatives of states concerned, whose citizens are the refugees." [73] The Polish delegate, Mr. Stanczyk, supported the Soviet proposal by pointing out that, since most of the refugees were nationals of the Eastern countries, a staff composed mostly of nationals of the countries of origin would be best qualified to deal with the displaced persons.

The implications of the Soviet draft resolution were immediately apparent to the members of the commitee. Such a resolution, if adopted, would place all refugee camps under the administration, and therefore policy, of the minority powers. The majority, visibly annoyed, was unanimous in its rejection. Mr. MacNeil of the United Kingdom explained the Western position on such a proposition when he said: "The Anglo-Saxon conception of law is based firmly on the principle that no one may be both judge and prosecutor in the same case. To what end does the Soviet delegate suggest that the administrator have the same nationality as the displaced persons?" [74] The same point was emphasized with even greater force by Mr. Fraser: "The proposal is almost frightening. The idea that refugees who are opposed to the governments of the countries of origin, should be placed under the authority of those whom they fear, cannot be considered even for a moment." [75] The Soviet draft resolution came to a vote without further discussion and was defeated. The division was the same as on the previous vote.

Shortly before the committee was scheduled to adjourn, the Yugoslav delegation attempted one further move to obtain control over refugee camp operations. Dr. Bebler in a draft resolution now implicitily admitted that there could be bona fide refugees not wishing to return. In the light of this assumption, the resolution was hardly taken seriously when presented to the committee:

> Those refugees who are not war criminals, quislings, or traitors and who do not wish to return to their countries of origin, should receive assistance in their early settlement in a new place with the consent of the

governments concerned — that of the country of their origin and the country of resettlement.[76]

Obviously such a resolution, if adopted, would give a veto power to the countries of origin on the question whether resettlement grants should be made to their nationals by the projected international organization. After a brief but lively debate along lines previously explored, the resolution was defeated by a vote similar to the vote on each of the two preceding Soviet proposals.[77]

The committee was now ready to report to the General Assembly. The delegates had labored hard and long. Many of the sessions had lasted far into the night. On the whole, the record shows a remarkable willingness on the part of most of the delegates to look for solutions acceptable to all. This was particularly true of the early sessions which produced unanimous agreement on two important policy issues which were to confront the future refugee organization — agreement that the refugee problem could best be solved by international action and that the preferable method of solution would be repatriation of the refugees to their countries of origin. The serious cleavage that began to emerge in the latter part of the committee sessions was due to differing convictions on the type of repatriation — voluntary or enforced. The majority decided in favor of free choice and speech for the refugee, but all the delegates agreed that the question deserved further scrutiny and exploration. The committee decided, therefore, to recommend to the General Assembly the establishment of a Special Committee on Refugees which would make a thorough survey of the problem under the auspices of the Economic and Social Council.[78]

THE SPECIAL COMMITTEE ON REFUGEES

The General Assembly, on 12 February 1946, adopted the report of its Third Committee including its recommendation to refer the question of refugees to the Economic and Social Council. On February 14 that organ decided to establish a Special Committee on Refugees as suggested, to meet in April and May for thoroughgoing consideration of the problem in all its aspects.[79] The sharp debate in the plenary session of the General Assembly closely followed the lines drawn in the committee, except that probably none of the speakers hoped for a tangible result from his rhetoric, save the publicity. That, indeed, was forthcoming. After Andrei Y. Vyshinsky declared that he could not accept the "tolerance of the West which is known in history by the name of Munich," the *New York Times* reported, "Voting at 1 A.M. after more than six hours of debate, the Assembly rejected the Soviet, Polish, and Yugoslav amendments which, Mrs. Roosevelt said, would restrict human rights and human freedom, and which Hector MacNeil of Britain said, would dim the lamps that light this assembly."[80] The same paper declared in an editorial on the following day that "the Russian attitude may seem odd in view of the fact that pro-Soviet propaganda, often viciously critical of one or another of the UN, not only sizzles out of Moscow on every air wave, but has free scope in all the democratic countries."[81] Within a few days, however, the refugee question seemed to disappear from the public eye, while, in the meantime, preparations were made by the delegates of twenty member governments to meet as an *ad hoc* committee on 8 April 1946.

The meetings of the Special Committee on Refugees, sitting from April 8 to August 15, may be considered as the second phase of the discussions leading to the birth of the International Refugee Organization. Its records are much less illuminating than those of the Third Committee of the General Assembly. The basic positions had been taken and it now remained to fill in the details. Discussions were long and often tedious, as well as repetitive. Brittleness, rather than flexibility, was the keynote. And a clear division between East and West was dominant throughout. On the whole, it may be said that there were only three matters which the committee in fact decided. The form of the proposed international organ was finally fixed; the organ's budget was determined; and it was decided to draw up a constitution. All other discussion was essentially a repetition of positions which had been debated exhaustively in the Third Committee. After a study of the *ad hoc* committee's sessions one might well state that the birth of the IRO was a painful process.

The question of the form of the new organization was resolved without much difficulty. It was the only decision on which voting cut across the East-West barrier. The United Kingdom delegation defended the creation of a commission responsible to the Economic and Social Council.[82] The Soviet delegate, Mr. Arutiunian, on the other hand, proposed the establishment of a "specialized, independent and temporary agency" to deal with the refugee problem.[83] George Warren of the United States agreed with the Soviet position. He felt that the United Nations was already overburdened and that the creation of an additional integral organ would not guarantee adequate attention to the problem.[84] Mr. Arutiunian expressed the fear that, by establishing an integral United Nations organ, the refugee problem would be perpetuated. Mr. MacNeil of the United Kingdom, on the other hand, made his plea for a commission under the Economic and Social Council, stating, "If we create an incomplete organization without the backing of the United Nations, I think we shall have failed in our task."[85] The Dutch delegate added caustically that "by the time a specialized agency would be set up, all deserving refugees would already be dead."[86] But the discussion was short, and reasonably temperate in tone. By a vote of twelve to six, with two abstentions,[87] it was decided to establish a nonpermanent specialized agency of the United Nations.

The reasoning of many delegates showed flaws which indicate that their minds may have been preoccupied with graver matters. Mr. MacNeil seemed to forget that under the United Nations Charter a specialized agency would enjoy "the backing of the United Nations" as much as a commission of the Economic and Social Council. And, by the same token, a vigorous specialized agency might accomplish more than a commission because of its greater freedom from the control of the Economic and Social Council.[88] Similarly, the logic of the Soviet delegate was open to question. The subsidiary organ arrangement might perhaps have been put into effect more quickly than the specialized agency plan and more broadly based financial support might have been obtained, thus liquidating the refugee problem more efficiently.

In general, the delegates developed no clear distinction between a specialized agency and a subordinate United Nations organ and no standards for the usage of one or the other method. But, by and large, all delegates were agreed on the essentially temporary character of the refugee problem, and proposed to deal with it accordingly. The solution finally adopted, namely the creation of a temporary specialized agency, was a reflection of that assumption.

A special subcommittee was set up to consider the budget for the new organization.[89] It had been agreed informally by most of the delegates that the scale of contributions to the proposed budget should coincide as closely as possible with the contributions of member governments to the United Nations. The subcommittee studied and debated for two weeks during July and finally emerged with what it called a "rock-bottom budget" of $193,954,000 for operational expenses during the first fiscal year.[90] In addition, the subcommittee stipulated an administrative budget of $4,800,000 plus a special fund for large-scale resettlement operations amounting to $60,000,000 for the first fiscal year.[91] This last figure was based on the eligibility report of another fact-finding subcommittee of the special committee. The total number of eligible refugees was estimated by the fact-finding subcommittee to be 1,391,000.[92] Thus the budget subcommittee estimated a daily per capita expense per refugee of roughly thirty cents. Most of the operational budget for the first fiscal year was expected to be spent on various aspects of care and maintenance for the refugees, ranging from food and clothing to medical supplies, while the organization was engaged in exploring repatriation and resettlement opportunities. In the debates of the budget subcommittee the Soviet bloc was consistently outvoted in its advocacy of drastic reductions in the budget. The Eastern nations opposed, of course, all care and maintenance expenses connected with large-scale resettlement.

While the per capita stipulation in the budget was pitifully low, the sum total represented a not inconsiderable amount. In view of this, the ease with which the subcommittee's report was accepted by the whole committee is somewhat surprising. Of course, it must be remembered that agreement did not necessarily mean actual commitment to the proposed outlay. Only final signature of the constitution and in most cases ratification by the legislatures of the participating member states would set the final stamp of approval on the proposed budget. The members of the *ad hoc* committee realized this difficulty in their deliberations. Two measures were taken to deal with the problem. First, the $60,000,000 for large-scale resettlement operations was reduced to $5,000,000 at the suggestion of the French delegate,[93] and was to be voluntary even after the constitution entered into force. Second, it was stipulated that the International Refugee Organization could come into existence only if 75 per cent of the proposed operational and administrative budgets was actually subscribed, and at least fifteen nations were actual contributing and fully participating members.[94] Thus, it was hoped that IRO, once born, would be an effective and financially solvent organization.

In the meantime, another subcommittee labored on a draft constitution for the new organization.[95] This subcommittee operated completely within the framework of the resolutions arrived at in the General Assembly's Third Committee and the Special Committee of the Economic and Social Council. There was no major change in policy, and the broad features of the constitution reflected previous compromises and cleavages.

On August 15, the special committee reported the fruits of its labors to the Economic and Social Council, which in turn transmitted its conclusions, in essentially the same form, to the General Assembly for its consideration.

The question came up for final decision at the second session of the General Assembly in December 1946. Since time was short, the delegates agreed to limit the debate to three speakers on each side of the problem. The final vote was to be taken on the constitution of the projected organization as it had been passed by a majority vote in the special committee and subsequently in the plenary session of the Economic and Social Council.

Mrs. Roosevelt delivered the most impressive address for the majority. She hailed the IRO constitution as "an expression of the high ideals and aspirations for which the United Nations stands," urging its signature and ratification on all member governments.[96] However, Mr. Gromyko of the Soviet Union had the final word, asserting that "we have tried to correct the Constitution with a series of amendments, but since they have been rejected, we consider the Constitution to be unsatisfactory."[97]

The dramatic final vote came on December 15. It showed thirty member nations in favor of the constitution, and five against, with eighteen abstentions.[98] A clear bifurcation between East and West was evident. The large number of abstentions illustrated significantly that many nations did not attach much importance to the refugee problem.

CONCLUSIONS

A year of legislative labor had finally produced a constitution. An analysis of the events throughout the year shows an initial flexibility on the part of most of the delegates which, however, hardened as the debates proceeded. Most of the actual decisions were taken in committee. The Economic and Social Council as well as the General Assembly did not in their plenary sessions contribute to a further meeting of minds. While in committee a consistent effort was made to reach decisions unanimously, the plenary sessions relied more on the technique of voting. Whatever harmony did prevail at the outset of the debates was quickly countered by the dissonant chords of the radically different definition of a "refugee" by the East and the West. The issue turned, finally, upon freedom of choice for the individual displaced person.[99]

The East's denial of such freedom was obviously rooted in its great reluctance to tolerate dissident elements. By definition, all dissidents were traitors and should be treated accordingly by their home governments. Enforced repatriation would have ensured that. Furthermore, to rebuild the Eastern countries after the vast devastation resulting from the Nazi occupation, a large reservoir of manpower was needed, to which the repatriated displaced persons would contribute. For the Soviet bloc, the political considerations were overriding ones. It had no stake in any international assistance rendered to its dissidents. To contribute funds to such a venture would be a profitless enterprise since such contributions would not be accompanied by an equitable return in terms of control. On the other hand, it might be argued that Soviet participation in the proposed organization would have ensured its election to the governing organs and thus guaranteed it an important voice in the administration of the refugee problem.

The unanimity prevailing on basic issues in the majority was doubtless rooted in the strong tradition of the right of asylum and freedom of speech and assembly prevalent in the West. The policy of the majority was dictated by a liberal conception of the scope of individual liberty and freedom of choice. However, it is significant that that tradition was often in grave jeopardy. Certainly, the West's adherence to the "ration bribe" must be considered a compromise on a matter of principle. Similarly, the great number of abstentions at the final vote showed a disturbing amount of indifference concerning issues on which a position would have to be adopted sooner or later.

The final result of the legislative debates was a somewhat paradoxical one. The influence of the Soviet bloc on the new organization was manifest, despite the fact that the Eastern countries refused to become active participants in IRO. The heavy emphasis on repatriation as a preferable mode of settlement, reinforced by a poorly disguised bribe in the form of a three months' ration supply to repatriates, certainly stemmed from Soviet considerations of policy. However, it would be erroneous to conclude that the Western powers were "outmaneuvered by the Russians into making concessions that weakened the IRO in the mistaken belief that by doing so they could induce the Soviet Union to join the organization."[100] As one of the American negotiators put it:

In the negotiations we were guided by a single aim: to obtain the approval of the United Nations Assembly for the constitution of an international refugee organization and its recommendation that all members of the United Nations should join it. After immense efforts the aim was achieved. It was to achieve it and not to persuade the Russians to join the IRO that concessions had to be made . . .[101]

The final vote created an international organization which – although originally intended for humanitarian purposes – exhibited many characteristics of an essentially political nature. The repudiation of the new organization by the Soviet bloc may be interpreted in two ways. It did portend greater efficiency in the discharge of the organization's responsibilities owing to an underlying harmony and agreement on fundamental considerations among the participating states. But to that end the universal character of the organization was sacrificed. In other words the establishment of IRO cannot be considered an unqualified success in terms of the evolution of habits of universal cooperation in international organization.

But the founding of the International Refugee Organization signified an about-face with respect to the refugee problem by at least a part of the international community. For the first time in history sovereign nation-states made a determined effort to come to the defense of the homeless and destitute. By their firm stand the Western powers probably saved hundreds of thousands of innocent human beings from a tragic fate in forced labor camps behind the Iron Curtain. The International Refugee Organization was destined to be the first great international humanitarian experiment to approach the refugee problem in totality. In that sense, the blood, tears, and despair of Buchenwald, Auschwitz, and Bergen-Belsen had perhaps not been entirely in vain.

PART II · THE INTERNATIONAL REFUGEE ORGANIZATION

6

The New Refugee Charter

> "Are great events not but the game of chance? And is history not the process of giving inherent meaning to an endless succession of accidents?" LESSING, NATHAN DER WEISE

THE ELIGIBILITY CLAUSES OF THE IRO CONSTITUTION

THE League of Nations, intent upon its search for new member states, had never dared to assert itself on behalf of refugees. The one international succor of the refugee, the High Commission, had been recognized only with extreme reluctance by the League of Nations; and it had to exercise the utmost care not to offend any member government of the League. Consequently the refugees eligible for protection by the High Commission were defined as narrowly and specifically as possible.

The newly established United Nations Organization, although setting the goal of universal membership, from the first was governed in practice by a more exclusive membership policy than the League and was less sensitive about offending a member or potential member state. Thus, the United Nations found it easier to enlarge the definition of refugees under its care and protection. By 15 December 1946, a refugee constitution guaranteed basic human rights to over one million human beings; the large majority of these were refugees from Communism.

Eligibility of refugees under the constitution of the International Refugee Organization was conceived broadly and in terms of general categories rather than specific groups. Assistance was not extended to refugees from natural disasters such as floods or earthquakes; the jurisdiction of IRO extended exclusively to man-made upheavals. Most of the persons eligible under the constitution were nationals of those states which had voted against it in December 1946. Eligibility entitled the refugee to a broad range of benefits including legal protection, care and maintenance in refugee camps, and the aid of the Organization in exploring repatriation and resettlement opportunities. There was no constitutional discrimination between refugees requiring material assistance and those needing only a legal confirmation of their refugee status.

Two categories of uprooted people were eligible for official aid. The first included "displaced persons," those who had been uprooted forcibly by German and Japanese occupations during the war. This made eligible victims of Nazi or Fascist regimes who had undergone displacement from their homes as forced laborers or who had been deported because of racial, religious, or political reasons. The second category included "refugees" who had voluntarily fled from the Nazi, Fascist, or Falangist regimes, as well as others who were unable or unwilling to avail themselves of the protection of their home governments. This latter definition was broadest of all. It included groups ranging from the remaining White Russian and Armenian refugees and Spanish Loyalists to refugees from Communism subsequent to World War II. The term "refugees" was also applied to orphaned children found by the Allies after World War II.

Because the determining criterion was the motive of flight, the constitution excluded a third category, that of simple migrants, from eligibility. Broadly speaking, if the motive was primarily political, that is, persecution or fear of persecution by the person's home government, the applicant was considered eligible. If, on the other hand, the motive was essentially economic and eligibility was requested in order to improve the applicant's standard of living, the IRO constitution did not grant refugee status.

While the distinction between "refugees" and "migrants" was theoretically plausible, practically the distinction was difficult to draw. Supporting documentation was inadequate in most cases and not infrequently forged, making an altogether objective evaluation of motives not an easy task. Moreover, even assuming good faith and adequate documentation, motives were often not as clearly defined as the constitution required. For example, since Communism is both a political and an economic doctrine, political reasons for flight might very well be given in an economic form, thus making a political objector look like an ordinary migrant.

In sum, the Organization was faced in matters of eligibility with determinants of an essentially subjective character. Every refugee was interviewed and registered individually, and those doing the interviewing had to exercise considerable discretion. A strong controlling factor was information supplied concerning a particular applicant by other refugees from the same area. When faced with a veritable flood of forged documents, IRO officials' only recourse was the archives of UNRRA and of the military authorities. In view of the fact that eligibility entitled the refugee not only to political and legal protection but also to material assistance, forgery was soon developed to a fine art.

The IRO constitution, in anticipation of such difficulties, had provided for an Eligibility Review Board consisting of five impartial judges, which provided a system of appeal whereby an applicant could request the review of a negative decision. However, because of the very technical nature of most of the applications, the role of the board became essentially one of endorsing the negative decisions of the field officers as constitutionally justified.[1]

The difficulty arising out of the constitutional distinction between "refugees" and "migrants" was only one of the problems which beset IRO in matters of eligibility. A second problem sounded grave political overtones, for "criminals, quislings, and traitors" were not eligible for aid under the IRO constitution.[2] This phrase, which had been inserted upon the strong insistence of the Eastern bloc, was intended to include persons defined as collaborators with the Nazi or Fascist regimes who actively assisted in persecuting the civilian populations of countries which were members of the United Nations, or who had voluntarily helped the enemy forces after the outbreak of World War II. On the insistence of the Eastern countries, who wanted to suppress all anti-repatriation activities, all persons who discouraged refugees from returning to their countries of origin were excluded from IRO jurisdiction. But only overt acts, not opinions or attitudes on the part of the refugees, were thus interpreted.[3] A second major group specifically excluded from IRO benefits were all *Volksdeutsche*, or ethnic Germans, including those who had been dislocated as a result of the "Potsdam Transfers." These people, who had never been eligible for the assistance of any United Nations organization thus became the responsibility of the German and Austrian authorities. Their presence in these countries was a cause of continual difficulty for IRO, which was responsible for only a minority of the total refugee population in each country. Finally, ordinary criminals extraditable by treaty were also excluded from IRO jurisdiction.

The major difficulty confronting the Organization was how to define "collaboration with the enemy." A striking example may be seen in the case of many of the Baltic refugees applying for eligibility who had been active on the side of the Nazi army during the war. A fine line had to be drawn by IRO officials in determining whether the applicant had been fighting in defense of his national liberties or whether his alliance with the enemy had been motivated by acceptance of the Nazi ideology. In many cases, Balts were conscripted by force into the German army and even into S.S. fighting units. Again, screening had to rely in most cases upon primarily subjective factors, although in most cases it was possible to determine whether participation in the German armed forces had been of a forcible or voluntary nature. On the whole, the Organization favored a generous interpretation of eligibility, partly because the Eastern countries were unrepresented in IRO, and partly because of fear that large groups would otherwise be left to wander about Europe uncared for and uncontrolled, bringing about further unfortunate political and social consequences.[4]

Another difficulty presented itself to the Organization in its definition of "criminal." The criterion used was the distinction between war crimes, on the one hand, and ordinary crimes, on the other. The result was that many persons who had committed petty offenses in the chaotic conditions of postwar Europe were sometimes eligible for IRO assistance. In this context, IRO officials often found it difficult in establishing motive for flight to distinguish between legitimate fear of persecution and mere fear of punishment for ordinary crimes committed in the refugee's home country.

The IRO mandate, on the whole, was unprecedented in its inclusiveness though exhibiting a markedly European emphasis. The definitions as laid down in the basic document, however, proved to be rather artificial and formalistic, particularly the distinction between "refugees" and "migrants" and the catch-all phrase "quislings, criminals, and traitors." In practical application, many of these definitions broke down completely. Interpretation of the constitution by IRO field officers as well as by the Eligibility Review Board was liberal and a spirit of justice tempered with mercy prevailed over the sentiment of retribution.

The Eastern countries, as we have seen, had succeeded in securing the inclusion of the provision in the IRO constitution that the primary aim of the new refugee organ should be "to encourage and assist in every way possible the early return to their country of origin of those persons who desire to return." [5] In view of this provision, a choice in favor of repatriation was taken for granted by the Organization unless the refugee registered "valid objections." Such objections might include compelling family reasons arising out of previous persecutions — as was the case with the surviving Jews who held strong feelings against returning to the scene of their suffering. A second reason which the refugee could advance in support of his desire not to be repatriated was an objection of a political nature.[6] This provision, included in the constitution over the adamant and repeated protests of the Eastern countries, was to shift the Organization's main task from repatriation to overseas resettlement notwithstanding the constitutional provision initiated by the Eastern countries which would supply only repatriates with food rations for a three-month period.

In summary, we may say that the eligibility clauses of the IRO constitution were a compromise between the Eastern and Western conceptions of a refugee. They were drawn up in an era which saw the rise of a totally new and complicated situation in which governments desired to have returned to their countries of origin persons who disagreed with them politically. These persons were in the majority refugees from Communism. IRO's experience in applying the constitutional definitions to individual cases reflected the contradictions inherent in those definitions. Since the Eastern countries refused to participate in IRO, most of the problems were resolved in an essentially Western frame of reference. This development was furthered by the form which the constitution prescribed for the new refugee organization.

IRO AS A SPECIALIZED AGENCY

IRO was one of the first intergovernmental bodies to test a new invention in the annals of international organization — the "specialized agency" device.[7] The other alternative, a United Nations commission for refugees directly responsible to the Economic and Social Council and to the General Assembly, had been rejected during the debates of the Special Committee on Refugees and Displaced Persons in May 1946.

The "specialized agency" technique was essentially an effort to enable the United Nations to deal effectively with the refugee problem without jeopardizing the Organization's basic aim: the maintenance of international peace and security. The League of Nations' answer to Soviet criticism of international assistance to Russian refugees had been the establishment of the League High Commission for Refugees as a quasi-autonomous organ. Although largely dependent upon the League for funds, only tenuous institutional links had connected Dr. Nansen's organization to the main international body. Similarly, IRO was placed on the periphery of the United Nations system. Under its constitution the International Refugee Organization as a specialized agency of the United Nations (and with the legal status of a United Nations organization) was permitted to have its own selective membership policy, which enabled it to operate without the participation of the Soviet bloc and to enlist the active adherence of "other peace-loving states,"[8] not technically members of the United Nations, as was later done by the admission of two states with valuable experience in refugee work—Italy and Switzerland. The formula had the further advantage of enabling the Asiatic, Arab, and other governments which had little interest in IRO's limited refugee problem to dissociate themselves from its work. The boycott of the Eastern countries promised a smoother, more harmonious discharge of the Organization's functions since the Western members agreed on basic policy issues, and the limiting of membership to those nations actively interested gave the Organization coherency and drive.[9]

As a specialized agency, IRO was not subject to operational supervision by the General Assembly. Such supervision might have resulted in difficulties and delays because of the hostile attitude exhibited by the Soviet bloc of that body, although specific acts of Soviet obstructionism might have been limited by the absence of any veto right. Policy decisions of IRO were made by its General Council composed of representatives of the eighteen members of the Organization.[10] This policy-making body delegated administrative responsibility to an Executive Committee of nine members under the authority of a director-general.[11] In accordance with the terms of agreement signed between the United Nations and IRO, only the administrative, not the operational, budget of the new organization was to be subject to review by the General Assembly.[12] This provision rendered IRO's large operational budget independent of the General Assembly. Furthermore, even review over the small administrative budget entailed no real authority.

During the debates of the Special Committee it had been the British view that a grant of the necessary funds would be easier to obtain if the new refugee organ were integrated fully into the United Nations system. Although this approach did not fully take into account the effect of Soviet hostility toward IRO if the Organization's budget were subject to approval by the General Assembly, it anticipated correctly the great difficulty which IRO would have to face in its appeal for funds as a specialized agency with a separate constitution of its own: parliamentary ratification of the constitution and of the budget by the member governments of the International Refugee Organization.

THE BUDGET OF IRO

The form of the new refugee organ to be created had been the only matter under discussion before the Special Committee in May 1946 on which voting had not followed the usual East-West division. Both the Soviet Union and the United States had argued for a specialized agency, the former with the hope that the temporary character of the new organization would thus be better safeguarded and the latter with the aim of reserving to the United States Congress the right to pass upon the merit of a separate IRO appropriation by the American government. When this view prevailed, the members of the Special Committee realized its dangers and provided that the IRO constitution would go into effect only upon the accession of at least fifteen states and the actual subscription of at least 75 per cent of the operational and administrative budgets of the Organization.[13] Thus it was hoped that IRO, once called into existence, would have sufficient funds at its command.

Shortly before the constitution was opened for signature, the Special Committee on Refugees and Displaced Persons reduced the annual operational budget of the Organization from $193,954,000 to $151,060,500, and fixed the administrative budget at $4,800,000.[14] A large-scale resettlement fund of $5,000,000 was placed by the committee on a voluntary basis.[15] The operational budget was divided among the member states following the pattern of assessment of the United Nations, and the administrative budget deviated only slightly from that norm. It is significant that the planning of the budget and the scale of contributions was built upon the assumption that all governments of the United Nations would join IRO.

In view of the stipulation that 75 per cent of the budget would have to be guaranteed before the Organization could come into existence, an intensive search for ratifications became the preoccupation of the Secretary-General of the United Nations. It was quite obvious that the ratifications of the United States, the United Kingdom, and France had to be secured if IRO was to see the light of day. When the constitution was opened for signature on 16 December 1946, eleven governments signed the document. While ten affixed their signatures *ad referendum*, only the United Kingdom, whose contribution to the operational budget constituted 14.75 per cent, signed without reservation.[16] Shortly thereafter, four more deposited their instruments of ratification, bringing the total percentage of the subscribed operational budget up to 19.47 per cent.[17] However, no more ratifications followed and it became obvious that the world looked to the United States to take the initiative. It was tacitly understood in United Nations circles that ratification by the United States, whose percentage of contribution was 45.75 per cent, would be followed by the accession of at least six other governments including that of France, thus virtually assuring life to IRO.[18]

Public opinion in the United States seemed badly divided on the refugee issue. Most of the arguments circulating throughout the nation made their appeal on an emotional plane; there was little objective research. Two strands of argument were predominant. In the first place, most of the sectarian pressure groups appealed to the humanitarian duty of the United States to ratify the constitution and take in a "fair share" of the refugees. On the other hand, a small but very articulate minority, spearheaded by military pressure groups such as the American Legion and the Veterans of Foreign Wars, appealed to traditional isolationist sentiment. When the issue of ratification finally reached the Senate on 1 March 1947, predictions as to the outcome were far from unanimous.

A team of two men, Under Secretary of State Dean Acheson and the Under Secretary for Occupied Areas, General John H. Hilldring, appeared before the Senate Foreign Relations Committee and defended the position of the State Department in recommending ratification. The first part of the hearing dealt chiefly with the humanitarian necessity of salvaging refugees scattered throughout displaced persons camps in Europe. Summing up his appeal, Acheson made a final observation which elicited the following significant exchange:

Under Secretary Acheson: Any member [of IRO] may at any time give written notice of withdrawal . . . Such notice shall take effect one year after the date of receipt . . ."[19]

Senator Vandenberg: "What would you say to the proposition that . . . we should give our notice of withdrawal the same day we start the thing?"

Under Secretary Acheson: "I should think that would probably insure the Organization would not be successful were [the United States] to give it notice before it started."[20]

The administration now tried a different tack. It pointed out to the committee that approximately 60 per cent of the total number of eligible refugees were located in the American zones of Germany and Austria.[21] Thorough research had shown that the expenses of the United States government for these refugees, through funds allocated to UNRRA, the IGCR, and the Army, amounted to $130,000,000 annually, while the proposed annual contribution of the United States to IRO was set at $73,000,000.[22] The conclusion—namely, that by decentralizing financial responsibility among a number of participating governments, the United States would save funds—was obvious. After an elaborate discussion of the administration's report, the following crucial exchange occurred:

Senator Vandenberg: "Then it is fair—I want to get this over-all relationship—it is fair to say that IRO involves a total expenditure of $73,000,000 for an operation which has cost and is costing $130,000,000 under existing auspices?"

General Hilldring: "That is correct, Senator."

Senator Vandenberg: "So we are saving, so far as dollars and cents are concerned, $57,000,000 by this switch over to IRO; is that correct?"

General Hilldring: "Based on the record alone."[23]

It was largely upon the strength of this argument that the Senate ratified the constitution by a vote of 63 to 13. Thus, American adherence and, by implication, the very life of the Organization itself depended upon an essentially fortuitous circumstance.

At this time the entry into force of the IRO constitution was assumed to be merely a question of time. When the accessions of Canada and Guatemala brought the number of ratifications to eight, it was decided to establish a Preparatory Commission of IRO which would take over the functions of UNRRA, the IGCR, and the Army, and itself assume operational responsibilities for refugees and displaced persons under IRO jurisdiction. Accordingly, on 1 July 1947, UNRRA and the IGCR terminated their activities after bestowing their residual funds and part of their personnel on the successor organization.

Pressure was now exerted by the eight member governments upon the French National Assembly to ratify the constitution. Accession by France, whose percentage of the total budget was 4.10 per cent, would make the Organization a reality. However, seven other governments deposited their instruments of ratification before the French Parliament finally ratified. Its reasons for ratification were rather similar to those of the United States: the French government, which had borne sole financial responsibility for over 200,000 Spanish Loyalist refugees, now saw a welcome opportunity to reduce its expenses since these refugees from Franco Spain were included under IRO's jurisdiction. Finally, on 20 August 1948, after more than a year of actual operational activities on the part of the Preparatory Commission, the IRO constitution came into force when fifteen governments subscribed 76 per cent of the stipulated budget.

In evaluating IRO budget provisions, we may discern an artificially formalistic approach similar to the constitution's eligibility claims. In the first place, the scale of assessments was based upon the erroneous assumption that all members of the United Nations would join IRO. This, of course, did not happen and at no time did the members' contributions total more than 78 per cent of the budgetary scale as it was originally agreed upon.[24] In addition, the constitution allowed for little flexibility and the member governments were confronted by recurring financial emergencies. Governments repeatedly defaulted on their contributions, the case of China being a notorious example. The official currency devaluations promulgated in the United Kingdom and France slashed seriously into the Organization's purchasing power. Many member governments met their obligations toward IRO in soft, nonconvertible currencies or even by payment in services or goods.[25] Also, appropriations to the Organization had to be renewed annually by most legislatures with the result that such renewals often were not forthcoming or were seriously delayed. As a result of such defaults, the American government each year actually contributed over 60 per cent of the total budget of IRO instead of the 45.75 per cent as originally stipulated. Since the IRO operational budget was a sizable sum, contributions to it constituted for most governments their largest single appropriation to any one international organization. In the case of the United

States, its contributions to IRO during the Organization's existence amounted to between 40 per cent and 70 per cent of the total American expenditures on membership in international organizations up to that time.[26]

The numerous financial crises to which the Organization was subjected were somewhat offset by the contributions of the German, Austrian, and Italian governments. The upkeep of the displaced persons camps and the supplying of certain basic staple foods were made the responsibility of these governments.[27] On the whole, however, it is hardly surprising that the IRO General Council found itself in a state of continuing financial emergency. It is remarkable that under such circumstances the integrity of the operational program itself was never sacrificed to the technicalities of the budget. A typical report of the General Council, after facing another financial crisis, read as follows: "Having reached certain conclusions with regard to the character of the Organization's operations, the Council turned to the budgetary aspects . . ."[28]

7

Rehabilitation

"When we shall no longer be mere numbers, categories and statistics, but men – unique and irreplaceable in our individuality – then only will our humanity be restored."[1] C. V. GHEORGHIU, *La Vingt-Cinquième Heure*

AGREEMENTS BETWEEN IRO AND COUNTRIES OF FIRST ASYLUM

THE assumption of operational functions by the Preparatory Commission of IRO in July 1947 signified the first international attack upon the refugee problem in its totality. The political and legal protection activity of the Nansen Office, the maintenance and repatriation functions of the Allied armies and of UNRRA, as well as the quest for resettlement opportunities by the IGCR, were integrated by the new organization. Duly constituted as a specialized agency of the United Nations and equipped with an operational budget three times as large as that of the parent organization, IRO set about discharging the task entrusted to it.

In order to assume effective responsibility for the million refugees under its jurisdiction, the Organization proceeded to conclude agreements with the Allied occupation authorities as well as with several sovereign governments.[2] Since two thirds of the seven hundred assembly centers to be operated by IRO were located in Germany and Austria, IRO officials took great pains in drawing up satisfactory agreements with the United States, British, and French military governments. During these negotiations the Organization constantly sought to obtain the most favorable terms possible for its wards – assuming a quasi-consular role for the refugees *vis-à-vis* the occupation authorities. In this endeavor the Organization profited from the sympathetic climate prevailing among the Western Allies toward the survivors of Nazi persecution. In all three Allied zones the Organization was successful in obtaining recognition of IRO eligibles as United Nations wards beyond the control of German and Austrian local authorities.[3] The occupation authorities agreed that some of the burden of maintaining the refugee assembly centers should devolve upon the German and Austrian economies as a token repayment for the hardships inflicted upon the refugees during the Nazi regime. Accordingly it was stipulated that the German and Austrian local governments would have to supply living accommodations, food, clothing, some medical services, and other basic necessities to the refugees, all of these contributions being calculated on the basis of the average consumption of an individual German or Austrian citizen.[4] At the same time, IRO fixed its own refugee maintenance standards — all somewhat higher than the norms calculated for the indigenous population — and considered itself responsible for supplying the differential from its own budget.[5] The effect of this policy was to accord a privileged status to IRO eligibles as opposed to the native German and Austrian population.

Hostility between these groups, already apparent when IRO assumed responsibility, was further fanned by the new policy. The steady influx into the area of the *Volksdeutsche*, expelled from the Eastern countries under the Potsdam Agreement, aggravated the situation considerably since these new refugees found themselves outside of IRO's jurisdiction and were accorded a cool welcome by their German brethren. On the whole, the IRO refugee became to the German a symbol of his defeat in the war and much of his latent aggression was projected upon the new elite, a constant reminder to him of a more glorious past and of a present onerous responsibility.

The agreements negotiated by IRO with the Allied occupation authorities were gradually adjusted to the changing political picture. As Germany was drawn more and more into the Western orbit, IRO felt constrained to give up most of the privileges it had secured for its refugees. The British were the first of the three Western Allies to request the Organization to reduce its food rations to a level equal to that of the indigenous population.[6] The French and American authorities soon afterward followed suit and IRO agreed to the request, although it justified the policy change not in political terms but by contending that a reduction in ration provisions would accelerate movement of refugees by making continued residence in the assembly centers somewhat less desirable.[7] Similarly, the extraterritorial privileges which the Organization had managed to secure for its wards began to disappear in 1948. Refugees were again placed for most purposes under the authority of the German and Austrian court systems subject to ever-diminishing supervision by the occupation authorities and IRO. Jurisdiction was at first delegated to the German and Austrian courts in minor criminal matters only, but by 1950 all vestiges of international supervision had disappeared in fact, if not in law.[8]

It is clear that IRO and the refugees under its jurisdiction in Germany and Austria were fundamentally affected by the gradual recovery of the local economy and the relaxation of Allied occupation controls. This process ended the privileged status of IRO refugees and hence contributed toward eliminating some of the hostility existing between them and the native population, paving the way for a humane policy to be adopted by the local governments toward the refugees remaining in their domains after IRO had ceased to exist.

As in Germany and Austria, IRO experienced little difficulty in establishing jurisdiction over its refugees in other countries. In France, the country of refuge par excellence, IRO met with a cordial reception and speedily concluded an agreement with the French government whereby the jurisdiction of the Organization over its eligible refugees was recognized.[9] Since France already had in operation a highly developed machinery for the maintenance of its Spanish Loyalist refugees, IRO merely took over responsibility for the smoothly functioning apparatus. Similar courtesy was, generally speaking, extended to the Organization in its negotiations with Italy, Greece, the Netherlands, Denmark, and Belgium.

In the Middle East, the only government to conclude an agreement with IRO was that of Egypt, where some Polish refugees were concentrated in a single assembly center.[10] However, the Organization faced a major policy decision as a result of the Arab-Israeli conflict. The General Council on 1 August 1948 unanimously voted against the inclusion of either Arab or Jewish Middle Eastern refugees under IRO jurisdiction, stating as its reason the "essentially non-political and humanitarian character of the Organization, unable to afford embroilment in a major political conflict."[11] It was also felt in IRO circles that the Arab refugee problem was a localized one and should be solved by the local governments.[12] The different nature of this new problem, together with the conviction voiced repeatedly by IRO officials that it would be unfair to expect only eighteen governments to shoulder the financial burden of a task which should be the responsibility of all United Nations members, convinced the General Assembly that a new and separate United Nations agency should be created for the Palestine refugees. The argument was strengthened by IRO's status as a "non-permanent specialized agency" and the Organization's impending dissolution. Nevertheless, it would seem that the General Council made the decision with an uneasy conscience and proceeded with a sigh of relief to divert various commodities, such as food, blankets, and medical supplies, to the newly created United Nations Relief and Works Agency for Palestine Refugees in the Near East.[13]

The fact that "a major political conflict" had been the crucible from which IRO itself had been born was not lost upon those IRO Officials who pressed for the assumption of international responsibility for the new Palestine refugees. The establishment of UNRWA in December 1949 was the direct result of such pressure upon the General Assembly and of the realization that a distinction between political and humanitarian considerations had become almost impossible.

While IRO neatly sidestepped a delicate jurisdictional problem in the Near East, it was confronted with a rapidly deteriorating situation in the Far East. The Organization had been given jurisdiction by the Nationalist Chinese government over 25,000 refugees,[14] mostly in Shanghai, but had hardly begun its operations there when the Communist forces neared Shanghai. Nine thousand of the Shanghai refugees were White Russians and the Organization attempted to evacuate these oldest enemies of Communism, but succeeded in shipping only half of them to the island of Samar in the Philippines.[15] When Communist forces entered Shanghai in May 1949, the IRO office expected the worst. To its great surprise, the new government took no punitive action against the frantic White Russians. Instead, an agreement between IRO and the new Chinese People's Republic was drawn up, permitting the evacuation by the Organization of all eligible refugees.[16] This was the only agreement between IRO and a Communist government and like those with other governments it was honored by the host country. The fact that evacuation proceeded at a snail's pace and remained incomplete at the time of IRO's termination was not due to obstacles placed in the path of the Organization by the Chinese government, but rather to the severe lack of funds besetting IRO during the last year of its existence.[17]

On the whole, wherever the Organization found refugees under its jurisdiction, it succeeded in negotiating agreements giving to itself a quasi-consular role, if not sovereignty, over the refugees. The Organization in fact functioned like a state without a territory and with all its citizens permanently abroad.

LEGAL AND POLITICAL PROTECTION

Rendering "legal and political protection" [18] to its refugees was not only one of the most important functions of IRO but also an integral part of its human rehabilitation program. There were essentially two types of stateless persons with which the Organization had to deal: first, those refugees such as the White Russians who had been deprived of their nationality and had thus become stateless in law; and, second, the refugees who had retained their nationality in law but in practice refused to have any contact with their home governments. All refugees who were stateless either by choice or by fiat became not only aliens but aliens unprotected by their countries of origin. Thus, the substitution of the protection of the international community for a national passport became one of the main concerns of IRO.

All eligible refugees were equipped with a "document in lieu of Passport" issued by IRO and finally recognized by thirty-two governments.[19] In no country did the IRO document become equal in value to a national passport. Its greatest usefulness was evident in the countries of first asylum, particularly Germany, Austria, and Italy, where the document clarified the refugee's status and enabled him to reside indefinitely, to work, to marry, to divorce, and finally to die, legally. The IRO document not only enabled the refugee to live within the law in countries of first asylum, but also legally clothed him to enter into a new life in a country of resettlement where the paper usually was required by immigration authorities as a first step toward naturalization.

The Organization was well aware of the responsibility which the issuing of such documentation entailed. Refugees were interviewed individually and their available papers scrutinized conscientiously by IRO officials, who realized that the contents of the document to be issued were crucial for the refugee's future. For example, the authenticity of a professional diploma presented by a refugee had to be tested before entry of that profession on the IRO document. Although extreme care was exercised by the Organization, some forged documents slipped through undetected as IRO later found out to its chagrin, when several "doctors" were shipped back from Canada as unacceptable.[20] The Organization exercised some discretionary power within the limits of its constitution, such as the expunging of minor offenses from the records of refugees under certain circumstances.[21] Viewed in perspective, the issuance of identity certificates by IRO to its eligible refugees was a carefully organized and thoroughly screened process with individual attention given each applicant.

The essential characteristic of the IRO refugee was not material need nor was it his desire to migrate. What distinguished him was his anomalous position before the law on which his material life depended. Naturalization—the acquisition of a new nationality—was a solution to the problem, and IRO's main contribution in its activity of legal and political protection was to bring that solution nearer.

THE INTERNATIONAL TRACING SERVICE

After jurisdiction over its eligible refugees had been established by IRO and provisions for legal protection made, the Organization launched a three-pronged rehabilitation program which was to prepare the refugee physically and mentally for a favorable adjustment in his new home. The first phase involved the work of the International Tracing Service of IRO which attempted to locate the missing members of those refugee families which had been separated during the Nazi holocaust. Second, the Organization played an active role in attempting to secure for Nazi victims adequate compensation and restitution from the German and Austrian governments. Finally, an elaborate care and maintenance program was developed to tide the refugee over the waiting period in IRO assembly centers.

The International Tracing Service consisted of a group of dedicated international civil servants and locally recruited personnel, devoted to the difficult task of tracing almost one million missing persons for whom enquiries had been made by refugees. The work achieved was truly enormous: "More than a hundred tons of documents were collected in three years concerning nearly one million persons. The checking of individual graves yielded information on 155,093 more."[22]

The main sources from which the documents were gathered were the German civil administration, national and international record offices where war crimes were listed, and IRO itself. No stone was left unturned by the IRO Tracing Service in its effort to determine the fate of missing refugees. Gestapo and criminal police records, urns, crematoria, and mass graves were all meticulously examined and in most cases, because of the thorough records kept by the Nazis, the Tracing Service found the information it needed. By the use of this material, hundreds of thousands of inquiries could be settled. The efforts of the Tracing Service made possible the reconstruction of vital statistics, and the clarification of the legal status of many refugees, as well as the validation of indemnity claims. The information gathered proved invaluable for various legal purposes in the life of the refugee, such as re-marriage, adoption, guardianship, succession, and the payment of life insurance. The comprehensive records of the International Tracing Service became the most extensive collection of refugee documentation in the world.[23] Unfortunately, while most of the refugees' inquiries could be answered with certainty, the reply was usually a notification of death.

A subsidiary branch of the Tracing Service was the Child Search Service which attempted to locate missing children, particularly those who had been kidnapped by the Nazis during the war and deported for Germanization purposes. Approximately 20,000 children were involved, but only a small percentage could be located and even fewer were willing to be reunited with their families, for they had formed deep ties with their foster parents.[24] The impotence of the Tracing Service in this respect underlined, perhaps more starkly than any other single phase of IRO's operations, the extent of the Nazi crime and the immense difficulties in making a partial salvage of the wreckage.

IRO, with the help of its International Tracing Service, exerted great efforts to assist refugees in indemnity claims and general restitution proceedings against the German and Austrian governments. The Organization played an important part in persuading the German authorities to pass the General Claims Law, guaranteeing certain payments to sufferers from the Nazi regime.[25] A great number of victims did not possess the evidence necessary to document their claims, but the International Tracing Service, in most cases, was able to furnish certificates of incarceration or other requisite documentation.

The General Claims Law, finally extended to all three Western zones in both Germany and Austria after intensive pressure by IRO, provided indemnification for damage to life, limb, health, and liberty as well as some restitution for loss of property. IRO operated on the principle that indemnification enabled the refugee better to re-establish himself, in addition to being an act of justice to the individual concerned. It was finally decided to compensate each former concentration camp inmate by a payment of 150 Deutsche marks for each month of deprivation of liberty.[26] In view of the fact that many refugees had spent more than a decade under such conditions, the sums paid were frequently not inconsiderable.

The Organization also approached the Allied occupation authorities about the gold, diamonds, and other valuables which had been confiscated from the Jews upon their entry into concentration camps. The Allied authorities readily turned over to the Organization $95,000 from the former Nazi coffers, a welcome addition to the IRO budget.[27]

CARE AND MAINTENANCE

While the Organization was doing all in its power to regularize the legal relationships of the refugees, to search for their relatives, and to press for their indemnification, the actual physical care and maintenance of the uprooted pending their re-establishment absorbed much of the energy of IRO workers in all its assembly centers.

Over seven hundred IRO refugee camps dotted the map of Europe, most of them located in Germany and Austria.[28] It was thought best by the Organization to continue the administration of the UNRRA camps. This facilitated administrative procedure, making refugees easily accessible to the Organization. Also, concentration in camps reduced to a minimum outbreaks of violence between the DP's and the native population since contact could be regulated easily by the Organization. On the other hand, an unpalatable similarity of the IRO camps to the refugees' former places of confinement could not be denied and continued camp life made it more difficult for the refugee to rid himself of his "concentration camp mentality."[29]

Most of the buildings had been requisitioned by IRO from the local authorities and were largely German army and S.S. military installations hastily renovated for the occupancy of the victims of their former inmates. Housing conditions were crowded although the Organization attempted not to exceed a maximum of five thousand refugees per camp. Wherever possible, IRO officials encouraged democratic self-government by the refugees in the centers, most of which were run much like little municipal governments.[30] A small number of refugees were living outside the camps and received cash grants from the Organization to defray their housing expenses. The great majority of the million IRO refugees, however, were part and parcel of the little DP communities in the midst of an alien and often hostile population.

It was the Organization's constitutional responsibility to provide adequate nourishment to the refugees under its jurisdiction. There had been much discussion in the General Council regarding caloric standards of the food to be provided. Since the food item constituted by far the largest single sum in the IRO budget in its first year of operations, the Organization faced a major dilemma. If food rations were pegged too high, the attractiveness of the DP camps would be enhanced and resistance to leaving the assembly centers would increase. On the other hand, if the quality or quantity of the nourishment fell below a given minimum, the resulting undernourished refugee might easily be rejected by the resettlement selection missions visiting the camps. It was thus of great importance to set a standard which would make life in the camp not too attractive, yet not one of deprivation. There was much disagreement on this issue in IRO's policy organ, but finally the American view favoring a standard substantially above that of the native population prevailed over the British position which had favored a daily ration of caloric content equal to that of the indigenous populace.[31] The progressive political emancipation of Germany and Austria was the main factor in the ultimate acceptance of the British view in 1949.[32] In sum, the General Council felt that the refugees' food ration had been accurately pegged, since food per se apparently was not a factor in the refugee's decision regarding his re-establishment.[33]

An important challenge was met by the Organization in its extensive health and sanitation programs in the assembly centers. IRO officials were well aware that concentration of large numbers of refugees in crowded quarters might easily lead to the outbreak of epidemics. Intensive preventive measures were taken by the IRO medical staff to forestall such a contingency and the centers remained completely free from epidemic disease.[34] A high health standard was very desirable since only refugees in good health were resettlement prospects. In view of the great rigidity shown by most of the selection missions visiting the camps, IRO attempted to enforce rigorous health standards among its wards. Since the past experience of most of the refugees had served as a brutal selection process, allowing survival only to the toughest and most durable constitutions, most of the refugee population was in fairly robust physical condition when IRO assumed responsibility. Generous assistance was rendered IRO by the World Health Organization, which supplied vaccination and inoculation teams that traveled from camp to camp to perform their services.[35] In addition to WHO's cooperation and the efforts of IRO's own medical staff, the services of many refugee doctors were enlisted with generally good results except that, in some instances, discrimination by the refugee doctors in favor of their own ethnic groups caused some difficulties.

There was some criticism on the part of the refugee population to the effect that the health program was conducted too stringently and that the IRO screening process excluded too many refugees from re-establishment opportunities on the grounds of ill health. This criticism, although understandable, was probably in the last analysis invalid since the prestige of IRO with the selection missions depended very heavily upon the rigor of its pre-selection health screening. Since the Organization had to adapt itself to the demands of the selection missions, a more lenient policy would probably not have resulted in better re-establishment chances for the refugees.

A final factor in preparing the refugee for a favorable re-establishment in a new home was the Organization's aim "that genuine refugees and displaced persons as far as possible should be put to useful employment in order to avoid the evil and anti-social consequences of continued idleness."[36] This constitutional provision was interpreted in the broadest possible sense in all assembly centers and by the time the new Organization had completed its first six months of operation, approximately half of the total refugee population was receiving vocational training.[37] IRO offered training courses in twenty different occupations, much of the teaching staff being drawn from the refugees themselves. The main contribution to this aspect of refugee rehabilitation, however, was rendered by the numerous voluntary organizations associated with IRO.[38] The response among the displaced persons was enthusiastic and by the end of the first year more than half of the 598,000 persons receiving such instruction were classified as employable.[39] IRO made it its business to register each refugee who had completed a training course and to seek employment for him either within the camp administration or in the local economy. Among the men, the occupations most frequently registered were those of tailor, shoemaker, carpenter, agricultural worker, and mechanic, while important groupings for women workers were seamstress, domestic worker, teacher, and nurse.[40]

Opportunities for employment within the camp administration were, of course, limited and IRO attempted wherever possible to find suitable job opportunities for its employable refugees in the local economies. The greatest obstacle to maximum results in these efforts was the unfavorable employment situation then prevailing in Germany and Austria. During the first year of IRO's operations the currency in the occupied areas was of little value and there was correspondingly little financial incentive to work. After the German currency conversion, employment opportunities for refugees decreased even more because of the influx of the *Volksdeutsche*, who were in most instances preferred over the refugees by the native employers. In addition, the attitude of many refugees reflected a disinclination to work for the German and Austrian economies, these feelings being particularly pronounced among the Jewish displaced persons.

On the whole, only about one fourth of IRO's refugees were employed, either by the Organization itself or in the native economy.[41] While a large number of the displaced persons developed an apathy toward employment as the result of protracted camp life, IRO's vocational training program promised to serve the refugees well when they re-established themselves in other countries. During the difficult waiting period, IRO did its best to reduce enforced idleness to a minimum and the vocational training schools went a long way toward the physical and mental rehabilitation of the refugee still in the "DP state."

An equally intensive language training program was launched by the Organization immediately after its inception. It was realized quite clearly early in 1947 that IRO's main challenge would ultimately be the task of resettlement in overseas countries.[42] Accordingly, courses in English, French, Spanish, and Hebrew were instituted and attended religiously by all refugees who had even a remote chance to be resettled by the Organization. Attendance of at least one such language course was made compulsory for all refugee children, and as a result, IRO had become by 1948 a unique educational institution giving instruction to children and adults of over eighty different nationalities.[43] In these efforts the Organization was generously assisted by a specially trained and equipped teaching staff loaned to IRO by the United Nations Educational, Scientific, and Cultural Organization.[44]

A considerable number of intellectuals, students, and professional people were found among the refugee population by IRO and efforts were made to utilize their abilities during their camp life. In most cases these attempts were not successful because of the great dearth of positions available, and the Organization as a result adopted the policy of encouraging such refugees to train in one or more of the vocational schools. The assistance of the voluntary agencies in the delicate job of "re-educating" the intellectuals and guiding them toward more menial occupations was invaluable to IRO.[45] This policy proved to be a sound one since most of the selection missions visiting the camps placed a premium on manual labor and in some instances went so far as to pronounce a virtual "embargo on brains."[46] Nevertheless, the Organization succeeded in placing a number of students in German and Austrian universities and UNESCO was persuaded to grant a few scholarships for particularly promising young refugees.[47]

In all the programs conducted by the Organization, IRO officials attempted to reduce the inevitable impersonal character of any large-scale operation to a minimum. The IRO staff had been instructed repeatedly that personal attention to the individual refugee was probably the most important single element in his mental rehabilitation. In the case of many refugees long years of concentration camp anonymity could only be neutralized by warm and personal attention. A special counseling program under the aegis of IRO attempted to fill this function although the heaviest burden fell on the voluntary agencies.[48] The complications of refugee life were so numerous that expert and friendly individual attention became necessary to lead the refugee through the labyrinth of difficult situations and decisions confronting him.

In an evaluation of IRO's policies in the seven hundred assembly centers under its jurisdiction, it must first be observed that such treatment of the refugee rehabilitation problem was without precedent. The phenomenon of the DP camp itself was nothing new, but until the advent of IRO such places had been at best congested centers of enforced idleness and semistarvation. This Hades-like quality was no longer characteristic of the average assembly center under IRO. The many efforts of the Organization to turn the centers into useful vestibules for rehabilitation might look rather prosaic on paper, but they added up to the re-human-ization of most of the IRO refugees. If some of the policies – the treatment of intellectuals, for example – fell short of what was desirable, it must be remembered that the Organization did not completely control the essential factors in the solution of a given individual case. It could do its best for a refugee by vocational training, medical treatment, and counseling, but the displaced person's immigration depended upon the laws of particular countries and the rules of their selection missions. Even within these limitations, which the Organization sought constantly to ameliorate, the IRO care and maintenance program in its assembly centers was of the greatest significance for the future favorable absorption of the refugees into the countries of their choice.

REPATRIATION

IRO was well aware that only by permanent reintegration of its refugees into nation-states willing to receive them could it hope to complete its work. In theory, three alternatives presented themselves to IRO: first, repatriation to the refugee's country of origin; second, resettlement in new national homes; and finally, settlement by integration into the local economy. In practice, of course, the IRO constitution bound the Organization to a definite priority policy in favor of the first alternative by the provision that directed IRO to "encourage and assist in every way possible the early return of the displaced persons and refugees to their countries of origin." [49] Despite the fact that the nations which had been mainly responsible for the inclusion of this provision in the IRO constitution had refused to join the Organization, the General Council felt in duty bound to honor the directive. The attitude of most of the delegates to the General Council toward this decision is reflected in a statement by the representative from the United Kingdom: "Well, after all, provided one is not forced to go there, there is no place like home." [50]

The main energy of the Organization upon its inception was therefore directed toward the encouragement of repatriation. A sizable portion of the IRO budget had been set aside for the three months' supply of food which the U.S.S.R. and Yugoslavia had insisted be issued to all repatriates. However, upon attempting to purchase the food rations from the United States military authorities, the Organization found that the cost would be far higher than originally anticipated and a practical compromise was agreed upon. It was decided to furnish every refugee returning to his homeland with a parcel containing approximately twenty days' supply of food to tide him over the period immediately following his return.[51]

The efficacy of the food rations as an incentive to return was negligible. Even before IRO began operations the UNRRA policy of granting a two months' food supply to all repatriates had begun to lose its effect because of the steadily increasing reluctance of refugees to return to countries where Communist regimes were in power. No abrupt change in repatriation statistics was observable after the inception of IRO: 12,000 refugees were repatriated in January 1947 under UNRRA auspices and 10,000 in July under the new IRO policy of reduced ration incentives.[52] After the close of the year, the monthly repatriation figures dropped sharply and never again exceeded 3500 refugees.[53]

As time went on and the political atmosphere between East and West increased in tension, the Organization found greater and greater resistance on the part of its refugees to repatriation. The reasons given were largely political. Repatriates did not wish to submit to the totalitarian regimes established under Soviet leadership and feared possible persecution by them. Actual or possible presence of Soviet troops in their home country, the increasing power of security police, gradual nationalization of land and industry, the way in which elections were conducted, lack of religious freedom — all acted as deterrents to repatriation. Also, many a refugee was reluctant to return to an area whose boundaries had been changed, thus changing his nationality from that held before his deportation or displacement to Germany. The correlation between the monthly repatriation statistics and the deteriorating international situation was quite evident to IRO officials. When Stanislaus Mikolajczyk was expelled from the Polish government, repatriation figures sank considerably, and after the Communist coup in Czechoslovakia they were reduced to a trickle.[54]

When the food incentive was recognized as inadequate and repatriation threatened to come to a complete standstill, a campaign was launched by IRO to develop among the refugee population a "state of mind favorable to repatriation." [55] Extra clothing was issued to repatriating refugees and it was suggested that the Organization, through liaison offices maintained in the countries of origin, should provide material assistance to the newcomers for a period of six months.[56] The latter was never put into effect for financial reasons, but it is questionable if this promise of assistance would have influenced repatriation to any considerable extent. It must be remembered that a refugee's decision to go home was indeed a crucial one. While in the case of resettlement, a refugee was always able to leave his new country if his adjustment was not a satisfactory one, a decision to repatriate was final. Each refugee was aware that, once his decision to return was made, there would be little possibility of leaving his country thereafter.

Part of the Organization's campaign to increase the rate of repatriation was the dissemination of information to the refugees about their home countries. Although the constitution had provided for distributing objective and unbiased material, the fact that most of the printed matter about the countries of origin was, naturally enough, prepared by the Eastern governments prevented an accurate total impression. The constitutional provision for "freedom of information" [57] allowed much material of a frankly propagandistic nature to enter the assembly centers. The Polish government, for example, under the auspices of IRO, provided more than 600,000 printed leaflets and documents among which the most effective was the *Repatriant*.[58] However, it is doubtful whether the efforts made by the Organization to create nostalgia among the refugees for their home countries met with success. Frankly biased films showing conditions in Poland were received with great skepticism and disbelief, although familiar scenes recognized by the refugees frequently caused outbursts of emotion.[59] Another part of the program, the dispatch of delegations of refugees to their home countries and return visits by repatriated refugees, was discontinued by the Organization because of adverse effects upon repatriation morale.[60]

The Organization dealt rather severely with refugees who attempted to impede repatriation movements by openly hostile acts or excessively aggressive propaganda techniques. Segregation of such offenders was usually the mildest penalty, and in most cases involving physical violence the refugee concerned was stricken from the Organization's eligibility list. On the whole, however, peaceful suasion against repatriation was freely permitted in the assembly centers.

IRO encouraged visits from representatives of the Eastern governments to the assembly centers. Such repatriation missions were usually composed of military personnel giving impassioned speeches in favor of return. When these missions first visited the DP camps, the representatives were greeted eagerly and showered with factual questions by the refugees. However, it soon became apparent that the main function of these repatriation officers was not the dissemination of information, but the indoctrination of the refugees with political propaganda. Soon the missions became extremely unpopular and far from contributing to the rate of repatriation, actually had to be protected from outbursts of violence against them by the camp population. Finally, the situation became so intolerable that the Soviet Repatriation Mission was ordered to leave the United States zone of Germany by the American occupation authorities.[61] The British followed suit soon afterward and by late 1949 all repatriation officers had disappeared from IRO assembly centers.[62] The Eastern governments replied to this move by stating that "nothing better could have been expected from an Organization dedicated to the protection of traitors [IRO]." [63]

Until 1949, IRO maintained liaison offices in Poland, Yugoslavia, and Czechoslovakia. These small IRO missions were tolerated by the Eastern governments "as long as there was actual evidence that IRO was assisting in the return of refugees." [64] The main function of these three offices was to help the returning refugee with his initial adjustment problems. Most of the work involved was strictly routine and even it was discontinued with the final expulsion of all three missions when they were informed that "their activities failed to achieve the expected results." [65] The closing of the IRO missions in the countries of origin was seen by IRO officials as a retaliation measure following the expulsion of the Eastern repatriation missions from the refugee assembly centers. The rupture severed the last remaining contact between IRO and the coutries of origin.

In the last analysis, repatriation did not prove even a partial solution. During its lifetime the Organization repatriated 72,834 refugees, a meager 5 per cent of the total number of displaced persons registered with IRO.[66] A great amount of energy was expended by the Organization in adhering to the constitutional provision defining repatriation as its primary responsibility, but to little avail. It is possible, but improbable, that budgetary considerations motivated these efforts. Although it was evident to IRO officials that the cost of repatriation per refugee was but a fraction of the cost of resettlement, this argument never appeared in the discussions of the General Council. It seems that the Organization was convinced of the inherent superiority of repatriation as a solution, provided freedom of choice was permitted. However, when resistance to repatriation reached such a degree that the Organization began to fear for the welfare of its refugees and when the countries of origin themselves exhibited a slackening of interest, IRO reoriented its policy completely.[67] In short, when the Organization found itself confronted with a situation totally different from the one faced at the time of its birth, it met the new challenge in a pragmatic and realistic manner. Through a multiplicity of programs ranging from the satisfaction of physical needs to intensive training of the mind, the refugee assembly centers had become more than mere "camps for persons, asocial and unemployed, who had become superfluous and bothersome,"[68] and the majority of the uprooted were ready, when the time was ripe, for the first organized mass resettlement of refugees in history. That time came when the Organization, untrammeled by the dead hand of the countries of origin and encouraged by increasingly positive attitudes in many nations of potential resettlement, directed its energies westward and across the sea.

8

New Horizons

> "Say not the struggle naught availeth,
> The labor and the wounds are vain
> The enemy faints not nor faileth,
> And as things have been, they remain . . .
>
> And not by eastern windows only,
> When daylight comes, comes in the light;
> In front the sun climbs slow, how slowly,
> But westward, look, the land is bright!"
>
> ARTHUR HUGH CLOUGH

RESETTLEMENT IN EUROPE

The absence of the Soviet Union and its satellites from the policy organ of the International Refugee Organization made it possible for IRO to meet the challenge of the hour. Although the basic document of the Organization had clearly stipulated the primacy of repatriation, resettlement had been left open as a possible alternative over the vigorous protests of the Eastern governments, and by the end of 1947, it had become abundantly clear that resettlement for over a million refugees was to be the major responsibility of IRO. In assuming this function, IRO became the first international organization devoted to the mass re-establishment of refugees.

When the policy shift toward resettlement was in process of crystallization, most IRO officials envisaged a solution of the refugee problem within the context of the European continent. A minority of ambitious staff officers dared to consider major overseas operations, but in view of rather unfavorable tentative reactions from the American, Australian, and Canadian governments, a concentrated effort was made to persuade western European governments to open their doors to IRO refugees. The refugees themselves, except for the Jews, who desired to migrate to Palestine, showed little enthusiasm for overseas resettlement early in the life of the Organization because of a reluctance to sever all connections irrevocably with their country of origin. Most of the refugees were still hoping for a change of governments in the Eastern countries which would permit them to return without fear of retribution. Some of the displaced persons did not hide their desire to contribute to the fall of the Communist regimes if at all possible.[1] In almost all cases, this ambivalence – love of country and hatred of the existent regime – effectively prevented the refugees from deciding to place a vast ocean between themselves and their native land.

In its negotiations to provide resettlement opportunities in Europe, IRO was able to build upon some groundwork already prepared by the Inter-Governmental Committee for Refugees. Before the IGCR was absorbed by IRO, it had opened negotiations with several European countries regarding the admission of refugees as manual laborers.[2] By the time IRO took over, prospects for resettlement had brightened considerably because of the postwar shortage of manpower and the need for reconstruction in most western European countries. This development placed the Organization in a favorable bargaining position *vis-à-vis* countries of potential immigration, a factor of which the IRO General Council was quite aware and which it attempted to exploit as much as possible.

Although the Organization attempted to outline basic policy principles which were to govern its resettlement negotiations, the unprecedented nature of the operation made it almost impossible to lay down specific rules to be followed throughout. In all its agreements with recipient countries, IRO tried to obtain for its wards as favorable conditions for admittance as possible. However, flexibility again was the keynote of the operation and policies were tested and shaped in accordance with constantly varying circumstances and trends.

The United Kingdom. The first country to conclude a resettlement agreement with IRO was the United Kingdom. Asylum had already been given by Britain to about 200,000 members of the Polish Army who had been stranded on British territory and had refused to return to Poland. This contingent of troops, known as the "Anders Army" or the "Polish Resettlement Corps," had been resettled in 1946 throughout the British Empire by its Ministry of Labour without the assistance of the IGCR.[3] Because of the good impression made by these first postwar refugee resettlers in Britain, opinion was favorable in Parliament toward an agreement with IRO. The Organization promptly concluded a trial agreement allowing the admission of 2500 Baltic refugees to the United Kingdom.[4]

This first formal accord between IRO and a country of resettlement did not enjoy the enthusiastic approval of the Organization. The scheme, known as "Balt Cygnet," allowed only for the admission of single refugees of Baltic origin and the General Council feared that the restrictive nature of the agreement might set an undesirable precedent for those to follow.[5] However, upon the assurances of the British government that its admission policy would be liberalized and expanded if the re-establishment of these first 2500 refugees as manual laborers proved successful, the Organization gave its blessing to the enterprise.

Fortunately, the most optimistic hopes of IRO officials came true when the British government in the summer of 1947 announced its great satisfaction with the "Balt Cygnet" operation and declared its readiness to embark upon a much more extensive resettlement program. Accordingly, the British House of Commons in early 1948 passed a measure granting admission to 50,000 single refugees for purposes of manual labor.[6] The scheme, publicized as "Westward Ho," applied to all three Western zones of Germany and Austria. No restrictive stipulation was made by the British authorities with regard to nationality or religion, but the refugees had to be unmarried and were recruited exclusively for purposes of manual labor.[7] The Organization recognized the United Kingdom's urgent need for reconstruction workers, but objected to the British government's rejection of married refugees. IRO officials pointed out that emigration of refugees in "whole economic units" would cushion the shock of initial adjustment and that, generally speaking, the economic value and productivity of married workers would be somewhat higher than that of unmarried refugees. The British government recognized the objections of IRO and stated that only lack of adequate housing facilities prevented the admission of family groups. The British delegate promised that, as soon as accommodations were available, dependents would be allowed to follow. In the meantime, only single men for factory work and single women for employment in textile industries could be admitted.[8]

Immediately after the signatures of the two contracting parties had been affixed to the agreement, large numbers of refugees began to trek toward the British islands. IRO assisted in the transportation of 50,000 refugees under the "Westward Ho" scheme, most of them arriving during the course of 1948.[9] It was part of the agreement that every refugee had to contract to undertake only employment selected by the Ministry of Labour and that the place of employment might be changed only with the consent of that Ministry.[10] Many refugees found this stipulation unbearably harsh and as a result of an increasing number of returns to IRO camps, these restrictions were gradually lifted by the British government. Finally, after the quota of 50,000 refugees originally agreed upon had been filled, a new agreement reduced the compulsory work contract period from two years to one, after which time the refugee was free to do as he pleased.[11] Also, in accordance with the promise given, dependents of the refugees within a very narrow degree of relationship were permitted to follow. According to the terms of both agreements, all refugees admitted were eligible for British citizenship after a period of five years provided the conditions of the work contract as set forth by the government had been carried out faithfully.[12] It was an integral part of IRO's policy to encourage naturalization procedures as rapidly as possible since only through the acquisition of a new citizenship could refugee status be effectively terminated.

Of a total of 81,000 displaced persons admitted under the two agreements, the great majority made a very favorable adjustment in the United Kingdom. Only 4000 insisted upon returning to Germany and Austria and the majority of these were people who had left behind dependents.[13] A small minority found the conditions of work too harsh and preferred continued refugee status to paying the price for British citizenship. With regard to returnees, the Organization adopted a rather strict policy of granting no further resettlement opportunities unless "extreme and unjustifiable hardship" could be proved by the refugee. In order to clarify this position, a memorandum was issued by IRO and distributed to refugees throughout the United Kingdom,[14] but it seemed to have no visible effect upon the number of refugees returning. Evidently those few who did go back to Germany and Austria found their maladjustments so intolerable that the factor of continued IRO eligibility hardly entered into the decision. Altogether the returnees amounted to only 5 per cent of the total number of refugees resettled in the United Kingdom.[15]

The British government was so pleased with the settlement schemes that it liberalized its conditions of admission further and decided to allow the entrance of 40,000 Polish families, mostly dependents of members of the "Anders Army" who were scattered throughout the British isles.[16] These families were widely dispersed throughout IRO assembly centers and a few thousand were located in Middle Eastern camps. However, through an efficient operation (nicknamed "Pole Jump" by IRO officials) the dependents of the Polish Resettlement Corps members were quickly concentrated and transported to the United Kingdom by the Organization.

Although the conditions of admission prescribed by the British government had been correctly judged as somewhat harsh by IRO, the Organization had considered it advisable to sign the agreement in order to break the ice blocking the paths of resettlement to other countries. The gamble was won by IRO when the British government considerably liberalized its immigration conditions. To the British government goes the credit of having been the first nation to grant asylum to large numbers of refugees in the postwar world. Not only did the British economy profit greatly from the influx of additional workers which it badly needed, but the British example set a pattern which, although defective in some ways, broke down much of the initial resistance of many countries to refugee immigration.

Belgium. An important legacy left to IRO by the IGCR was the opening of negotiations with Belgium. In fact, a tentative agreement had been concluded between the Inter-Governmental Committee and the Belgian government regarding the admission of an indefinite number of refugees to Belgium as miners.[17] The encouraging example of the British experiment, and the fact that Belgium, which had suffered grievously during the war, was sorely in need of manpower, disposed the Belgian government favorably and an agreement was concluded with IRO on 11 June 1948.[18] Again, as in the British precedent, the Belgian government exacted a price for its permanent asylum: it agreed to admit as manual laborers 50,000 refugees who had to contract for a two-year period of work in coal mines designated by the government.[19] Belgium, in turn, guaranteed equal working conditions for the refugees, the right to social security benefits, and Belgian citizenship after a period of five years. After the expiration of the two-year contract, the refugees were allowed to follow any occupation they chose to adopt. No nationality restrictions were included in the agreement and although preference was given to single migrants, family units were also deemed eligible.[20]

The Belgian scheme, on the whole, was a failure. Although the agreement contained very similar provisions to those in the agreement with the United Kingdom, the Belgian government adhered rigidly to the conditions of the contract. When the British found that the two-year work contracts were the cause of much hardship, the enforcement of that provision was watered down considerably in practice. The Belgian government, on the other hand, did not reduce the two-year term of indentured servitude, and furthermore the conditions in most of the mines to which refugees had been assigned were very unsatisfactory. It became obvious that the Belgian government had reserved the most difficult areas of mining operations for the refugee workers.[21] Belgian selection missions were so eager to recruit workers that medical standards often erred on the side of liberality whereas the British criteria had been extremely high. Many weak, aged, and infirm persons, and many others who were physically or mentally unable to perform this hard and unpleasant work, agreed to go to Belgium for lack of other resettlement opportunities. The result was that recruitment of refugees to Belgium became more and more difficult as the word spread, and a considerable percentage of the resettled refugees wanted to leave Belgium. By the end of 1948, 20 per cent of the 22,000 refugees resettled in Belgium voiced a strong desire to return to IRO assembly centers in Germany and Austria.[22] This began to pose a serious policy problem for the Organization.

Whereas it had been relatively easy to establish in the British experiment that the desire to return on the part of some refugees was not due to the culpability of either IRO or the British government, the case was somewhat less clear in the Belgian example. Clearly, the Belgian government had not kept some of its promises of "equal working facilities" for the refugee workers. By implication, IRO carried part of the guilt since it had been a party to the agreement. A cleavage emerged in the General Council on the question of whether returning refugees from Belgium should be re-eligible for IRO assistance or whether IRO should categorically refuse to resettle a refugee twice. A decision was postponed for the time being while the Organization attempted to persuade the Belgian authorities to improve living and working conditions for the refugees as well as to relax some of the most stringent provisions of the work contracts. Although a few minor steps were taken by the government in response to these requests, the total picture remained unchanged, and IRO was faced squarely with a decision which would become a precedent for the future.

A conscientious course was adopted by the Organization, which refused to attempt a blanket solution of the problem. The case of every returning refugee was considered on its merits and if the cause of return was deemed "unreasonable," no further IRO assistance was given him.[23] If, on the other hand, the Organization decided that the behavior of the Belgian government in a particular case had been wanting, the services of the IRO to that refugee were not denied. In case of negative decisions, each refugee had recourse to the semi-judicial Eligibility Review Board which would then serve as a court of appeal.[24] By this meticulous procedure it was determined that the great majority of the returning refugees had valid reasons for leaving the Belgian mines and they were reinstated in IRO assembly centers.[25] About one thousand refugees who were refused renewed IRO status complained bitterly and with some justification that they who had had to earn their living in discomfort and had aided the Belgian economy should now be penalized at the expense of others who had in the meantime consumed the bread of charity.[26] But the Organization decided that each individual act of resettlement was final and that only exceptional circumstances would warrant a second opportunity.[27] In principle this was probably the only course IRO could adopt since too lax a policy might easily have resulted in chaos. The excessive rigidity that might have resulted from this policy was avoided to some extent by the personalized approach that characterized all aspects of the Organization's operations.

The contrast between the British success and the Belgian failure was instructive to IRO officials. It showed how a flexible and a rigid application of essentially similar agreements could render almost diametrically opposite results. It also brought home painfully to IRO officials the fact that the Organization had but little control over the refugees once they had entered the territory of a sovereign state. And perhaps most important, the Belgian failure began to convince the members of the IRO General Council that a permanent solution of the refugee problem could be found only through overseas migration.

Other European Countries. Several other agreements were signed between the Organization and European countries, most notably with France, Sweden, and Turkey. The French scheme was patterned largely after the Belgian precedent and allowed the entry of 40,000 refugees as miners and agricultural workers.[28] No nationality restrictions were stipulated and IRO succeeded in persuading the French government to admit family groups provided the family head agreed to work for a two-year period as a miner or agricultural worker. Although contract conditions were not as rigidly enforced as in Belgium, working conditions in the French mines were little better than those in the neighboring country. While the Belgian experience enabled both IRO officials and the French government to avoid some of the crass mistakes committed in the past, the scheme nevertheless was hardly successful, partly because of an increasing reluctance of the refugees to go into mining, and partly owing to the growing attraction of overseas resettlement. Approximately 30,000 refugees found a new home in France and a further 5000 subsequently accepted employment offers by the French government in Morocco, Tunisia, and French Guiana.[29]

An offer by the Swedish government to accept 10,000 single Baltic refugees found little favor because of its restrictive clauses and only 4330 displaced persons decided to re-establish themselves in that Scandinavian country.[30]

Perhaps the most significant agreement between the Organization and a European power was that signed with the Turkish government. Among the million refugees under IRO jurisdiction there existed, despite all national differences, one basic cultural unity: the Judeo-Christian heritage. Only a small minority of Moslems, about 3000 Albanians and Yugoslavs, were outside this bond. While determined not to return to their homelands now dominated by Communist governments, these people were equally reluctant to seek resettlement in traditionally Christian societies. Realizing their plight, the Organization approached the Turkish government and requested it to permit resettlement on its territory of the Moslem refugees. The Organization was well pleased when the Turkish government declared itself ready to admit all such refugees irrespective of sex, marital status, health, or profession.[31] When IRO followed up its advantage and negotiated for favorable naturalization conditions, the Turkish authorities caused a sensation in Geneva by announcing to IRO officials that Turkish nationality with all attendant rights would be conferred upon the refugees immediately after their arrival on Turkish territory.[32]

The Turkish scheme was probably the most humane of the agreements which the Organization concluded with European powers. Although only 2358 refugees were actually resettled in Turkey,[33] it must be remembered that the success of resettlement cannot be measured solely in quantitative terms. The generosity of the Turkish government, which laid down no restrictions, but showed understanding for the plight of its co-religionists, was lauded by IRO's director-general. Unlike many other governments, the Turkish authorities admitted that every community including a refugee community had its dependents, its sick, and its infirm and that in the long run it was neither humane nor wise economics to break up these family units by attempting to "skim the cream." In fact, in the report submitted by the Turkish government to the director-general in March 1950, the government of Turkey "was pleased to report the successful integration of the overwhelming majority of IRO refugees into the life of the Turkish Republic." [34]

The exemplary behavior of Turkey marked the conclusion of mass refugee resettlement on the European continent. The steadily deteriorating international situation, the ousting of Stanislaus Mikolajczyk from the Polish government, and the Communist coup in Czechoslovakia seemed to extinguish in most refugees the last hope of ever being able to return. Most were now ready to sever irrevocably the bond which held them to their homeland by placing between it and themselves a symbol of permanent divorce — the ocean. To reinforce this trend, many overseas governments were more favorably disposed toward refugee immigration than they had been at IRO's inception. A total resettlement of 170,000 refugees in European countries was, on the whole, a creditable achievement and this lesson was not lost upon many countries overseas. In addition, propaganda efforts by IRO, coupled with the need for manpower in order to exploit vast, still underdeveloped areas in the Western hemisphere, began to place refugee immigration in a favorable light. By early 1948, the stage was set for IRO's greatest responsibility — overseas migration.

OVERSEAS RESETTLEMENT

Australia and New Zealand. The Organization was thoroughly attuned to the prevailing desires of its refugee population and when the ranks of those wishing to emigrate overseas began to swell, the IRO Department of Public Information undertook a vigorous "selling" campaign for the refugees. Hundreds of thousands of pamphlets were circulated to overseas countries by the Organization, IRO officials went on extended lecture tours, films were produced and widely shown, radio time was bought, and contacts were made with countries of potential resettlement. The primary efforts of the Organization were directed toward breaking down long-standing stereotypes of DP's held by many persons otherwise friendly to immigration. IRO held a trump card in the successful resettlement experiment in the United Kingdom which had made a deep impression throughout the British Commonwealth. IRO was able, on the strength of the British precedent, to dispel many common misconceptions about refugees such as their alleged subversive tendencies, economic unproductivity, unassimilability, and poor state of health. The Organization's intensive efforts were rewarded when Australia, encouraged by the British example, declared herself willing to admit up to 100,000 IRO refugees.[35]

The Australian Parliament decided to pattern its admissions policy after the initial British "Balt Cygnet" scheme. It was widely contended that the only justification for refugee immigration would be their "economic value" in the exploitation of the vast inner regions of the Australian continent. It was also deemed desirable to preserve the essentially Anglo-Saxon character of the Dominion by limiting the admission of refugees to those from northern Europe, preferably the Baltic countries. Although preference would be given to single refugees, family groups would not be totally excluded.

While the Organization was pleased to receive its first concrete offer from an overseas country, it was not particularly happy with the substance of the proposals. During protracted negotiations, IRO attempted to break down the severe nationality restriction, and finally succeeded in securing the admission of some non-Baltic refugees.[36] However, it could do nothing to mitigate the severity of the contractual agreement on which the Australian government insisted, namely a compulsory two-year term of government-designated labor as the price for Australian citizenship after five years. Finally, the agreement stipulating the admission of 100,000 refugees to Australia was signed with some misgivings by the Organization in March 1948.[37]

The Australian government promptly sent selection missions to the many European IRO assembly centers and even dispatched some to the Near East and to the Philippines. In choosing eligible refugees, the selection missions made little effort to disguise the strictly utilitarian purposes for which the refugees were recruited. Strong preference was given to single male displaced persons of Baltic origin, and there was a noticeable emphasis on seeming fitness for heavy manual labor. Although the agreement with the Organization did not include a stipulation granting preference to Baltic refugees, it quickly became clear to IRO officials that they were, in fact, at the mercy of the selection missions. The Australian officers seemed to enjoy much discretionary power and made numerous apparently arbitrary decisions concerning eligibility. Although refugees of other nationalities were accepted in small numbers, the overwhelming majority consisted of nationals of the Baltic states.[38]

Despite these rigid conditions, the Australian scheme proved extremely popular with the refugees. Despairing of ever being able to return home, disillusioned with conditions in western Europe, fearful of an indefinite prolongation of their refugee status, most of the displaced persons grabbed eagerly at the chance to emigrate to Australia. Only lack of shipping slowed movements to the new continent and, as IRO's fleet grew to meet the challenge, ever greater numbers of refugees made the long voyage to Australia. The government, very pleased with the initial adjustment of the first 50,000 refugees, announced to IRO that it was willing to admit a further 100,000 to its shores.[39]

The Organization now requested a liberalization of the admissions criteria. After repeated and often somewhat heated protestations to the Australian government, the latter agreed to admit all nationalities indiscriminately, to raise the age limit of admissible refugees to fifty years, and to admit families with more than two children.[40] However, the government remained adamant on a continuation of the two-year work contract clause.

With the new agreement signed, immigration continued steadily, but an increasing number of disturbing reports from refugees in Australia began to worry IRO officials. It was learned that most of the refugees were employed in unattractive types of work, such as construction work in the desert and road building. There was much dissatisfaction and some despair, but the hope for freedom of movement at the end of the two-year labor contract kept most refugees in Australia. This hope was dispelled for many refugees when they discovered at the end of their contract periods that intensive trade union opposition prevented them from securing more attractive employment or entrance into one of the professions. A typical letter from a refugee in Australia to IRO contained the following striking paragraph: "It seems almost impossible to get a respectable job here even after expiration of the government contract. And I am afraid that even Australian nationality will only give us a kind of second class citizenship."[41] By 1950, the program had tapered off, partly because of unfavorable reports to refugees in the assembly centers from those who had emigrated to Australia, and partly because of competing offers of a more attractive nature from other countries.

When IRO had finally resettled 182,159 of its refugees on the Australian continent,[42] it was unanimously agreed that the British Dominion had exacted a severe price for the conferral of its citizenship. The Australian experience developed a kind of cynicism in IRO officials who were from then on genuinely surprised if other than strictly economic reasons motivated a given country to send its selection missions to the Organization's assembly centers. IRO realized, of course, that it had to choose between defective agreements or none at all. And preferring unsatisfactory contracts to an indefinite refugee status for its wards, the Organization did all in its power to eliminate some of the most glaring defects from the stipulated agreements.

When Australia's little island neighbor, New Zealand, noticed the favorable effects of refugee immigration, it offered to open its doors to 5000 of IRO's refugees under conditions similar to those laid down by the Australian government.[43] However, IRO was successful in eliminating all the objectionable clauses in the New Zealand offer with the result that 4837 DP's—including all dependents—of mixed nationalities, found a haven in New Zealand.[44] Only the smallness of the islands prevented the government from admitting a greater number of the people whom it called "excellent potential citizens."[45] IRO officials were proud of their success in turning the New Zealand contract into a model agreement, and the director-general announced publicly that he hoped all other potential refugee-receiving countries would pattern their agreements after the "generous terms" of the New Zealand government.[46]

The wide divergence between the policies of these neighboring countries, both members of the British Commonwealth, caused much speculation in IRO circles. It was widely believed that the small number admitted to New Zealand made generous terms easier to adopt. However, the proportionate refugee influx into New Zealand was equal to that of Australia. At any rate IRO's success in the New Zealand venture showed that its powers of persuasion as an international organization could have real effect upon the policies of sovereign governments.

Canada. Encouraged by its success with the New Zealand government, the Organization in its negotiations with Canada attempted to secure the most favorable conditions possible. Although tentative negotiations with the IGCR had already come close to agreement on immigration criteria, IRO found the conditions too stringent and after a series of protracted conferences the final agreement with the Canadian government stipulated the entrance of 100,000 refugees as manual laborers irrespective of nationality or religion or marital status.[47] Upon the insistence of the Organization, the Canadian government renounced its original plan of a two-year labor contract patterned after the British precedent, and contented itself with placing definite "orders" with the IRO to fill the labor needs of that vast and underpopulated country.

Although the "work orders" placed by Canada were mostly for heavy manual laborers, such as hard-rock miners and construction and track workers, there was no legal compulsion to stay at the job if it caused undue hardship to the refugee.[48] The role of the Organization in the Canadian venture became essentially that of a huge employment agency. Every month, IRO officials received quotas for twenty different types of labor from the Canadian Department of Labour which the Organization then filled as rapidly as possible. No attempt was made to separate family groups provided the breadwinner was in one of the work categories. However, few of these opportunities included any of the intellectual or professional occupations and no amount of protest by the Organization was able to modify this one aspect of Canadian refugee policy.

The actual process of resettlement in Canada was a very successful one. Largely because of generosity on the part of the Canadian authorities, a great amount of mobility existed among the refugee workers and there were only a few attempts to bind the displaced persons to jobs which seemed to them unbearable. By December of 1949, over 120,000 refugees had settled in the Canadian Dominion and according to the last summary report of the Canadian government, 97 per cent of the settlers had made favorable adjustments; only 3 per cent had turned out to be problem cases.[49] When Canada decided to terminate the program in 1951, the general impression in both IRO and Canadian circles was that the immigration scheme had benefited the Canadian economy enormously while granting rather generous terms to the refugees. The director-general praised the Canadian scheme highly for its humane policy, but regretted the government's avowed "embargo on brains." [50] It was this last problem which began to disturb IRO officials increasingly as the work of the Organization proceeded.

Since organized mass resettlement of refugees was an unprecedented activity, the policy of the Organization had evolved in a pragmatic fashion as the main problems with which it had to grapple became clear. Thus, in carrying out its responsibility for European resettlement and in its agreements with the British Commonwealth countries overseas, IRO learned to apply ever increasing pressure in order to eliminate as many prejudicial stipulations as possible from the contracts signed. Nationality restrictions, marital, age, and health standards, all were progressively relaxed owing to the Organization's efforts. But one factor consistently eluded control, namely the exclusive recruitment by all countries of manual labor. This problem had not been anticipated by IRO, which had in fact expected great demand for specialists and intellectuals, particularly for reconstruction and engineering purposes.[51] Now, for the first time, the Organization became seriously concerned about the possibility of its best people being left behind as undesirable residue. Accordingly IRO set itself to give special attention to this factor in any future agreements which it might negotiate.

Latin America. While the Australian and Canadian operations were in progress, a lively interest in refugee immigration was developing in Latin America. Many Latin American countries had carried on negotiations with the IGCR and it was one of them, the Dominican Republic, which alone had offered mass asylum to the persecuted Jews in Hitler Germany. Ten of the Latin American governments expressed their further interest by signing the IRO constitution although only three of these, Guatemala, the Dominican Republic, and Venezuela, actually ratified the document and contributed to the Organization's operational budget.[52] The Organization began to give its full attention to Latin American countries when it received requests from them for refugee technicians and specialists to be settled in areas not yet exploited. IRO's department of Public Information immediately prepared a brochure, *The Forgotten Elite*, listing the professions (more than a hundred) and various intellectual achievements among the refugee population. This booklet was widely circulated by IRO officials and found a favorable response in many Latin American countries.[53]

In April 1948, the Venezuelan government approached the Organization with a request for a number of refugee engineers and doctors to be settled in the interior of the country. An agreement was drawn up stipulating the admission of 20,000 refugees of all nationalities including a small contingent of 400 specialists.[54] Most of the immigrants were recruited as agricultural laborers and guaranteed employment and mobility by the government.

On the whole, agricultural refugee colonization in Venezuela disappointed the hopes of IRO officials. The completely strange environment and language, the absence of voluntary societies to aid the refugee in his initial adjustment, and an inhospitable climate as well as difficult conditions of work, all made assimilation and integration of the refugees into the Venezuelan economy very difficult. However, the adjustment of the few refugee specialists, the first such group to be resettled under IRO auspices, surpassed all expectations. Not only did the majority of them contribute significantly to the wealth of their new country, but they became the protégés of the government and were given special privileges and social and economic benefits.[55] The statement of the IRO mission at Caracas, in evaluating refugee settlement in Venezuela, neatly summed up the situation by reporting that there were but two classes of refugees in Venezuela – those who owned Cadillacs and those who washed them.[56]

Chile, which had also negotiated tentatively with the IGCR and had expressed a desire to absorb refugee intellectuals as early as March 1947, sustained that interest and signed an agreement with IRO in which the government agreed to guarantee placement to 2000 refugee specialists, mostly engineers and technicians.[57] The agreement with Chile stipulated a preference for Baltic refugees and, while the Organization looked askance at this clause, the consideration of resettling professional refugees hitherto almost impossible to re-establish outweighed the restrictive part of the agreement. When the Chilean selection missions began to operate in the IRO assembly centers, it became evident that they had been given instructions to reject refugees of the Jewish faith.[58] In repeated instances, Jewish specialists whose non-Jewish counterparts were eagerly processed by the Chilean personnel were arbitrarily rejected. When IRO officials protested against this policy, they were advised that the terms of the agreement did not preclude a selective religious admissions policy.[59] Finally, 5108 refugees, mostly of Baltic origin, including 2000 engineers and technicians, were resettled in Chile.[60]

Again, as in the case of Venezuela, the overwhelming majority of farmer immigrants made a poor adjustment and a great number of them moved to the cities in search of factory employment. On the other hand, the refugee specialists who had migrated were for the most part eminently successful. The letter of appreciation written by the Chilean government to IRO's director-general,[61] praising the contribution of the refugee engineers, technicians, doctors, and teachers to their new country, was widely circulated in potential refugee-receiving countries in order to stimulate further resettlement of specialists.

The diminutive Dominican Republic, which had made headlines by offering asylum to 100,000 persecuted Jews from Hitler Germany, had continued its negotiations after the war with the IGCR. While President Rafael L. Trujillo's offer in 1939 had come too late for large-scale Jewish immigration because of Hitler's refusal to allow his victims to escape, the IGCR in 1946 had concentrated its efforts upon that little Latin American country. The committee had managed to resettle 1000 Jewish refugees in an agricultural colony near Sosua, an area granted for resettlement purposes by President Trujillo.[62] However, the enterprise did not seem to be blessed with success — water supply, roads, and fertile soil were lacking and an inhospitable climate prevented a favorable adjustment — and the IGCR, after extensive studies, recommended against further colonization of refugees in the Dominican Republic.[63]

IRO agreed with the conclusion of its predecessor organization and, although it was difficult to pass up a generous offer to resettle 100,000 refugees in a farming colony, the Organization decided not to sign an agreement. Only in an hour of emergency, when the Philippine government threatened to evacuate forcibly 2000 refugees to whom it had granted asylum from Communist China, did IRO permit a Dominican selection mission to recruit 800 of the refugees.[64] As events proved, the decision not to resettle large numbers of refugees in the Republic was a wise one, since by 1953 almost all the refugees, who had been fighting great physical hardships and almost insuperable natural obstacles in the arid Sosua region, had given up the attempt and emigrated elsewhere.[65] It is bitterly ironical that the only generous offer to resettle persecuted

Jews was later deemed by international migration experts as the only totally unacceptable one and had to be rejected as a settlement possibility for all refugees.

The largest single refugee-receiving country in Latin America was Argentina. This is of particular interest since no specific agreement had been signed between that country and the Organization. Although Argentina had offered to admit up to 40,000 refugees, it had stipulated as a condition the virtual exclusion of refugees of the Jewish faith.[66] IRO was not willing to sign such an agreement, but it publicized the Argentinian offer throughout its assembly centers. Since the Argentine government did not limit its recruitment to manual laborers, but promised employment mobility to those wishing to emigrate, the scheme proved to be quite popular and 32,712 refugees found new homes in Argentina during the life of IRO.[67] Even though no formal agreement existed, the Organization paid the cost of transportation to the point of the refugee's disembarkation and provided each immigrant with $10 as landing money.

A similar situation prevailed in the case of Brazil, which offered an agreement to the Organization whose terms excluded all Jews and persons of Asiatic origin.[68] Although many protests were made by IRO officials to the Brazilian authorities, the government remained adamant and refused to alter immigration restrictions which had been on the statute books for over three decades. No formal agreement was forthcoming, but individual migration to Brazil proceeded at a rapid pace for reasons similar to those of the Argentinian resettlers. A large contingent of refugee specialists was recruited for engineering purposes and even some university professors found positions at the University of Rio de Janeiro. Finally, in May 1948, the Organization decided to conclude a limited agreement with the Brazilian government covering the admission of 500 specialists.[69] However, the overwhelming majority of refugee immigrants to Brazil went there without the official blessing of the Organization. Because of extensive employment opportunities in both Argentina and Brazil, most of the refugees found the adjustment somewhat easier than in other Latin American countries. Most reports reaching the Organization from these two countries gave favorable accounts of refugee re-establishment.

The only other agreement concluded by the Organization with a Latin American government was that with Paraguay. It is of special interest because it covered the migration of only one particular religious group — Ukrainian Mennonites. These people had been unable to find resettlement opportunities elsewhere because of their strongly pacifistic leanings and the severe secular limitations which their religion imposed upon them. The Paraguay government was the only one which declared itself ready to admit these refugees as agricultural colonists; it even offered to reserve an area of land for them where they could live their separate community life somewhat apart from the tribulations of the modern world. The settlement of 5887 Mennonite refugees was successful and a prosperous enclave of Ukrainians began to flourish in the midst of that Latin American country.[70]

The settlement of over 100,000 IRO refugees in a dozen Latin American countries presented a mixed picture but, on the whole, could be evaluated as a moderate success. Although a heavy premium was placed upon manual labor, a small number of specialists were welcomed to the continent. While these specialists made excellent adjustments, most of the farming refugees did not, and many moved to establish permanent homes in the cities. This they were able to do because of the lenient policy of most of the Latin American governments. Perhaps the only reprehensible characteristic of Latin American refugee policy was the exclusion of Jewish refugees by all these nations except Venezuela and the Dominican Republic. Since the Australian and, to a lesser degree, the Canadian policy had also preferred non-Jewish immigrants, the Organization began to be concerned about the resettlement opportunities of the 200,000 Jewish refugees under IRO jurisdiction. However, the birth of a new state solved this problem.

Israel. For three thousand years, since the Jewish Exodus, the Jews had hoped that they might once more assemble in Palestine, their Promised Land. During Hitler's years of power, the Zionist ideal had gained rapidly in strength since it had become clear to the Jews that in a world of national states their rights as human beings could be effectively guaranteed only by a nation-state. It was contended that if the Jews had had an official spokesman for their cause in the League of Nations, the catastrophe of annihilation might have been averted. However, since immigration into Palestine was regulated by the mandatory power, Great Britain, and was limited to a monthly quota of 1500 Jewish refugees,[71] most of the Jewish population of Europe had been doomed to perish in Hitler's crematoria.

From the beginning of its operation IRO was well aware that the overwhelming majority of its Jewish refugees fervently desired to emigrate to Israel. However, despite repeated appeals by Jewish voluntary agencies and by IRO itself, the British government remained adamant. Only illegal shipments of refugees sponsored by various Jewish organizations were able to enter Palestine and in some cases these were intercepted by the British authorities and quarantined in Cyprus. IRO was careful to support only legal immigration into the territory of the British mandate.[72]

When the independence of the new State of Israel was proclaimed on 15 May 1948, the rejoicing of the Jewish refugees throughout the IRO camps knew no bounds. Fulfilling their most optimistic hopes, the new Israeli government promptly informed the Organization that immigration of all Jewish refugees would be welcomed with no limitations whatsoever.[73] The Organization was only too pleased to see in the offing a solution of its Jewish refugee problem, but then it was suddenly confronted with the outbreak of hostilities between Israeli and Arab troops.

The Israeli government requested the Organization to begin with the transport of Jewish refugees regardless of the war situation. Similarly, Jewish voluntary organizations pleaded with the Organization not to hesitate any longer since the Jewish population in the camps was becoming increasingly restless. The General Council went into emergency session and decided unanimously to adopt a policy which made the Organization extremely unpopular with its Jewish refugees. IRO announced that its task was to sponsor the "genuine resettlement of individuals and families to enable them to lead a normal existence." [74] However, since a state of open warfare existed in Israel, it was inconceivable that "a humanitarian organization should send women and children into a war zone." [75] Similarly, the Organization did not consider it part of its function to send single men to fight as soldiers on either side. Therefore, IRO's policy organ decided that no IRO funds or facilities could be used for the emigration of Jews to Israel until the United Nations Palestine Conciliation Commission should report the restoration of peace in the area.[76]

This principled stand on the part of the Organization was attacked vigorously by most of the Jewish organizations, but it is significant that the nonpolitical character of the decision was recognized and honored even by those who criticized it most heatedly. Two of the most active

Jewish voluntary organizations, the Jewish Agency for Palestine and the American Joint Distribution Committee, then decided to organize and finance the transportation of the refugees themselves. All available shipping space was provided by the Israeli Navy and movements progressed at a rapid pace, tolerated but not aided by the Organization. By April 1949, when finally the Palestine Conciliation Commission declared the question of the support of emigration to Israel as not within its competence,[77] the two Jewish agencies had moved 96,500 Jewish refugees to the Promised Land.[78]

The decision of the Palestine Conciliation Commission not to advise IRO on Jewish emigration to Israel was interpreted by the director-general to mean that conditions had sufficiently improved to warrant a resumption of IRO responsibility.[79] Accordingly, the Organization declared itself ready to share in the task, but found that most of the job had been completed by the two Jewish organizations in the space of one year. Since the operation had almost exhausted the resources of the Jewish agencies and since the Israeli economy was tottering under the strain of unlimited immigration, the IRO General Council considered the question of reimbursement for the work already done. Finally it was decided that a lump sum of $10,250,000 would be paid by IRO to the two Jewish agencies.[80] The figure was based on a calculation of the savings accrued to the Organization owing to the diminished caseload in Germany, Austria, and Italy. The funds were used to facilitate the adjustment of the newcomers to Israel and IRO's generous move went a long way to make the initital hardships of many Jewish refugees easier to bear.

Israel's immigration policy, heartily supported and acclaimed by IRO subsequent to April 1949, was unique in its liberality. Based upon the assumption that unlimited Jewish immigration was the *raison d'être* of the new state, the government tried its utmost to gather in all those Jews who expressed a desire to come to the Promised Land. The young and the old, the healthy and the thousands of crippled and sick concentration camp survivors, men and women of all occupations and professions, streamed toward the shores of the little country. The arrival of every ship laden with Jewish refugees was celebrated as a new triumph. IRO officials could not help but compare Israel's policy with that of other countries which had negotiated agreements with the Organization. The highest tribute paid to any country by IRO's director-general went to Israel: "Almost alone among the nations of the world, Israel has consistently based its immigration policy upon the highest humanitarian ideals. No Jewish refugee has ever been considered too poor, too destitute or too ill to be admitted to Israel."[81]

The total number of IRO's refugees who found a haven in the new state finally reached 132,109.[82] Only the United States and Australia exceeded this figure; proportionate to population, no other country was as generous. But perhaps the greatest triumph was Israel's nonselective, humane immigration policy which made the achievement not only quantitative but qualitative as well.

The United States. The Organization could justifiably look with satisfaction upon the results of its intensive efforts to lower the immigration barriers of most of the potential refugee-receiving countries of the world. By mid-1948, IRO had succeeded in opening the doors of two dozen nations to its wards, but one country, the very nation which had contributed so decisively to the birth of the Organization itself, refused steadfastly to admit more than a small trickle of refugees to its shores.

Since 1924, the United States had adhered to the "quota principle of national origins" in matters of immigration. Under this system, which made no legal distinction between refugees and ordinary immigrants, approximately 150,000 quota numbers were divided annually among the countries of Europe in proportion to the corresponding ethnic components of the United States. Birthplace was the single criterion of quota allocation and a quota number made available to any given country in any given year was declared forfeited at the end of that year if not used. Quota numbers from so-called undersubscribed countries, such as Great Britain, could not be transferred to one of the many oversubscribed nations, with the result that only about half of the theoretical 150,000 immigrants were able to enter the United States each year.[83]

Throughout its existence, the IGCR had urged the American government to liberalize its immigration laws, but to little avail. The intensive efforts of the committee had produced only the so-called Truman Directive, under which the United States President, through an executive order, had made available thousands of Baltic, Polish, and southern European quota numbers which had remained unused during the war years.[84] This order, promulgated in December 1945, was the first American reaction to international pressure. Under the provisions of the Truman Directive, approximately 30,000 immigrants were able to enter the United States, but only about half that number consisted of refugees and displaced persons.[85]

When the International Refugee Organization became seriously concerned about the possibilities of overseas migration as a solution for its refugee problem, it was not unnatural that the Organization turned to the United States. Seen by IRO as a country of practically unlimited immigration opportunities, the United States was inundated during 1947 with a large variety of brochures, pamphlets, films, and radio broadcasts, all sponsored by the Organization in order to "sell" the idea of refugee immigration to the American people. Both IRO officials and the many voluntary organizations in the United States which assisted the Organization in its endeavors realized that much publicity would be necessary since a major liberalization of immigration laws could be effected only by the United States Congress. Accordingly, IRO's Department of Public Information during 1947 and 1948 spent most of its energies upon the American people.

It is interesting to note in this connection that the decision to employ IRO as a "pressure group" was made by its Executive Committee under the Preparatory Commission's broad directive to "encourage resettlement opportunities as widely as possible." [86] George Warren, the United States delegate, voted against such lobbying in the United States, but his negative vote remained the sole dissent.[87] In this instance, the IRO staff, at the initiative of the Executive Committee, came close to operating as an independent body.

The response of the American public surpassed the Organization's expectations. Where indifference and apathy if not hostility had prevailed before, a definite trend became discernible in American popular opinion favoring the passage of special legislation for the immigration of refugees. Many leading magazines and newspapers took up IRO's battle by pointing to the political wisdom and humanitarian necessity of taking in a fair share of the world's refugees. The following editorial comments constituted a fairly representative segment of the American reaction:

> Our fighting men displayed during the war a devotion to human liberty. Their relatives at home felt the same devotion. For Europe's displaced populations the war is not yet triumphant. We can speak more convincingly of freedom everywhere when we have done our fair share – even more than our fair share – to bring real freedom to those who have suffered most.[88]

This newspaper feels that our country can afford to make some limited exceptions in order to help care for people whose plight has too long been on the conscience of the world.[89]

We have exhorted the British to admit a considerable number of them [refugees] to Palestine. Yet we have done nothing on our own account to afford refuge to them here. The failure to practice what we preach ill becomes us and robs our exhortation of all its moral force.[90]

Let Americans prove their concern for free peoples by giving a few of these hapless and hopeless refugees a chance to be free.[91]

At the same time, however, a strong and determined opposition began to form against special refugee legislation. A powerful group in both houses of the American Congress, backed by two determined pressure groups hostile to refugee influx, the American Legion and the Veterans of Foreign Wars, was fighting against any "tinkering with basic American institutions." [92] In addition, a segment of the American press, led by the *Chicago Tribune*, consistently opposed special legislation. The grounds for such opposition comprised racial and generally anti-foreign prejudices as well as the belief that "most refugees were politically subversive elements." [93]

The opposition in Congress based its case squarely and frankly upon a defense of the racial principle of the quota system of national origins. It was argued that, since this principle had been in operation for a quarter of a century, it was *ipso facto* a sound one and should not be changed. The following expressions were typical of the opposition:

It seems to me that the question of racial origins — though I am not a follower of Hitler — there is something to it. The fact still remains that the peoples of Western Europe have made good American citizens. I come from there . . . I believe that possible statistics would show that the Western European races have made the best citizens in America and are more easily made into Americans.[94]

If we scrap the national origins formula, we will in a course of a generation or so, change the ethnic and cultural composition of this Nation. The times are too perilous for us to tinker blindly with our basic institutions.[95]

The advocates of special legislation, including most hyphenated American voluntary agencies and IRO itself, proposed the admission of 400,000 refugees under IRO jurisdiction, with no nationality or religious restrictions.[96] But in the face of the virulent opposition to these suggestions, it seemed for a while during the congressional debates that no refugees at all would be admitted. *Newsweek* opined editorially in early 1948 that "in any case, the United States seems certain to remain closed to all but a minority of those who dream of entering it as a promised land." [97]

Finally, after repeated exhortations by President Truman, a compromise was reached in the Displaced Persons Act of 1948, which became law on 25 June 1948. This piece of legislation provided for the admission to the United States of 205,000 refugees by 30 June 1950 but enumerated certain preferences and priorities. These limitations elicited vehement criticism from the majority of the American public, from IRO, and from President Truman who described the act which he had signed reluctantly as "a pattern of discrimination and intolerance wholly inconsistent with the American sense of justice." [98]

Compromising with the demands of the opposition, the act of 1948 discriminated in favor of immigration from western and northern Europe and, in effect, against Jewish and Catholic refugees. Thus, 40 per cent of all available visas were given to refugees from Esthonia, Latvia, and Lithuania.[99] IRO had informed the legislators repeatedly that its supply of Baltic refugees was nearly exhausted, but to little avail. Furthermore, Congress succeeded in maintaining the national origins principle through a somewhat circuitous device. The quota system was not changed in essence, but quota numbers allocated to the refugees over and above the regular annual quota would in fact be borrowed from quotas for the years ahead, or, as it was appropriately called, "mortgaged." Thus, some quotas under the DP Act were subscribed until the twenty-third century, in theory rendering it impossible for ten future generations of that particular country to send a single immigrant to the United States.[100]

A second restrictive provision in the DP Act required that at least 30 per cent of all refugees admitted to the country must have been engaged in agricultural pursuits previous to emigration and must be guaranteed similar employment upon their arrival in the United States.[101] Again, protestations by IRO to the effect that most of its farmer refugees had already emigrated to other countries, owing to the tardiness of the United States, did nothing to prevent the inclusion of the restrictive clause.

When a specially appointed United States Displaced Persons Commission left for Europe in order to administer the new act in conjunction with IRO, the *New York Times* exclaimed vehemently: "The DP Bill just approved by the Senate is a sorry job. Every liberalizing amendment which would have treated DP's equally as members of the human race was voted down." [102]

IRO officials set to work conscientiously to fulfill the requirements of the DP Act. Under the act every adult or family was required to have a written invitation from a sponsor in the United States in the form of a sworn assurance of adequate housing and a job that would not displace another person, as well as a guarantee that the refugee would not become a public charge.[103] These assurances, or "affidavits," as they came to be called, were supplied by relatives, church groups, civil organizations, and social agencies. It was IRO's responsibility to maintain a constant flow of these guarantees in order that movements could continue as steadily as possible under the restrictive provisions of the act. The collaboration of almost fifty voluntary agencies in the securing of assurances was invaluable to the work of IRO.

However, by mid-1949 it had become evident that there were not enough refugees who met the requirements of the act to fill the quota. Moreover, IRO experienced very great administrative difficulties in setting criteria for "past agricultural employment." Accordingly, the Organization made repeated protestations to the United States government. Both the President and the United States Displaced Persons Commission were in fundamental agreement with the Organization's desire to see the act liberalized and the preferential clauses eliminated.[104] As a result of concerted pressure upon the Congress, a Senate Subcommittee of Relations with International Organizations investigated the possibilities of liberalization. After an extended trip through many of IRO's assembly centers, the subcommittee reported favorably upon the question of amending the DP legislation:

> It is quite manifest that unless the countries of the world, which are able to do so, assume their full responsibility with respect to displaced persons, the IRO may have to continue indefinitely. Accordingly, the subcommittee feels that it is in the interest of the United States to take steps to admit a higher number than are admissible under the Act.[105]

It was evident that physical proximity to the situation and actual contact with the refugees had changed the outlook of many congressmen. Furthermore, the prospect of extending the life of IRO and having to foot two thirds of the bill was repugnant to the legislators. The favorable report by the subcommittee was able to prevail upon the floors of both houses and a substantial liberalization of the original legislation resulted.

In the DP Act as amended on 30 June 1950 the offensive Baltic preference clause and the agricultural priority provision were removed and the total of eligible refugees was raised to 341,000.[106] Of these, 287,000 were under IRO jurisdiction and 54,000 visas were allocated to *Volksdeutsche* refugees not under IRO.[107] Although the number of admissible refugees was increased, the quota system itself remained in force, quota numbers now being "mortgaged" even farther into the future than before. The life of the Displaced Persons Commission was extended to 31 August 1952.[108]

The amended act had hardly become law when the wheels of IRO began to turn with a heretofore unknown velocity. All the resources and energies of the Organization were thrown into the mass movement of refugees to the United States during 1950 and 1951. The Organization developed a regular assembly line system, yet never neglected its personalized approach in dealings with the refugees. It was during this period that IRO commanded the largest civilian fleet in history. Forty vessels flying the IRO flag, a blue life buoy against a white background, ploughed the sea, bound for the Statue of Liberty. There was a special sense of urgency because IRO was scheduled to go out of existence in December 1950. The life of the Organization was subsequently extended for one year, but even so, great speed was necessary if the full quota of refugees was to be processed and admitted to the United States under IRO's auspices. Finally the task was accomplished. By the end of 1951, 328,851 refugees had been admitted as future citizens to the United States.[109]

The results of the American refugee policy were most satisfactory to all but the "irreconcilables" in the American body politic. The United States Displaced Persons Commission called the complete program a successful "Citizens' Foreign Policy" and expressed its appreciation for IRO's contribution to the American culture.[110] The fact that the overwhelming majority of the refugees made a good adjustment to the American scene [111] was attributable partly to the generous policy of the American government in allowing complete social and economic mobility to the displaced persons and partly to the fact that every refugee found enclaves of his own people in the multi-cultural structure of

American society, thus enormously facilitating his acclimatization. The criticism of the opposition, which seemed to believe that a refugee immigrant was by definition guilty until proven innocent, was somewhat weakened in the light of the official records of the Displaced Persons Commission reporting that "not a single person admitted under the DP legislation had to be deported for reasons of security." [112]

THE "HARD CORE"

When IRO's General Council met for its final plenary session in January 1952, it was able to report the resettlement of 1,038,750 refugees in sixty-five different lands.[113] In sheer quantitative terms, this was an unprecedented accomplishment. No organization, national or international, had dared dream in terms of mass overseas migration for refugees prior to the International Refugee Organization. Not even the great prophet of refugees, Fridtjof Nansen, had ever conceived of so bold a venture. But IRO had not been content with an accomplishment measurable in mere numbers and statistics. It had exerted itself unstintingly on behalf of a relatively small group of its wards, those rejected by the selection missions. Two categories of DP's fell into this class of rejected people, officially known as the "hard core."

It was a sad reflection upon the immigration policies of most refugee-receiving countries that intellectuals were given little if any chance for resettlement. It was undeniable that opportunities for refugees to emigrate were inversely proportional to their intellectual achievements. Since "economic value" was primary, chiefly the manual laborers among the refugees found a ready market. IRO was undaunted despite the seeming impossibility of finding a solution for 26,000 refugee intellectuals biding their time in IRO assembly centers.[114] In October 1949, a special Resettlement Placement Service was put into operation by the Organization. This unit collected individual dossiers on each such refugee and then attempted to locate a sponsor for him. Through intensive efforts, most of these people, ranging from doctors to opera singers and engineers, were successfully resettled all over the world and for the most part made valuable contributions to the communities which offered them a new home.[115] Only a highly organized and individualized attack upon the problem could have achieved the results which the Organization was able proudly to record at the end of its operations.

The second part of the "hard core" posed an even more difficult problem for the Organization. They were the sick, the maimed, and the old, those whom the selection missions had rejected for reasons of health. Sometimes a family with excellent chances for resettlement refused to leave an IRO camp because an aged mother would have to be left behind forever. It was for 16,000 such people that IRO officials all over the world sought a haven in which they could find peace and some stability.[116] The French delegate to the IRO General Council expressed the thoughts of most of his colleagues when he commented: "The family is all a refugee has left. Must a family be doomed because it has one infant too many? Has a man a right to one parent, but not to two? Is an amputation like a contagious disease?"[117]

During difficult and protracted negotiations, the Organization was successful in finding resettlement opportunities for some of these unfortunate people on a purely humanitarian basis. When Sweden agreed to accept one hundred blind refugees, and Switzerland declared her willingness to take in two hundred tubercular displaced persons, and Norway gave asylum to fifty aged refugees,[118] the Organization cherished these accomplishments perhaps more than many a large-scale resettlement scheme for healthy refugees, since these achievements made the Organization's success qualitative as well as quantitative.

CONCLUSIONS

Throughout all its resettlement operations, IRO attempted to safeguard and protect the human rights of its refugees. By turning the DP camps into educational centers, the IRO trained the refugees to become useful future citizens. Before actual movement took place, the Organization made sure in its agreements that the recipient country's conditions of immigration met certain minimal standards of human decency and justice. All governments with which the Organization concluded agreements liberalized their conditions during the negotiations although the Organization had no power of enforcement once the refugees had left its assembly centers. In the case of Israel, conditions were already sufficiently generous to be more than satisfactory to the Organization.

Although IRO always attempted to "sell" its wards for as high a price as possible, it recognized the fact that nations exacted a price, sometimes a heavy price, for the bestowal of their citizenship. None knew better than the IRO officials that refugee status could effectively come to an end only with the acquisition of a new nationality. Since the Organization itself could not interminably protect the human rights of its refugees, it sometimes had to compromise with those nation-states which saw in the refugee nothing but an economic asset to be exploited. But the record is a mixed one. If some governments agreed to admit refugees only on purely utilitarian grounds, there were others who offered a haven out of undiluted humanitarian considerations. In all cases, the Organization attempted to show the recipient countries that humanitarianism and economic utility were not necessarily incompatible, that it was in the national interest in the broadest sense to offer homes to the refugees.

In the final analysis, the Organization could not take the place of a nation-state. The IRO passport, though greatly respected, could not guarantee the human rights of a refugee once he had entered a sovereign state. The resettlement operation of IRO, if viewed in perspective, was but the successful functioning of a huge international transport agency dedicated to the endeavor of transferring refugees away from areas where the fundamental human rights of the dignity and inviolability of the individual human being were not recognized, to those areas of the world where such rights were still held in esteem. But the magnitude of the task accomplished bears testimony to the fact that at least a part of the international community showed political wisdom and sufficient social consciousness to gather its resources in a concerted attempt to find new homes for the uprooted throughout the free world.

9

From Many One

"Seldom has so much been accomplished for so many by so few." [1]

POLICY AND ADMINISTRATION OF IRO

THE accomplishments of the International Refugee Organization were due in large degree to the extraordinary unity of purpose prevailing in its policy and administration organs.[2] Since the Eastern countries did not participate in IRO's program, a fundamental harmony on basic policy issues was evident throughout IRO's life. While the differences between East and West sounded the keynote in most United Nations discussions and stamped with a political hue most of the allegedly nonpolitical social and technical agencies, the great majority of the policy discussions of IRO's General Council were notable for their objectivity and constant quest for the greatest benefit to the refugees. When the French delegate declared during one of the last sessions of the General Council that "IRO's policy organ had been but the collective will of the governments of which it consisted," [3] he came rather close to the truth.

Only one major schism on policy was evident among the eighteen member governments of the General Council. While the Continental members of the Organization constantly sought to extend IRO's authority and life, the Anglo-Saxon countries were more interested in curtailing the scope of the Organization. The Continental countries, which constituted the major areas of first asylum for the refugees, were of course eager to relieve themselves of responsibility for the DP's by widening IRO's sway. The Anglo-Saxon nations, on the other hand, especially the United States which shouldered the greatest part of the financial burden, were reluctant to commit themselves to even greater expenditures. This disagreement, prevailing throughout the life of the organization, resulted in parliamentary compromises in most instances, but finally the determined refusal on the part of the United States to contribute further funds to IRO hastened the organization's premature death.

Policy making in the General Council evolved in a pragmatic fashion. The task of the organization was not one for which firm rules could be laid down at the beginning and adhered to consistently thereafter. The refugee problem was in constant flux: new groups of refugees were arriving; the attitudes of national governments were changing; and new methods were made necessary as the work proceeded and the composition of the refugee population changed. The council was continually preoccupied with a mass of current business and on some occasions the need for a policy decision became apparent only when conflicting actions had already been taken in the field. Many policy decisions were taken in haste during an emergency and did not lend themselves to long and thorough staff work. However, the very informality of policy formulation provided a safeguard against disastrously arbitrary decisions and, since the future of human beings was at stake, it was probably wiser to proceed in this tentative way than to make far-reaching mistakes and put them smartly into execution. Roughly speaking, the General Council was guided in its decisions by the following broad principles: assistance to all genuine refugees under IRO jurisdiction, freedom of choice between repatriation and resettlement, and equality of opportunity for each refugee regardless of age, sex, family status, or profession. Within these broad aims, the conscientious efforts of the organization were circumscribed only by the policies of recipient governments, by the budget, and by the short duration of IRO's existence.

The General Council was represented between its semiannual sessions by the Executive Committee of IRO.[4] This body, which never made any important policy decisions without the authorization of the plenary body, consisted of the delegates from Australia, Belgium, Canada, the United States, France, Italy, Norway, the United Kingdom, and Venezuela. These nine states were elected in September 1948 for a period of two years on the basis of their respective contributions to IRO's budget, and were re-elected in 1950.[5] The Executive Committee took the responsibility of putting the resolutions of the General Council into execution, and reported back on the results to its parent body.

However, as time went on, most of the responsibilities of the Executive Committee were taken over by IRO's chief administrative officer, the director-general.

The connection of the Organization with the United Nations was only a tenuous one. The agreement between the United Nations and its specialized agency stipulated a review of the administrative budget, exchange of information, proposal of agenda items, and the exchange of statistical services.[6] When these relatively unimportant items periodically reached the Economic and Social Council and the General Assembly of the United Nations, the suggestions of IRO were always heeded by the two United Nations organs. Only the determined opposition and often vicious criticism of the Organization by the Soviet bloc prevented, in most instances, unanimous approval of IRO's reviewable agenda items. The Soviet bloc, although it had refused to associate itself with the Organization, was quick to condemn its policies from a safe distance. IRO's resettlement program was called a "slave labor enterprise" by the Eastern delegates and its Child Tracing Service was defined as an "outfit of organized kidnappers." [7] A broadcast from Radio Moscow in January 1950 alleged that four hundred American students had been brought by the Organization to Geneva in order to carry out espionage in the "peoples' democracies." [8] The alleged spies turned out to be a few girls from Smith College who visited IRO installations as part of their "finishing" process. The Organization's report to the United Nations considered the Soviet assertion as too ridiculous to be dignified by refutation, although IRO's director-general, a former educator, was inclined to think that Radio Moscow had unwittingly made a valuable contribution to the education in world affairs of the Smith College girls then in Geneva.[9]

The administrative apparatus of the International Refugee Organization was unique among the secretariats of the United Nations' specialized agencies. In the first place, the responsibilities of IRO's staff were essentially operational whereas the functions of the other secretariats were primarily of an administrative and "housekeeping" nature. Perhaps the most significant aspect of these operational responsibilities was control over the largest civilian fleet in the world. As we have already noted, at the peak of IRO's activity forty ships, all but three of them rented from the United States government, plied the seas, carrying refugees to their destinations.[10]

In order to accomplish its huge task, the administrative machinery of the Organization was ten times as large as that of the average United Nations specialized agency and comparable in size to the United Nations Headquarters Secretariat. The hierarchy of IRO's 5600 international civil servants [11] had its apex in the organization's director-general. Although the organization could boast an annual budget three times as large as the United Nations itself and a staff similar in size to that of the parent body, IRO's membership base was the most narrow of all the international organizations affiliated with the United Nations. With a membership of only eighteen nations, IRO was the least universal of the specialized agencies. Thus, IRO was at once the largest and yet, internationally speaking, the narrowest of all United Nations organs.

The conflict between national and international loyalties which constantly plagued the United Nations in theory and in practice never seriously entered into IRO's debates regarding personnel policy. Although every staff member of the organization had "solemnly to swear to exercise . . . the functions entrusted to [him] as a member of the international service of the IRO and . . . not to seek or accept instructions from any government," [12] it was implicitly understood by the fathers of the constitution that IRO's director-general would have to be of American nationality. Since the United States contributed by far the largest amount to the Organization's budget, a "national viewpoint" of the director-general was almost a condition of appointment, as appears from the following testimony before a subcommittee of the American House of Representatives:

Representative Javits: "Is it a fact that no official would be in a position to either be designated or accept such a designation [the director generalship of IRO] without the approval of General Marshall [then Secretary of State]?"
Assistant Secretary of State Hilldring: "That is correct, Sir."
Representative Javits: "That should seem to be a pretty good guaranty of the man's caliber." [13]

The three directors-general at the helm of the organization during its lifetime were all American citizens of the highest caliber, excellent administrators and men of profound humanism. IRO's first chief administrator was J. Arthur Altmayer, who had been chairman of the Federal Security Agency and had also been active in the work of the Social Commission of the United Nations' Economic and Social Council. Mr.

Altmayer left, however, a few months after IRO's Preparatory Commission was established, and the post of director-general was then filled by William H. Tuck. The new incumbent had had extensive experience with refugee work as a member of the Hoover Commission in Belgium during World War I and had been active in the international public service ever since. Under him, the Organization geared itself for its biggest job, mass overseas resettlement, but in June 1949 Mr. Tuck, who had won the respect and good will of all of IRO's member nations, felt that it was time to have a younger and fresher man at the helm. Accordingly, upon his resignation, a man not yet forty years old took over IRO's leadership. J. Donald Kingsley's contribution to IRO's work was mainly that of a brilliant and efficient administrator. Mr. Kingsley had taught public administration at Syracuse University, had occupied responsible positions in the American government, and was thus eminently well qualified for the huge task awaiting him. Through a reorganization of IRO on a functional basis, the new director-general was able to increase the organization's efficiency beyond all expectations.[14]

Although the only formal authority granted the director-general was that of chief administrator,[15] in practice he frequently came to fill the function of a policy adviser on relatively minor issues.

Mr. Kingsley was the only one of IRO's three directors-general who attempted to make suggestions concerning basic policy to the General Council. It is perhaps significant that toward the end of the Organization's existence, Mr. Kingsley, although himself an American, came out more and more strongly against the United States' position favoring the dissolution of the Organization.[16] On repeated occasions, IRO's last director-general recommended an extension of the Organization's life.[17] In sum, it may be said that the three chief administrators of the organization during their incumbency always considered their actions in terms of the best interests of the refugee community. In the case of Mr. Kingsley, the conflicting loyalties to his own country and to the international civil service were resolved in favor of the latter by placing first the interest of the refugees as he conceived it.

The composition of IRO's staff was the direct responsibility of the director-general. Guided by the constitutional provisions that in the choice of personnel the paramount considerations should be to secure the highest standards of efficiency, competence, and integrity and that recruitment should be spread over an appropriate geographical basis,

IRO's directors-general sought to gather a truly international staff.[18] Mr. Altmayer had felt that "it would be a crime to deprive refugees and displaced persons of the assistance and care of the experienced personnel of the IGCR and of UNRRA" and had placed on IRO's payroll approximately 50 per cent of the staffs of the two predecessor organizations.[19] Many of the transferred officials had become acknowledged experts in their specialized fields, and it was highly desirable to keep them as permanent members of IRO's staff. The Organization's personnel procedures were carefully developed with the result that there were far fewer injudicious appointments by IRO than had been made by UNRRA and the IGCR.[20] The turnover of the transferred personnel was almost nil and IRO never indulged in haphazard hiring and firing like UNRRA, which was said to have recruited five thousand and dismissed three thousand employees in one sixty-day period of its European operations.[21]

During the peak of IRO's operations, the Organization's international, or so-called Class I, staff, taken over from the predecessor organizations, together with those newly recruited by the director-general reached 2600 people from forty-one countries.[22] Nationals from the member states of IRO were most heavily represented, roughly in proportion to the financial contribution of the particular country concerned.[23] There was only one exception to this rule: United Kingdom nationals held 38 per cent of the international staff positions while the United States, which contributed by far the largest single sum to the Organization's budget, had only 18 per cent.[24] However, even this exception was one in appearance only. At and above Grade 11, the United States held 36.5 per cent of these leading appointments while Britain provided only 25 per cent.[25] The conditions of employment and salary scales were largely patterned after the American civil service with additional bonuses and per diem allowances for most employees to compensate for the temporary nature of the Organization.

In addition to the Class I staff, approximately 3000 people, most of them drawn from the refugee populations in areas of IRO operations, were on the payroll of the Organization. Their work sometimes overlapped with that of the international staff, refugee doctors working side by side with international medical officers for example, but on the whole the activities of these local employees, or Class II staff as they were called, were confined to technical and housekeeping responsibilities. They constituted an invaluable point of contact between the international staff and the refugee population.

The 5600 civil servants of IRO did their job with extraordinary zeal and devotion. Although the staff members came from many different lands and spoke many different languages, their dedication to a common worthy cause developed an *esprit de corps* which came close to transcending petty national jealousies. The common devotion to the salvation of people in distress lent a certain romantic flavor to the enterprise and helped to forge a remarkable solidarity and camaraderie. A former high IRO official described a typical scene as follows:

> An urgent policy problem regarding assembly centers in Germany was being weighed and discussed. Around the little table there sat an old Indian army colonel and his American assistant, their Danish secretary, a French doctor, a Dutch information officer, a Belgian nutrition expert, an Australian social worker and a British resettlement officer. In this little room in a small German town, international harmony and cooperation were being accomplished with no effort at all.[26]

It was just this common devotion which made possible the accomplishment of the gigantic task which IRO had posed for itself. Only by submerging their national differences and concentrating upon the humanitarian responsibility which animated them all, did it become possible for this handful of men and women to achieve their goal. Always of first interest to the staff was the welfare of the homeless stepchildren of human society, those who had been deprived of their human and national rights. In extending to these unfortunate people the protection of the international community the men and women working under the emblem of the symbolic life buoy did full justice to the humanitarian task for which they had been recruited. This essentially international spirit also caught the directors-general of the organization who, although ostensibly national appointees, nevertheless placed their parochial loyalties in the background in most instances when conflicts arose. The staff of the International Refugee Organization probably came closest of all the United Nations agencies to achieving the ideal of an international civil service as set forth in the United Nations Charter.[27]

In an evaluation of the remarkable harmony prevailing among the staff members of IRO, it must be repeated that the agreement upon fundamental principles, which made smooth administration possible, depended in large measure upon the exclusively Western membership of the Organization. If the aim of international organization is essentially the building of habits of universal cooperation, IRO fell far short of attaining that goal. Rather than effecting a rapprochement between East and West, the political nature of the refugee problem even accentuated the rift between the Soviet Union and the Western world. IRO, having embraced the Western principle of individual dignity and freedom of choice, irrevocably alienated the Communist Eastern governments. But no compromise was possible on this issue since the fundamental conceptions of the East and the West concerning the relationship of man to the state were poles apart.

If, on the other hand, the aim of international organization is primarily the successful discharge of a task at hand which is of international proportions, the work of IRO was an eminent success. Over one million refugees were resettled by IRO in the democracies of the West. Eligibility screening by the Organization and the selection missions ensured that few refugees hostile to democracy were resettled.[28] Many of the newcomers rendered immeasurable services to the countries which opened their doors to them.

In the last analysis, the Organization was not able to resolve the "means versus end" dilemma with which it was confronted. It had to choose between universality and paralysis on the one hand, and selectivity and effectiveness on the other. By taking the latter course, IRO emphatically reaffirmed the Western concept of man as a free agent.

THE VOLUNTARY AGENCIES AND IRO

The International Refugee Organization, like the preceding intergovernmental agencies established on behalf of refugees, was conceived as a temporary organization. The only permanent factor in international work on behalf of refugees had been the activity of many diverse voluntary agencies, national and international. No evaluation of the refugee problem could be complete without taking into consideration the invaluable contribution to IRO's work of over one hundred such "nongovernmental organizations." [29] The permanent nature of the voluntary societies gave them a certain superiority over IRO and prompted the latter to solicit their collaboration, for only the voluntary societies could pursue and attempt to conclude those tasks which IRO would not be able to complete.

By the end of 1947 the IRO administration had concluded agreements with 128 voluntary organizations.[30] The societies collaborating with IRO fell into three main categories. In the first place, there were the denominational organizations which were based upon religious considerations and gave their support to refugees of their own particular faith. Among the Roman Catholic groups, the most powerful agency was indisputably the National Catholic Welfare Conference, while Protestant refugees looked for assistance to the World Council of Churches and the Church World Service. The Jewish societies which played a particularly remarkable role in refugee work comprised among others the American Jewish Joint Distribution Committee, the Jewish Agency for Palestine, and the Hebrew Immigrant Aid Society. Second, nondenominational organizations such as the International Red Cross, the International Social Service, and the International Rescue Committee gave considerable aid to displaced persons. Finally, a large number of private organizations, mainly national groups whose normal activities were performed almost exclusively on a local scale, were called upon to collaborate with IRO. Most of these societies, such as the United Lithuanian Relief Fund and the Polish Red Cross, rendered additional services to their countrymen.

In general, religious, ethnic, and national communities in the countries of first asylum, as well as in the countries of final resettlement, responded generously to appeals by the voluntary agencies in favor of their co-religionists and compatriots. A remarkable degree of cooperation was evident among the private agencies themselves, resulting in a natural allocation of responsibility rather than an exclusion of beneficiaries by definition.

In most instances, the agreements between IRO and the voluntary agencies limited the activities of the latter to basically supplementary services. If IRO decided that a particular voluntary agency negotiating for an agreement was of reputable and reliable character, the Organization usually advanced a certain amount of money to the agency for the provision of complementary services to the refugees under IRO jurisdiction. In that sense, "the voluntary agencies rendered particular and personal the necessarily general and impersonal services provided by the public international organization." [31] Since most of the activities of the voluntary societies did not touch on questions of national sovereignty or require intergovernmental accord, it was easier for these societies to cut the red tape in such matters as nutrition standards, health and medical care, and refugee vocational training and employment. They were less hampered than the Organization in matters involving protocol and were less susceptible to criticism by national governments.

The importance of these supplementary services should not be underestimated. IRO sheltered, fed, and clothed the refugees while they were awaiting either repatriation or resettlement. The Organization afforded the displaced persons its legal protection and transported them to their final destination. But the refugees also asked — and this was not much less important in their eyes — to be able to live through this waiting period like human beings, like people with requirements other than the strictly indispensable material needs for existence. They wanted something more which IRO could provide only superficially. This "something more" was precisely what the voluntary societies offered by making available their supplementary services. These included contact with their compatriots, their co-religionists, or groups from the population of the country that was going to welcome them. The voluntary services also provided individual help, not from an administration which was obliged by the nature of its task to consider general problems and to search for collective solutions, but from teams or individuals for whom welfare work was a vocation and who brought into the camps and even into individual homes long experience as well as the warmth of human sympathy. These organizations also gave the refugee the opportunity to renew his contact with the cultural and intellectual world, to read, to study the languages and customs of unknown lands, to take part in meetings, games, entertainments, and to see his children forget their privations and regain their strength. Visits to the sick, little gifts and letters to cheer the life of the aged and infirm, food parcels, clothing, all these added a little luxury to the refugees' existence. IRO was able to supply such goods and services only in a very limited degree and the complementary services of the voluntary agencies went a long way in bringing the refugees those pleasures that men often prize more highly than the very staples of life, helping them to possess their souls in patience and restoring their hope and strength.

The $40,000,000 invested by IRO in the 128 voluntary organizations [32] was money wisely spent. The agencies could draw on a fund of experience that no intergovernmental organization could possess — experience that in some cases went back twenty or thirty years. IRO, although blessed with an outstanding staff, was not able to demonstrate the competence of the Organization for Rehabilitation and Training (ORT) in vocational training, of the International Social Service (ISS) in the welfare field, or of the YMCA in organizing young people's cultural and sporting activities.

During IRO's existence, the voluntary agencies on two major occasions even assumed responsibility for services which might be considered basic to the task of the Organization. The first such instance was the emigration movement sponsored by the Jewish organizations to the new State of Israel. The Jewish agencies, by handling migration movements of refugees to Israel, relieved the Organization of a very heavy task and freed a large part of its resources for other operations. The financial reimbursement finally paid by IRO to the two main Jewish agencies was a tacit admission of that fact.[33] The second major single accomplishment of the voluntary agencies was their invaluable cooperation with IRO in the Organization's efforts to resettle a large number of displaced persons in the United States. In order to unleash the generosity that was destined to carry the United States to first place among the countries of refuge, American citizens had to be acquainted with the problem, told of the existence of the Displaced Persons Act and of its conditions of application. Interest had to be kept alive and active by a constant stream of news on the progress of the gigantic undertaking of rescuing the homeless. This work of providing information and stimulating and collecting the "affidavits" and sureties put up by the American public fell almost entirely upon the numerous voluntary agencies in the United States. They alone could handle successfully a task of such magnitude, thanks to their moral and material backing and their manifold and direct contacts with every level of American society.

Both IRO and the United States Displaced Persons Commission voiced their appreciation of the efforts of American voluntary societies in collecting the affidavits which enabled more than 300,000 refugees to emigrate to the United States:

> Although every agency did not necessarily engage in all phases of the displaced persons program, the joint contribution to each of several phases was enormous and was crucial to successful operations. The extent of this work and its importance in making for the successful

completion of the program is indicated by the single fact that of the 311,645 assurances filed, almost 90 percent were submitted through voluntary agencies.[34]

The tireless efforts of these American agencies helped shape an initially apathetic public opinion in the direction of an enlightened self-interest which finally resulted in a genuine "Citizens' foreign policy." The organizations were in advance of public opinion, were able to mold it, and thus could stimulate public action.

It should not be concluded from the foregoing that the advantages of collaboration between the voluntary agencies and IRO operated exclusively to the advantage of the latter. The societies themselves gained from this cooperation and saw their potential scope increased by virtue of IRO's support. The Organization extended to them the benefits of its own international status and it was from IRO or through its good offices that they were able to obtain the facilities indispensable to their activities. Finally, had the voluntary societies been left to their own devices, they would in most cases not have been able to develop their activities beyond the limits of emergency aid. Only agreements between them and IRO made possible the launching and financing of the great operations that led to the resettlement of more than a million refugees. It was only by becoming the agents and associates of IRO that the societies could transcend their own limitations and establish their magnificent record.

The work of the voluntary agencies showed the indispensability of public and private cooperation in the field of refugee migration. The voluntary agencies did much to stimulate the creation of IRO, but became dependent upon it once the Organization had been established. IRO, in turn, became to a large extent dependent upon the agencies' cooperation. But perhaps the main value of the voluntary agencies for the displaced persons was their permanence. Like the refugees themselves, they were here to stay. And since the world so easily tended to forget the refugee, these voluntary organizations filled the ever present need for a "public remembrancer."[35]

THE END OF IRO

Notwithstanding their foresight and devotion to the refugee cause, the fathers of the International Refugee Organization had labored under one persistent illusion: the temporary nature of the refugee problem.

The experience of centuries had not yet taught these men that the problem was a reflection of the malaise of the international body politic. Neither the phenomenon of Nazi Germany nor that of Soviet Russia had been sufficient to illustrate that refugees would continue to exist until the inhumanity of man to man had been eradicated from the face of the earth. IRO had been established as a "nonpermanent specialized agency."

Most member governments of the Organization were willing to extend its life provided that the United States, bearing the largest financial responsibility, would continue to meet the same obligation as heretofore. All the major contributors to the Organization's budget, including the United Kingdom, seemed convinced by the appeal made by the French delegate to the General Council:

We have done well indeed. But the refugee problem is far from solved. Look about you and what do you see? Intolerance of man to man has not abated, but is increasing in ferocity. Tens of thousands of refugees from the Soviet countries await our aid, a million Arabs are languishing in the Middle East, hundreds of thousands of Korean refugees wander aimlessly over that peninsula. And our own original task even is not yet done . . . we cannot stop now . . .[36]

However, the United States delegate, George Warren, steadfastly refused to make any further financial contributions to the Organization:

The IRO has cost my Government a tremendous sum of money. The Organization was not established to function indefinitely and the time has now come to attempt solutions to the problem through bilateral negotiations.[37]

The prolonged and sometimes heated debates during the last session of the General Council reflected a clear-cut cleavage between the United States and the other members of the Organization. Finally, one minor concession was made by Mr. Warren:

Although the problems inherent in the situation are clearly not of sufficient magnitude to justify the maintenance of the IRO, they are so grave in terms of human suffering that they call for urgent consideration by the United Nations.[38]

But the United States adhered to its decision to contribute no further funds to IRO and in February 1952 the activities of this international experiment in humanitarianism came to a standstill.[39]

The International Refugee Organization was, then, another link in a procession of temporary agencies dealing with the problem of refugees. It was unique in the sense that it had irrevocably proved that the resettlement and favorable absorption of large quantities of refugees in the democracies was in the realm of the possible. But even while the Organization was closing its doors, thousands of new refugees were crossing the borders of countries where freedom had become extinct. The refugee was evidently a lasting phenomenon and IRO, instead of achieving—as it had hoped and intended—a complete solution of a temporary problem, only succeeded in achieving a partial solution of a permanent one.

PART III · AFTER IRO

10

Divided Counsels

"There is a tendency in the world to tackle problems piecemeal rather than at their roots." G. J. VAN HEUVEN GOEDHART, UNITED NATIONS HIGH COMMISSIONER FOR REFUGEES [1]

THE POST-IRO REFUGEES

As THE colossal operation of the International Refugee Organization came to a standstill at the end of 1951, most of its leading officials could see but little ground for optimism. Neither the remarkable efficiency of the Organization nor its great dedication to the task of human salvage had been able to effect a substantial reduction of the world's refugee problem. Even while IRO was engaged in the physical and psychical rehabilitation of the refugees under its jurisdiction, new torrents of uprooted and dispossessed human beings bore witness to the fact that the floodgates of man's intolerance had not yet been sufficiently dammed by rationality.

Hardly had IRO's mass resettlement program begun when the partition of the Indian subcontinent in August 1947 precipitated a fratricidal slaughter between Indians and Moslems which resulted in a mass migration. The fifteen million people thus permanently uprooted were not considered refugees by IRO in the technical sense since the movement of Moslems to Pakistan and of Hindus to India was not accompanied by loss of nationality.[2] Nor were there any serious efforts on either side of the conflict to reverse the population exchange. However, by the close of 1951 more than half of the transferees were still living a shadow existence in makeshift camps and had been unable to integrate themselves into their new environments.[3] These millions of people thrown upon the meager resources of the two recipient countries without any external aid, national or international, continued to be a formidable stumbling block to a permanent *rapprochement* between India and Pakistan.

A year after the Indian catastrophe, IRO officials were appalled at a new outburst of violence emanating from the birth of the state of Israel in May 1948. The Arab population of the British mandate of Palestine had attempted by every means at its command to prevent the creation of the Zionist state. When after protracted violence on both sides of the conflict the Zionist ideal was finally realized, most of the Arab population, fearful of Jewish reprisals, took to headlong flight into the neighboring Arab states.

Approximately 880,000 Arab refugees poured into the adjacent territories of Jordan, Lebanon, Iraq, Syria, and Gaza, creating a social, economic, and political problem of formidable proportions in the Arab lands surrounding Israel.[4] During 1948 and 1949, extensive debates centering on the two alternative solutions of repatriation to Israel or resettlement in the Arab lands produced no agreement. When IRO, which had never assumed responsibility for the Arab refugee problem, closed its doors, even the efforts of the United Nations Relief and Works Agency for Palestine Refugees in the Near East, a separate United Nations organ established to deal with the question, had been unable to effect a solution.[5]

The third major source of refugees during IRO's lifetime was the Korean war, which broke out in June 1950. The subsequent bloody war of attrition with its continually seesawing front line produced approximately seven million civilian refugees from North Korea seeking political asylum in the southern half of the peninsula.[6] IRO found its resources already too severely taxed to contribute substantially to salvaging Korean refugees. However, shortly before it concluded its operations, IRO made available to the newly created United Nations Korean Reconstruction Agency all the blankets, food, and medical supplies that it could spare.[7] By this token contribution the Organization attempted to express its concern for a new refugee problem with which it was unable to deal on a more comprehensive basis.

While IRO was able to contribute little more than its sympathy to a solution of the new refugee problems throughout the world, it was seriously concerned about the future of the residual displaced persons under its own jurisdiction. Notwithstanding the Organization's efforts to effect a solution within the life span allotted to it, approximately half a million IRO refugees remained scattered throughout camps in Germany, Austria, Italy, Greece, the Middle East, and faraway Shanghai in December 1951.[8] The majority of these displaced persons were in the so-called hard-core group, which implied that their opportunities of resettlement were limited for such diverse reasons as family composition, age, profession, and state of health. Only about thirty thousand of these were considered "unresettleable" by the Organization because of old age or ill health.[9] The overwhelming majority of the hard-core refugees consisted of men and women hoping for resettlement and eager to make their contribution to the country which opened its doors to them. Only the lack of time and of sufficient resources prevented IRO from eventually securing resettlement for them.

Before its dissolution, IRO exerted all its authority upon the local governments in an effort to render the legal and political status of these remaining refugees as favorable as possible. The cordial relations which IRO had painstakingly nurtured with the local authorities throughout its life now bore fruit. Germany, Austria, and Italy, which harbored 90 per cent of all IRO refugees, declared their intentions of granting the refugees the rights of employment and legal naturalization.[10] Most of the Organization's residual funds were divided between the local authorities and the voluntary agencies who were assuming responsibility for IRO's former wards. Under the circumstances, this was probably the best result the Organization could hope for. For the great majority of the refugees, however, local settlement was an unacceptable solution because of their antipathy toward their former Axis oppressors and their continuing fervent desire to emigrate overseas. And, whatever the good intentions of the European governments in granting rights to the refugees, reintegration of the non-German displaced persons into the native economy was made almost impossible by the continued presence of almost ten million *Volksdeutsche* expellees in Germany and Austria.[11] These people had never benefited from international assistance, but had nevertheless managed to assimilate themselves gradually into the German scene.[12] A student of the problem estimated in early 1953 that "about forty-five per cent of the expellees have been integrated, about twenty-five per cent have been enonomically 'placed,' and thirty per cent still constitute a marginal population." [13] This "marginal population" consisted of about three million people who had found it impossible to establish themselves permanently in the German economy. Although the chances of the *Volksdeutsche* to secure employment in the local economy were somewhat better than those of the non-German displaced persons, discrimination against them by the native German population was nevertheless marked. For these three million people, as for the five hundred thousand remaining IRO refugees, resettlement seemed the only alternative.

A particularly bleak fate was the lot of six thousand refugees still remaining in Communist Shanghai. These displaced persons, who had been receiving IRO assistance via Hong Kong, now were faced by the grim prospect of physical starvation. All IRO refugees, however, whether in Europe or in Asia, regarded the death of the Organization as a tragedy robbing them of the opportunity to rebuild their lives afresh in a new and more hospitable environment.

Finally, the dissolution of IRO coincided with a steady influx of refugees from the Communist-occupied areas into the Western zone of Germany. Perhaps this group more than any other made many IRO officials think that the death of the Organization was premature. These escapees pouring into West Berlin and West Germany at the rate of fifteen thousand a month [14] had left their homes, possessions, and friends, convinced that the chance to rebuild their lives afresh in the free world was worth the price. Although the Soviet-controlled border patrols managed to seal the frontiers in an almost hermetic fashion, the refugees only became more resourceful. Incredible tales began to reach the newspapers describing astonishing feats of refugees escaping from behind the Iron Curtain:

> Escapee rescued, unconscious from beneath a load of coal, as a railroad gondola car from Czechoslovakia was unloaded in Germany . . . Czech student tunneled out of a uranium mine and escaped to West Germany . . . Lithuanian fishermen imprisoned a Russian crew in the hold and escaped in the ship's longboat to Sweden . . .[15]

By the middle of 1952 almost two hundred thousand such escapees were crowded into reception centers in West Berlin and throughout West Germany.[16] Since IRO was out of existence, only the very meager resources of the German voluntary societies were available to alleviate somewhat the appalling conditions prevailing in the camps. An official spokesman of the United States State Department expressed his concern in the following words:

The situation in which they [the escapees] found themselves was demoralizing to these refugees who had risked their lives to escape to the free world, and failed woefully to reflect the hospitality which the Western democracies would desire to accord to those willing to sacrifice so much to regain self-respect and to live in a free and democratic society.[17]

All the preceding groups of uprooted people, diverse though they were, had one factor in common: they had fled from their countries of origin because of persecution or fear of persecution.[18] This common denominator became in fact the stamp of their refugee status. Although technically large numbers of them, such as the Moslem and Hindu transferees as well as the *Volkdeutsche,* were not defined as refugees since they either had not lost their nationality or had acquired a new one, their *de facto* status differentiated them but little from those who had no claim to any nationality, such as most of the Arab refugees, the IRO residual displaced persons, and the new waves of escapees from behind the Iron Curtain.

A conservative estimate would place the figure of refugees at the time of IRO's closure at fifteen million people.[19] It was clear to the United Nations General Assembly that some international organization would have to succeed IRO if a general calamity was to be averted. A world which was emotionally exhausted with the refugee problem saw itself confronted with a figure of refugees ten times as large as that which had come under IRO's jurisdiction.

They were men and women of all ages and many nationalities. They were children of no nationality who were born refugees. They had skills and professions that they could not practice. They had the will to work, but the law denied it. They could not travel because they had no passports and could not work because they had no labor permits. They sometimes could not marry because they lacked the necessary legal documents . . . These then were the refugees, not wrecks of humanity, but the wrack of Man's inhumanity. Rumor got around and they had heard of the Declaration of Human Rights.[20]

POST-IRO UNITED NATIONS REFUGEE AGENCIES

These ominous developments did not fail to make their impression upon the United Nations. In view of the categorical refusal of the United States to contribute any further funds to the International Refugee Organization, alternative means had to be found to cope with the problem. This was done through the establishment of three separate United

Nations organs to continue refugee operations in the period after IRO. First, the United Nations High Commissioner's Office for Refugees was set up as the successor organ to IRO in order to deal with the world refugee problem in general. Second, in answer to a specific challenge, the United Nations Relief and Works Agency for Palestine Refugees in the Near East was created to deal with the Arab refugees in the Near East. Finally, the Korean war gave birth to the United Nations Korean Reconstruction Agency, an integral function of which was to be the salvage of millions of Korean refugees wandering over that ravaged peninsula.

The United Nations High Commissioner's Office for Refugees (UNHCOR). In August 1949, the United Nations Economic and Social Council had commissioned a Special Committee on Refugees and Displaced Persons, consisting of thirteen governments, to draft plans for post-IRO refugee operations by the United Nations.[21] Poland and the Soviet Union walked out of the first meeting of the committee to protest the seating of a delegate from Nationalist China, thus reducing that body to eleven governments, all of which were members of IRO. Although most of the delegates were in favor of continuing and broadening IRO's jurisdiction, the strong weight of the United States delegation swung the balance in favor of an American alternative, the creation of a High Commissioner's Office under United Nations auspices, patterned to a large extent after the Nansen Office.[22] The committee's report was subsequently approved by the Economic and Social Council and reached the General Assembly on 11 December 1950. Here the Statute of the Office of the United Nations High Commissioner for Refugees was accepted by a vote of 36 to 5 with 11 abstentions.[23]

To fill the post of High Commissioner, the General Assembly chose Dr. G. J. Van Heuven Goedhart of the Netherlands, former Minister of Justice of the Dutch government-in-exile and on repeated occasions delegate of the Netherlands to the General Assembly. The Statute of the High Commissioner defined as a refugee "any person who had been thus defined in the Constitution of the International Refugee Organization" with one significant additional paragraph. At the insistence of Dr. Van Heuven Goedhart, the definition was broadened to include

any person who is outside the country of his nationality or, if he has no nationality, the country of his former habitual residence, because he has or had well-founded fear of persecution by reason of his race, religion, nationality or political opinion and is unable or, because of such fear, is unwilling to avail himself of the protection of the government of the country of his nationality, or, if he has no nationality, to return to the country of his former habitual residence.[24]

This latest redefinition of a refugee was the broadest and most comprehensive yet made by any international organization. It was inclusive enough to cover all refugees in existence at the time, estimated by the High Commissioner at approximately twenty million.[25]

However, the new definition of refugees which was inscribed into the statute was probably the sole progressive element in the new refugee organ. The very inclusiveness of the clause became a mockery in view of the fact that the High Commissioner's Office was stripped of all operational functions. Its annual administrative budget was fixed by the General Assembly at $300,000 and no provision was made for any operating expenses.[26] The functions of the new refugee organ were visualized as merely protective in nature, limited to the issuance of legal identity certificates and travel documents. It was emphasized by the General Assembly that responsibilities for care and maintenance as well as for resettlement would have to be borne by those governments in whose territories the refugees found themselves.[27] The High Commissioner's Office would not fill the function of an international authority for the protection of refugees, but rather the role of a mediator who would make his good offices available to both refugees and governments.

In view of the stringent limitations imposed upon him by the General Assembly, Dr. Van Heuven Goedhart gave up all hopes for major resettlement and economic reintegration programs. Within the limited means at his disposal he was able only to encourage the assimilation of refugees in countries of first asylum. He was realistic enough not to spread his sparse assistance too thin although under his jurisdiction the refugees in Asia were as eligible as those in Europe. Rather he preferred to concentrate upon the most desperate cases of IRO residual refugees. Among these the most unfortunate were singled out for the little assistance the Office was able to give: the remaining IRO refugees in Communist Shanghai. During the years of 1950 and 1951 most of the High Commissioner's scanty funds were used to purchase much-needed staple foods which reached the Shanghai refugees via the Hong Kong office of the High Commission.[28] The remainder of the funds available to the Commission was used to equip refugees in Germany, Austria, and Italy with travel and identity documents. The total staff employed by Dr. Van Heuven Goedhart comprised ninety-nine men and women.[29]

It had not been enough for the General Assembly to tie the hands of the High Commissioner by its refusal to grant him even a nominal sum for operational expenses, but it was expressly stipulated in the statute that "the High Commissioner shall not appeal to governments for funds or make a general appeal without the prior approval of the General Assembly."[30] At the beginning of 1952 desperate pleas reached the head office of the High Commission reporting that starvation was facing the remaining Shanghai refugees as well as most of the old and sick refugees formerly under IRO jurisdiction. On the strength of this information, the High Commissioner decided to follow in the footsteps of his great predecessor, Dr. Nansen, and appeal for an emergency fund in order to bring the most necessary relief to the refugees.

The protracted debate that followed in the Third Committee of the General Assembly, considering whether permission should be given the High Commissioner to appeal for an emergency fund, was a sorry sequel to the discussion which had taken place in the same forum six years earlier. Mrs. Roosevelt, the American delegate and the same person who under similar circumstances a few years before had passionately defended the interests of the refugees, now declared that "she could not vote for the resolution which would set the precedent of authorizing the United Nations to collect funds for a rather indefinite program to which her government would not contribute . . ."[31] The Soviet bloc seemed to have changed little in its approach since the 1946 debate:

> The Byelorussian delegate condemned the policy of IRO which is being continued by the United Nations High Commissioner for Refugees, of substituting for repatriation the forced resettlement of displaced persons in other countries. He also condemned the attempts of the Western states to recruit displaced persons by all possible means for subversive and diversionary activities in the territory of the U.S.S.R. and the peoples' democracies. He charged that the High Commissioner was perpetuating and legalizing the plight of refugees in order to provide cheap labor and cannon-fodder to further the imperialist aims of the Western states through compulsory resettlement.[32]

The Eastern countries, in other words, considered the High Commissioner's request for an emergency relief fund amounting to three million dollars the height of impudence. The United States delegate spent most of her time refuting the Soviet arguments, but seemed to evince little interest in the subject at hand, namely the approval of the fund appeal. Finally, late in the proceedings, the Norwegian delegate reminded the assembled representatives that no useful purpose was served by repetitive accusations. He, for one, supported the idea of establishing a relief fund to be maintained by voluntary contributions.[33] The Norwegian example was followed by the majority of the delegates and finally the committee recommended to the General Assembly that permission should be given the High Commissioner to appeal for the fund.[34]

The General Assembly followed suit and authorized the High Commissioner to become an international mendicant. In this role Dr. Van Heuven Goedhart was not very successful—only twelve governments responded to his appeal and their total contributions by August 1956 amounted to only $3 million.[35] This, besides his administrative budget, was the only sum the High Commissioner ever received from national governments for operating expenses.

The only significant contribution made to the High Commission came from the private source of the Ford Foundation, in October 1952. The $2,900,000[36] granted by that organization reached the High Commission in the time of its greatest need. Three conditions were stipulated by the donor, all of which were in harmony with the philosophy of the High Commissioner. First, the money was to be used to help the refugees help themselves; second, no discrimination was to be shown among refugee groups; and finally, no funds were to be allotted as pure relief without a view toward a solution.

Dr. Van Heuven Goedhart made maximum use of these funds. They enabled him for the first time to fulfill some vitally necessary operational responsibilities. Wisely he decided to allocate portions of the grant to various qualified voluntary agencies which would then act under the supervision of the High Commission. A very modest yet remarkable program was thus launched:

> A total of 108 projects submitted by the voluntary agencies have been approved which cover such enterprises as agricultural integration, housing schemes, vocational training, education, employment, counselling, youth and community centers, medical rehabilitation and overseas resettlement.[37]

The economy forced upon the High Commission compelled it to use its funds with the greatest possible circumspection; the result was a little refugee "Point Four" Program. The Ford Foundation registered its approval by contributing another $200,000 in April 1954.[38] The Statute of the High Commissioner, originally covering a period of three years, has recently been extended by the General Assembly for another five years and the administrative budget increased to $685,000 annually.[39] The Nobel Peace Prize awarded to the Commission on 3 November 1955 for having "best promoted the fraternity of nations" is testimony to the yeoman service rendered by Dr. Van Heuven Goedhart's organization even within the severe restrictions imposed upon it by the General Assembly.[40] However, the Commission's funds have again been exhausted and little further aid is in sight. With no financial support the Office of the High Commissioner might become a travesty of even the limited purpose for which it was established and the mere time extension a hollow triumph.

Dr. Van Heuven Goedhart died in July 1956. By and large his hands were tied in much the same way as were those of Fridtjof Nansen toward the end of his life. An emotional exhaustion with the refugee problem and particularly the failure of the United States to provide the leadership which it provided for IRO have now led the United Nations to emulate the League by embracing a series of short-term expedients to deal with a long-term problem. Thousands of displaced persons have already suffered grievously because of this shift in policy, and the valuable experience of most of the IRO staff in overseas migration has been dissipated. The hopes of many refugees were raised high by IRO only to be shattered again by the stringent limitations imposed upon the High Commissioner's Office. However, a fair evaluation of United Nations work for refugees subsequent to the IRO experience must include the contributions of two agencies created specifically to deal with the refugee problems in the Near East and in Korea.

The United Nations Relief and Works Agency for Palestine Refugees in the Near East (*UNRWA*). Soon after the Arab exodus from Israel the General Assembly decided to make the Arab refugee problem a United Nations responsibility. Adopting an American resolution, it established the "United Nations Economic Survey Mission" in order to determine the extent of the new problem.[41] The mission, under the leadership of Gordon R. Clapp of the Tennessee Valley Authority, estimated the number of Arab refugees at 881,000 distributed among

Lebanon, Syria, Iraq, Jordan, and Gaza,[42] and recommended a work-relief program as the only possible solution. Repatriation to Israel was considered inadvisable by the mission since the homes and farms left behind by the Arabs had by now been occupied by Jewish refugees coming to the new state, and the *status quo ante* could not be restored. The mission drew up a blueprint for the consideration of the General Assembly recommending economic development and settlement projects which were to make the refugees self-sufficient in as short a time as possible with a minimum expenditure.

In accordance with the mission's recommendations, the General Assembly established the United Nations Relief and Works Agency for Palestine Refugees in the Near East (UNRWA), which under the leadership of Howard Kennedy of Canada began operations in May 1950.[43] Unlike the High Commissioner's Office of the United Nations, UNRWA did not at first suffer from a severe shortage of funds. The General Assembly had allotted to the new organization a sum of $66.3 million over an eighteen-month period.[44] Seventy-three per cent of this amount was pledged by the United States, 20 per cent by the United Kingdom, and the remainder by twelve other countries including Israel, which contributed $2.8 million.[45]

The new organization launched a program of public works in the areas in which the Arab refugees were massed. Road-building, afforestation, reclamation, and irrigation schemes were begun, all with the hope of making the refugees self-supporting and thus integrating them into the local economies. However, in spite of the generous funds allotted to UNRWA, after a period of one year only twelve thousand refugees had been employed and it was discovered that it was five times as expensive to put a refugee to work as it cost to keep him on relief.[46] The arid strips of land on which the refugees were situated did not lend themselves well to development projects. Only a few such "pilot projects" proved to be viable without continual financial support and most of them had to be abandoned altogether. It was generally conceded that the work-relief program was a failure which could be attributed mainly to two circumstances. First, the inexperienced UNRWA personnel attempted to create oases in areas which had been officially designated by the Arab states as "dead and waste." Thus, much money had been sunk into projects which were doomed for failure from the very beginning. In the second place, the governments of the neighboring Arab states had given the projects a decidedly cool reception and, together with most of the refugee population, had favored repatriation to Israel as a solution to the problem. Finally, in December 1950, the General Assembly voted to end the "work-relief program" and after a thorough investigation of the circumstances recommended a new policy of "reintegration."[47]

Israel had retracted an initial offer to readmit one hundred thousand of the Arab refugees[48] and beginning in January 1951 steadfastly refused to accept any of the displaced people. The Israeli position remained adamant despite strong American pressure and was justified in terms of already overcrowded conditions caused by the "open door" immigration policy espoused by the new state. Also the Israelis were afraid that Arab repatriation might be used as a Trojan Horse maneuver to blow up the Jewish state from within. In support of this argument Israel's Foreign Minister Moshe Sharett quoted the following excerpt from a leading Lebanese weekly:

> Our first urgent request must be the return of the refugees. Let us try to make them our fifth column in the struggle yet before us. Up to now the Jews argued that there was a state of war between us and one could not ask them to accept soldiers, enemies, into their midst. But at present, if we shall appear in the guise of peace-seekers, they will have no argument.[49]

The Jewish argument carried weight and the General Assembly accordingly voted a "bold and dramatic reintegration program" of the Arab refugees into the neighboring lands.[50] A sum of $250 million was allotted by the General Assembly to UNRWA with the aim of "making the refugees economic assets" of the countries extending their hospitality to them.[51] Through this sizable investment, it was hoped, the reticence of the Arab states could be overcome. Again, the United States contributed almost three fourths of the total while the United Kingdom's share was 20 per cent. Ten other countries made smaller contributions, again including Israel.[52] An American, John B. Blandford, Jr., was named as new head of UNRWA. He approached his task with remarkable energy and immediately set to work building small villages for the refugees, setting up small enterprises for them in the cities, and launching a multitude of rural development projects. UNRWA endeavored to coordinate its program with all other United Nations efforts in the Near East, thus seeking the reintegration of the refugees within the framework of general regional development. The organization was careful not to represent the refugee, despite his misery, as a symbol of privilege due to United Nations support. In the words of Mr. Blandford, "the solution of the problem of the poverty and unemployment of the refugees is inseparable from the problem of poverty and hunger which already affect the Middle East." [53]

The "bigger and better" Blandford program had some limited success. Alone among the Arab states, Jordan had expressed its willingness to absorb the refugee population upon its territory, and the reintegration program made particularly good progress in that country. By the end of 1952, approximately half of the 470,000 refugees located there were on their way to self-sufficiency and complete assimilation.[54] The remaining Arab states, however, including Syria, Lebanon, Iraq, and Egypt-controlled Gaza, retained their hostile attitude, thus hindering UNRWA's progress. Nevertheless, the organization's director was able to report about those regions that "the first stage of breaking trails was past," and "although there is no pretence of breathless speed or sudden miracle, there are now some grounds for cautious optimism." [55]

However, even this "cautious optimism" proved premature when suddenly, beginning in January 1953, all the Arab states with the single exception of Jordan again demanded "absolute repatriation" of all Arab refugees to Israel. While UNRWA doggedly went ahead with its program, the Arab delegates to the General Assembly denounced the organization's efforts in the most vehement terms as a "Jewish inspired policy to root the refugees in the Arab countries and thus weaken their claim for repatriation." [56] Furthermore, the Arab representatives in the General Assembly continued, the plight of the refugees was to be laid at the door of the United Nations which had helped create the state of Israel and hence the United Nations must be held responsible for the refugees' repatriation. The $250 million would be accepted as a temporary palliative pending repatriation, but permanent resettlement of Arab refugees outside of Israel could never be tolerated.[57]

The resulting impasse dealt a severe blow to the Blandford plan and the attitude of the Arab governments augurs ill for the future of the refugee problem. In January 1956, UNRWA reported to the General Assembly that there were still 835,986 refugees requiring assistance and that "the urgency of the problem increases every day." [58] It is clear to both UNRWA and the General Assembly that the reintegration program can never succeed without genuine Arab cooperation as exhibited in Jordan.

The Arabs seem to be interested in perpetuating rather than liquidating, the refugee problem; to maintain the expatriates as refugees and by so doing, to hold a trump card in their political game aimed at the destruction of Israel. Reintegration and resettlement, they fear, would mitigate [*sic*] against the refugees' demand to return to Israel; it would deprive them of their only means of arousing sympathy in the West. Consequently, it is not beyond the bounds of probability that they may see to it that the $250 million allocated for reintegration will not actually help further that objective.[59]

The Arab demand for repatriation is somewhat unrealistic in the light of the developments in Israel. Long experience has shown that population exoduses are not reversible. If the work of UNRWA is recorded as a failure in the annals of history, the blame will probably not be placed at the door of the United Nations. The Blandford plan was generous and sweeping in its conception and was a concrete response to a specific problem. It is a tragic irony that millions of dollars were wasted by a United Nations agency in the Near East while the same parent organization was jealous of every dollar given to the High Commissioner who made every penny count. The tragedy of UNRWA is the fact that a humanitarian organization simply cannot operate in an explosive political situation and expect to be able to ignore it. A painful and expensive stalemate has been reached with respect to the Arab refugee problem and only a prior political settlement of a permanent nature will enable the United Nations to resume a fruitful approach.

The United Nations Korean Reconstruction Agency (*UNKRA*). The last of the three United Nations heirs to the International Refugee Organization was the United Nations Korean Reconstruction Agency (UNKRA) which was established in early 1951 upon American initiative in order to conduct relief operations including the care of displaced persons in the war-torn peninsula.[60] Most of the funds were again subscribed by the United States, which shouldered 75 per cent of an annual budget of $100 million.[61] The remainder was borne by twenty-three other governments of which the United Kingdom had the largest share.[62] As agent-general of the organization the General Assembly designated J. Donald Kingsley, who brought with him to Korea his invaluable experience as director-general of IRO as well as a seemingly inexhaustible fund of energy.

For over two years, the new organization carried on its activities on behalf of displaced persons in a war situation, often immediately behind the front lines held by United Nations forces. It operated under immense difficulties since military supplies invariably had precedence over UNKRA material and frequent shortages of vital material occurred. Under existing circumstances it was hardly possible for UNKRA to supply more than emergency relief assistance to displaced persons. Unavoidable though it was, this policy brought the organization in for severe criticism of "its hand-out operations conducted at arm's length." [63]

In May 1953, Mr. Kingsley was relieved of the post of agent-general of UNKRA, and the vacancy was filled by a retired United States Army officer, Lieutenant General John B. Coulter.[64] The new chief entered upon a new phase of UNKRA's activities when, with the signing of the truce in Korea on 27 July 1953, the organization was able to carry out its operations in a situation of at least temporary peace. The United States immediately pledged $200 million for postwar reconstruction purposes in Korea, a not inconsiderable part of which was placed at the disposal of UNKRA for the rehabilitation of Korean refugees.[65]

As the guns were silenced, the focus in Korea shifted to the problem of peaceful reconstruction through the medium of UNKRA, and the organization embraced a constructive and long-range policy toward the six million refugees in South Korea. It seems safe to predict that the role of UNKRA will continue to increase in importance in the future.

In an evaluation of post-IRO United Nations work on behalf of refugees and displaced persons, three factors are in evidence. First, whereas the United Nations was extremely reluctant to provide for the High Commissioner who had a wide and general responsibility for refugees, the organization quite generously and without hesitation made specific plans to deal with specific problems in Palestine and in Korea. Like the League, the United Nations was unwilling to plan *in vacuo* and was ready to grant its assistance only when a clearly definable problem was in evidence. Second, the leadership of the United States was crucial to all three ventures sponsored by the United Nations. American refusal to support the High Commissioner's Office in its time of need guaranteed its failure just as American support of UNRWA and UNKRA made possible the limited successes these two organizations were able to achieve. Finally, the United Nations chose to abandon the unified and integrated approach to the refugee problem which had been characteristic of IRO, thus regressing to the pattern of "permanent processions of temporary agencies." And, further decentralizing international work on behalf of refugees, a quest for solutions outside the framework of the United Nations was beginning to gather momentum.

POST-IRO NON-UNITED NATIONS REFUGEE AGENCIES

The Inter-Governmental Committee for European Migration (ICEM). Concerned about the growing problem of European overpopulation and wishing to preserve at least some of the valuable experience of the International Refugee Organization, the United States government in December 1951 took the initiative in calling an intergovernmental conference in order to discuss methods of alleviating overpopulation through overseas migration. The result of this conference at Brussels was the establishment of a Provisional Inter-Governmental Committee for the Movements of Migrants from Europe (PICMME) with a membership of twenty-one nations.[66] The purpose of the new organization was to be "the transport of migrants from certain European countries having surplus populations to countries overseas,"[67] but the following stipulation was included in the basic document: "Among the migrants with whom the Committee will be concerned will be included refugees and new refugees for whose migration arrangements may be made between the Committee and the governments of the countries affording asylum."[68]

The new intergovernmental committee was established independently of the United Nations system. The financial contribution to the committee by the United States had been made only with the proviso stipulated by Congress that neither the Soviet Union nor any of the satellite states should be represented in the new organiaztion or take part in any of its deliberations.[69] In view of the fact that the American appropriation was fixed at $10 million out of a total of $34 million, the other governments, none of which desired to establish the committee outside the framework of the United Nations, reluctantly agreed to the American condition.[70]

Three hundred members of IRO's staff were put on the new organization's payroll and an American, Hugh Gibson, was elected director-general. Twelve ships from IRO's fleet were absorbed by the committee which hoped to be able to commence migration operations immediately.[71]

The history of the committee since its inception in 1951 is not a particularly inspiring story. Using the extensive experience in migratory movements of the staff which it took over from the defunct IRO, the committee has operated strictly in the capacity of a transport agency. It has merely paid and arranged passage for those migrants and refugees who have been unable to meet this expense from their own resources. No effort has been made by the committee to adopt the course so successfully followed by IRO of attempting to liberalize qualitatively and quantitatively the immigration restrictions of the recipient countries.

From the birth of the committee until May 1955, 106,399 persons were moved under its asupices, including 37,284 refugees.[72] No effort was made to give priority to the refugees over ordinary migrants in resettlement although the former suffered from homelessness in addition to mere poverty and hunger. The United States has headed the list with over one third of the total admissions, followed by Australia, Canada, and Brazil in that order. The admissions policies of the recipient countries have been of the most stringent variety. Heavy priority has been placed upon manual labor, an almost complete exclusion of "uneconomic family groups" has been the rule, and selection missions have been able to proceed in an almost completely arbitrary manner. Some weak protests against this policy have been made by the countries of first asylum such as Germany, Austria, and Italy, but although they are members of the committee, the recipient countries have turned a deaf ear. Finally the situation became so serious that Queen Juliana of the Netherlands on 18 March 1953 addressed the following lines to President Eisenhower of the United States:

> Discontent, frustration and even despair is felt by millions of uprooted people, dislocated all over the world. The free world cannot tolerate so much suffering in its midst without having to suffer itself. To preserve their human dignity and restore their self-respect, the right psychological and spiritual approach is of overriding importance. How could refugees ever trust free society if it shows interest only for trained muscles but lacks respect for the higher values of life; if it looks at refugees only as labor potential, and refuses those who cannot work; if it separates them from their families? [73]

The only answer of the committee to Queen Juliana's communication was to constitute itself in April 1953 as a permanent "Inter-Governmental Committee for European Migration" (ICEM). However, there is little evidence to indicate that in the immediate future the committee might transcend its sole function of an overseas travel agency. The only instance of active collaboration by the committee with a United Nations agency has been the establishment of a joint office with a representative of the High Commissioner in Hong Kong.[74] Heeding an appeal by Dr. Van Heuven Goedhart, the committee agreed to extend its jurisdiction to those European refugees still stranded in various parts of China. But apart from this exception, ICEM continues to divorce its activities from those of the United Nations and pursues its own narrowly defined and executed task.

The United States Escapee Program (USEP). The final post-IRO effort to bring succor to refugees is not an international one, but a program conducted unilaterally by the United States government. In March 1952, President Truman, acting under the authority of the Mutual Security Act, established the United States Escapee Program. The beneficiaries of this new operation, to which $4.3 .million had been allocated by the United States government,[75] were to be those refugees who had escaped from the Iron Curtain countries, including East Germany, since 1 January 1948.

The chief objectives of the Program are to establish better facilities of reception for escapees in the countries of first asylum; to supplement the care and maintenance already provided by the governments of those countries and by voluntary agencies; and to assist the new escapees either to emigrate abroad or to establish themselves in the free European countries.[76]

The program's contribution has not been insignificant since it has assisted 10,000 refugees to leave the German Displaced Persons Camps by emigrating overseas.[77] However, in view of the fact that over 250,000 escapees eligible for USEP assistance are still languishing in more than 200 camps in the Western zones of Germany and Austria,[78] the following appraisal by a leading United States official seems somewhat overoptimistic:

The Program's significance lies in the rebuilding of hope among the refugees when they become aware that they are no longer forgotten by a free world preoccupied by other concerns. They no longer need to remain without prospects in overcrowded camps where the will to exist is threatened by frustrations and the skills previously acquired through industry are lost through disuse. Equally important, ways and means are now provided to give practical and constructive expression to the good will and hospitality which the free world desires to extend to those whose faith in democratic ideals has induced them to flee from the Iron Curtain countries.[79]

Most of the program's efforts are in fact directed toward making the escapees' stay in the camps somewhat more bearable by supplementary services and the provision of luxury items otherwise unavailable. As one observer put it, "An over-all and most laudable political objective of the Program would appear to be to make arrival in the free world a somewhat warmer and more hospitable process than the mere allocation of a pallet in a refugee camp." [80]

In sum, neither the Inter-Governmental Committee of European Migration nor the United States Escapee Program has contributed decisively to a solution of Europe's refugee problem. Neither organization has made any effort to induce recipient countries to liberalize their immigration restrictions and in view of the fact that most overseas countries have further reduced immigration quotas and tightened qualifications for the admission of refugees, the activities of both organizations have been reduced to a minimum.[81]

PROBLEMS OF COORDINATION

In surveying the post-IRO scene, one may discern a mosaic of international organizations purporting to deal with the refugee problem. In all these bodies, whether operative within the framework of the United Nations system or independent of it, the leadership or lack of leadership of the United States government is playing a decisive role. The attitude of the American government may make or break the post-IRO agencies just as it vitally influenced the course of IRO itself.

It was an American decision to establish ICEM and USEP outside the United Nations system. The official reason given by the United States government for its desire to stay aloof from the world organization was a reluctance to admit Soviet or satellite representatives to deliberations on the fate of refugees from behind the Iron Curtain. Information on such refugees might be used by the Soviet representatives against the escapees' relatives still under Soviet jurisdiction. Allegedly for this reason the United States government also refused to discuss refugee matters in the forum of the International Labour Organization since a few Soviet satellite states were represented in that body.

In view of the fact that operational matters, let alone details about individual refugees, had never been brought by IRO to the attention of either ECOSOC or the General Assembly and that no obligation to that effect had ever existed, the official American explanation is hardly satisfactory. It seems much more likely that the decision to bypass the world organization was due to domestic considerations, mainly generated by the United States Congress. Its mood by 1952 was violently anti-Communist and many congressmen operated on the unexamined hypothesis that the United Nations was not only inherently inefficient, but also too easily exploited by Communist machinations. Besides, it was felt that the Soviet bloc had done nothing but attempt to sabotage the work of IRO and that therefore no reason was indicated not to create strictly Western organizations to deal with a refugee problem which at any rate was largely an anti-Communist phenomenon.

The United States has not only chosen to establish ICEM and USEP outside the United Nations orbit, but has in addition used its leadership to discriminate among various categories of refugees. All the escapees eligible under the United States program also fall under the jurisdiction of the United Nations High Commissioner. Furthermore, as one student has noted, "It cannot escape notice that the main and admirable reasons advanced for initiating USEP are precisely those which prompted the United Nations High Commissioner for Refugees to appeal for his Emergency Refugee Fund—a fund to which the United States had made no contribution whatsoever." [82] Only about one third of the refugees under the High Commissioner's jurisdiction are also eligible for USEP assistance. The inescapable conclusion to be drawn from the above is that American generosity has in this instance not been motivated by disinterested humanitarianism, but rather by a political pragmatism based upon the unexamined assumption that refugees who had escaped after 1 January 1948 constituted better potential material for American citizenship than those who had fled from Communism before that date. The resentment against this American policy by most residual IRO refugees, many of whom are spending their tenth year in a displaced persons camp, has been considerable.

On the whole, the American leadership has been willing to establish generous refugee programs under the aegis of the United Nations in instances where the problems were clearly definable in ethnic and geographic terms. UNRWA and UNKRA are cases in point, but where jurisdiction has been vague and indefinite as in the case of the High Commissioner, the United States has refused to commit itself. It was deemed unwise to legislate for a refugee problem the scope and extent of which were so difficult to determine.

The striking inconsistency displayed by the American government in its post-IRO refugee policy has thus given birth to a confusing array of international organizations sadly in need of coordination and integration. The deputy High Commissioner for Refugees, James M. Read, for example, wrote the following report from the Commission's Hong Kong office to Geneva: "Despite repeated entreaties, the Migration Committee refuses to place at my disposal any of its twelve ships. Even if I can get the Shanghai refugees out, I probably could not evacuate them for lack of shipping space." [83] Hugh Gibson of the Migration Commitee, in turn, had the following complaint to register: "Attempts are made by the Committee to provide stateless persons with identity documents. These documents are obtained from the High Commission, but owing to a shortage of personnel, they are often slow in forthcoming." [84] The director of a prominent voluntary agency expressed his concern with the situation in the following words:

> With IRO, things were pretty clear cut. We had an agreement with them which worked and avoided unnecessary waste and duplication of effort. Now there are so many refugee organizations around that I feel safer not to commit myself. As a result, we are veering more and more towards social work within the borders of the United States.[85]

A prominent UNKRA official had this to say: "The UN refugee programs in Palestine and Korea are not as dissimilar as many people think. Reintegration and rehabilitation are the main aims of both. It might be very helpful if some liaison office would be established. Yet, so far as I know, nothing of this kind had been done." [86] The need for rationalizing the existing confusion was stressed by Dr. Van Heuven Goedhart:

> There is something paradoxical in the present situation concerning international action relating to the refugee problem. The United Nations has only recently undertaken to accept responsibility for the problem. Yet, very shortly after the resumption of responsibility by the United Nations, some governments have taken initiative in the Migration Committee and on behalf of new refugees which cannot fail to lead to a dissipation of effort and a certain confusion.[87]

THE REFUGEE AND HUMAN RIGHTS: MORAL ASPIRATIONS AND POLITICAL REALITIES

It is, of course, a truism that refugees are produced as a result of the abuse of fundamental human rights. A universal observance by states of these "natural rights which have been said to comprise life, liberty, freedom of religion and conscience and the like"[88] might eliminate most of the causes of refugee status by undercutting its roots — intolerance in its various forms and manifestations. In this sense, an examination of the United Nations' record in the field of human rights pertaining to refugees might contribute to our analysis by "avoiding the Scylla of a pessimistic cynicism and the Charybdis of mere wishful thinking and superficial optimism."[89]

The general framework is provided by Article 55 of the United Nations Charter which pledges "universal respect for, and observance of, human rights and fundamental freedoms for all without distinction as to race, sex, language, or religion."

The Genocide Convention. The first specific project of the United Nations to safeguard human rights was the formulation of a Convention on the Prevention and Punishment of the Crime of Genocide initiated by the Economic and Social Council in April 1948. The secretariat which had prepared a draft convention for consideration by the *ad hoc* Committee on Genocide had defined the crime to be proscribed according to a threefold classification:

Physical genocide — the destruction of groups by the actual destruction of individuals; biological genocide — the prevention of births within a group; and cultural genocide — the brutal destruction of the specific characteristics of a group by various measures designed to undermine its cultural and linguistic traditions.[90]

After protracted battles in the Legal Committee of the General Assembly, the cultural genocide provision was deleted and genocide narrowed to "the denial of the right to existence of entire human groups."[91]

While it may be argued that the omission of the cultural genocide provision from the convention seriously circumscribed the application of the covenant, the prohibition of physical destruction, by guaranteeing the basic right to life itself in the literal sense, was an ambitious effort to mitigate some of the most flagrant abuses of human rights producing refugees.

With its ratification by twenty-three states — three more than the required number — the convention went into effect in January 1951 rendering acceding states liable for genocide against their own citizens under international law. It may be argued with some cogency that the fairly high number of ratifications does not necessarily represent the most accurate criterion for judging states' attitudes. While the Soviet Union has ratified with reservations, the United States has not acceded to the Convention on Genocide. As one American student, deeply concerned with the problem of human rights, declared:

> In America, as elsewhere, the ghost of national sovereignty intrudes to scare off support for an international commitment to protect the rights of man. No one would dare to suggest that genocide be tolerated in this country. But we hesitate to obligate ourselves before the rest of the world to prevent it.[92]

In sum, the convention was probably motivated by an international guilt complex over the genocidal projects of the Nazi regime in the immediate past as well as a desire to contribute to a more humane system of international law in the future. While the observance of the convention by the ratifying states remains primarily within their domestic jurisdiction, this fact does not detract from the ambitious attempt by international law to proscribe the most basic threat of all to potential refugees — the threat of physical destruction.

The Universal Declaration of Human Rights. After two and a half years of debate in the Human Rights Commission of the United Nations, the General Assembly adopted the Universal Declaration of Human Rights on 10 December 1948 by a vote of 48 to 0 with the six nations of the Soviet bloc, Saudi Arabia, and the Union of South Africa abstaining. The declaration was intended as a statement of principles representing a common standard of achievement among nations rather than a legally binding instrument. Its thirty articles set forth certain inalienable personal and civil rights of the individual as well as rights in the economic, social, and cultural spheres.

The drafters of the declaration were confronted specifically with the refugee problem during their consideration of the questions of asylum and nationality. Article 14 of the declaration pertaining to asylum guarantees everyone "the right to seek and to enjoy in other countries asylum from persecution." Article 15 claims that "everyone has the right to a nationality" and that "no one shall be arbitrarily deprived of his nationality." These two provisions are deserving of closer scrutiny.

Upon examination of Article 14, an ambiguity of language, if not deception, becomes evident. According to the article, there is a right *to seek* asylum, but no corresponding assurance that the seeking will be successful. Clearly, such a right seems redundant in international law. To grant the *right of asylum* itself might have necessitated fundamental revisions in the immigration laws of most countries as well as an incursion upon their sovereignty. Such a right was opposed both by the West and the Soviet bloc as implying an interference in matters exclusively within the domestic jurisdiction of states.[93] Lauterpacht cites the British delegate suggesting that "such an application might actually lead to persecution by encouraging states to take action against an undesirable minority and then invite it to make use of the right of asylum."[94] Article 14 might be interpreted not as the duty of granting asylum, but that of respect for it on the part of the state of which the refugee is a national. However, such a right would once more be redundant in customary international law on the basis of long-standing tradition.

A similar ambiguity is apparent in Article 15 of the declaration. It proscribes arbitrary deprivation of nationality and, by implication, aims at eliminating statelessness. The equivocation rests in the word "arbitrary." No state would admit to arbitrary denationalization measures, but would certainly, as the record shows, justify such action in terms of *raison d'état.* Article 9 of the declaration proscribing arbitrary exile suffers from similar ambiguity. A French proposal in the Human Rights Commission to bring all stateless persons under the aegis of United Nations protection was rejected by the Third (Social, Cultural, and Humanitarian) Committee of the General Assembly.[95]

No one may claim any legal limitations upon the freedom of states based upon Articles 9, 14, and 15 of the declaration. Their moral force, moreover, seems seriously diluted not merely on the basis of their redundance but also on the basis of their obvious ambiguity. The framers of the declaration, while concerned with abuses of human rights in general, left in abeyance the search for specific solutions to the refugee problem.

Conventions Relating to Refugees and Stateless Persons. Encouraged by the Declaration of Human Rights, the United Nations High Commissioner for Refugees in June 1951 summoned a conference at Geneva to formulate a "Convention Relating to the Status of Refugees." Twenty-six states participated in this conference which was officially greeted by the General Assembly as a "New Magna Carta for Refugees."[96] The main items on the agenda were the definition of refugee status, international legal protection of refugees, and implementation of the rights to asylum and nationality as set forth in the Declaration of Human Rights.

In their attempts to arrive at a uniform definition, the delegates, hypnotized by the past, decided to recognize no persons as genuine refugees who had become homeless after 1 January 1951. Having thus narrowed its definition, the convention then stipulates that it leaves it up to individual governments whether to include only European refugees in their definitions or "others" as well. The convention grants various rights to refugees, including freedom of religion, employment, residence, access to courts, education, and social security. The rights to asylum and nationality are conspicuous by their absence and there are no provisions for uniform legal protection. The substantive human rights granted to refugees by the convention, defined by some observers as its only concrete achievement, seem to lose much of their efficacy in the light of the fact that by July 1956 only fifteen of the participating governments had chosen to ratify the instrument incorporating the "Magna Carta."[97]

On 11 August 1950, the Economic and Social Council requested the International Law Commission to prepare a draft convention for the elimination of statelessness. The commission initiated its work in late 1951 and at length submitted to the Economic and Social Council two draft conventions: one on the Elimination of Future Statelessness and the other on the Reduction of Future Statelessness.

The preambles of both instruments base the provisions of the draft conventions on the fact that the Universal Declaration of Human Rights proclaims that "everyone has the right to a nationality." The Draft Convention on the Elimination of Statelessness is based on a thorough study of the roots of statelessness seen in a world divided by profound spiritual and political conflict. The Draft Convention on the Reduction of Future Statelessness is the more specific of the two. It suggests legal remedies for the problem. The most significant provisions include these:

A child who would otherwise be stateless shall acquire at birth the nationality of the country in whose territory it is born.

Loss of nationality in consequence of marriage, termination of marriage, or adoption is to be conditioned upon the acquisition of a new nationality.

No person is to be deprived of his nationality on racial, ethnic, religious, or political grounds, nor shall the transfer of territory automatically result in the loss of nationality on the part of the inhabitants.[98]

While it is clear that most of the above provisions are within the classification of *de lege ferenda,* the effort of the International Law Commission clearly indicates the desire to clarify and implement the provisions pertaining to refugees proclaimed in the Declaration of Human Rights.

The Covenants on Human Rights. Having framed the declaration, the Commission on Human Rights turned its attention to the more difficult task of drafting an International Covenant on Human Rights. This instrument, unlike the declaration, was to be in the nature of a treaty and therefore legally binding upon ratifying states. Confronted with insuperable difficulties, the General Assembly in 1952 decided to break the projected covenant into two independent parts, one to be called a Covenant on Civil and Political Rights and the other entitled a Covenant on Economic, Social, and Cultural Rights.[99]

The projected Covenant on Civil and Political Rights includes the right to life; to protection against torture, slavery, arbitrary arrest, and detention; to fair trial by an impartial tribunal; to protection against *ex post facto* laws; to freedom of religion, expression, and assembly; and to equality before the law. The Draft Covenant on Economic, Social, and Cultural Rights, defined as a group of "objectives to be achieved progressively," contains provisions with respect to employment, conditions of work, trade unions, social security, the family, food, clothing, housing, health, education, science, and culture.[100]

During the drafting stages it was decided to omit rights to asylum and nationality from the Covenant on Civil and Political Rights. Delegates in the Human Rights Commission were almost unanimously agreed that the inclusion of such provisions would reduce chances of ratification by those states who might see an implied threat to sovereignty in the necessity of having to revise their immigration laws.

While it was the opinion of some observers that a separation into two independent covenants would enable most states to ratify at least one of the instruments, an impasse has been reached. Governments have been less willing to pledge action than to subscribe to ideals in this field. No sensitive observer can fail to be aware of the distances which separate states in their concepts of what constitute human rights and how they should be sanctioned. This distance seems abysmal particularly in matters directly concerning the refugee problem. The deletion of rights to asylum and nationality from the Draft Covenant on Civil and Political Rights lends weight to the observation that sovereignty reaches its most absolute form in matters of immigration.

The European Convention on Human Rights. While the project of a Universal Covenant on Human Rights has so far met with little success, more concrete results have been achieved on the regional level. On 4 November 1950, at Rome, the fifteen members of the Council of Europe signed the Convention for the Protection of Human Rights and Fundamental Freedoms.[101] The convention went into effect on 3 September 1953 in the traditional form of a treaty.[102]

The covenant as finally adopted includes the following rights already contained in the Universal Declaration of the United Nations:

Security of persons; exemption from slavery and servitude; freedom from arbitrary arrest, detention or exile; freedom from arbitrary interference in private and family life, home and correspondence; freedom of thought, conscience and religion; freedom of opinion and expression; freedom of assembly; freedom of association, freedom to unite in trade unions; the right to marry and found a family.[103]

As in the Universal Covenant, the framers of the European instrument chose to omit rights to asylum and nationality for essentially similar reasons. Moreover, the drafters of the convention claimed to represent states already harboring considerable refugee populations.

Implementing the provisions of the convention, a European Commission on Human Rights, the first international body established by governments competent to receive and to act on individual petitions concerning violations of the rights set forth in the Convention, is presently functioning. At its third session, in September 1955, the commission acted upon eighty petitions registered up to that date.

A European Court on Human Rights, whose function would be the adjudication of infringements of the convention, has been proposed should the commission fail in its task of friendly settlement. The machinery governing this second organ of implementation is presently in the formulation stage.

The fact that the European Convention, despite the omission of rights to asylum and nationality so pertinent to the refugee problem, goes far beyond the Universal Declaration in its recognition of the need for legal remedies under the law of nations, may be attributed to its regional rather than universal character. This development may lend additional emphasis to the contention advanced in our analysis of the International Refugee Organization that functionalism may find more fertile application at the regional level. It seems that "the recognition of obligations in the matter of these rights and freedoms is the principal – or perhaps the only – condition of membership in the Council of Europe." [104]

CONCLUSIONS

The conclusion seems reasonable that the dissolution of the International Refugee Organization was premature. The vacuum following its end was not adequately filled by the present galaxy of organizations dealing with the problem. The creation of these agencies was simply an admission that the refugee problem is an emergency of a long-term nature. An integrated and coordinated approach to the problem by an experienced international staff was able significantly to influence the policies of refugee-receiving countries and succeeded in liberalizing most immigration requirements. The post-IRO agencies had little such power of persuasion and by late 1952 had to curtail their operations to a minimum.

There are two main arguments which may be advanced in favor of a regional approach as typified by UNRWA and UNKRA. First, it is claimed that it is easier to obtain funds for a specific program than for a single refugee organization. Although this may be true, it would be difficult to prove that the funds allocated to the post-IRO agencies have been used more efficiently or economically than those granted to IRO. It has been estimated that the futile efforts of the inexperienced UNRWA staff to cultivate "dead and waste" Arab territory cost that United Nations agency close to $100 million.[105] No similar wasted sums are to be found in the books of the International Refugee Organization. Second, the argument that regional refugee programs could be used as "pilot projects" for further study of the problem seems to have little merit. IRO operated on all five continents and during its existence amassed a body of experience far outweighing that of any presently existing regional organization. In fact, its collective experience, as set down in its official history, has been published as a study in international administration.[106] Perhaps the dispersal of the IRO staff with its unique experience in the international refugee problem has been the greatest loss to the uprooted throughout the world.

Given the existence of a refugee problem much more extensive than at the time of IRO's inception, it would seem that a collaborative effort under the aegis of the United Nations might be indicated. The record of IRO might be cited in support of such an argument. Moreover, the contradictions between the relevant provisions of documents pertaining to human rights and the actual practice of states in respect to exile, right of asylum, and right to nationality, seem to suggest that the international community, for the immediate future at least, will be limited to symptoms rather than causes in its dealings with the refugee problem. The ambiguity of these provisions in the documents themselves, particularly those pertaining to asylum and nationality, lend further weight to this contention.

However, the amalgamation of existing organizations into a unified United Nations agency would not alone suffice to hasten a solution. Such a step would have to be accompanied or even preceded by a relaxation of immigration restrictions comparable to those effected through the influence of IRO.

The United States has taken a first hesitant step toward a realistic solution by providing for the admission of 214,000 persons to America over a period of three years.[107] This law, which was passed by the American Congress on 30 July 1953 over strenuous and bitter opposition, permits immigration to the United States of 106,000 refugees under the jurisdiction of the United Nations High Commissioner.[108] Because of the vehemence of the opposition which inveighed against "turning the United States over to a European horde,"[109] the quota system governing immigration to the United States has been retained. Numerous administrative difficulties have made immigration under the act slow, but recent joint policy pronouncements by President Eisenhower as well as leading United States State Department officials indicate that almost the full quota of refugees admissible will have entered the United States by the end of 1956.[110] Thus, the American government has again assumed the initiative, albeit in a cautious and restricted manner.

The assumption of American leadership in the establishment of a single permanent international organization to deal with the refugee problem might also reap rewards. Many of the refugees are inveterate enemies of totalitarianism, but, if crowded into camps for indefinite periods of time, may come to provide ammunition for ideologies hostile to those of the democracies. Careful screening, patterned after the IRO precedent and reinforced by domestic security regulations, could easily exclude politically undesirable elements from the democracies. The argument that the relaxation of immigration restrictions leads to undue economic competition has long since been invalidated.[111] Objective studies as well as the experience of IRO have shown the beneficial effects which the newcomers have consistently had upon the political life and economies of the recipient countries.

The loss of valuable human resources through flight from oppression is one of the inherent weaknesses of any totalitarian regime. Albert Einstein and Sigmund Freud, fleeing from tyranny, rendered immeasurable services to the arsenal of democracy. There are more homeless prophets today hoping to end their wanderings. Their potential contributions to a democratic society must not be dissipated.

11

The Community of Exiles

"Normal men do not know that everything is possible." DAVID ROUSSET [1]

THE preceding chapters have largely dealt with the efforts of one or another international organization to cope with a permanent refugee problem. However, the refugees themselves have so far been regarded as objects of institutional attention rather than as human beings with their own particular problems and difficulties.

An analysis of the peculiar psychological effects arising from prolonged refugee status might contribute to an intelligent approach to the problem. At best, such an analysis might help equip a future International Refugee Organization with relevant psychological material to assist it in its task, and at the least, it might indicate to the United Nations the urgency of establishing such an organization.

It must be stated at the outset that such psychological probings constitute an excursion into what is still largely *terra incognita*. Most of the literature on the subject is either of a highly emotional, polemical nature sadly lacking in objectivity, or merely statistical with little attempt at analysis. Even the warmest sympathy must be combined with clear-sighted objectivity if it is to be helpful; on the other hand, refugees should not be treated as a stagnant pool of statistics. An approach employing the tools and insights of social psychology, while it would have to exercise great care in any generalizations, might nevertheless avoid these two extremes and shed needed light on certain underlying factors common to human beings exposed to prolonged refugee status.

In his brilliant analysis of man's inherently destructive drives, *Civilization and Its Discontents*,[2] Sigmund Freud adumbrated the great battle of the twentieth century, the war between the forces of Eros — the societal and "civilized" instincts — and the forces of destructive sadism. But even in his most pessimistic moments Freud never imagined that his prophetic words would within the next few years be given such horrible demonstration. Never before had the still small voice of conscience been reduced to so spectral, so ineffectual a whisper as in the period of totalitarian concentration camps. It is not surprising that years of concentration camp existence should leave their mark upon the souls of the liberated prisoners of yesterday who are the displaced persons of today. Most psychiatrists agree that readjustment of concentration camp neurotics to a comparatively normal existence has been favorable in most instances, provided that the security of re-establishment followed in a relatively short time.[3] While estimates vary, there seems to be agreement on the fact that, if a displaced person is exposed to the insecurities of refugee camp existence for a period exceeding three years, basic personality changes take place.[4]

This chapter will not deal with those fortunate displaced persons who were able to emigrate to a new country comparatively soon after liberation. In these cases, the record speaks for itself, showing that they were capable of regaining their balance and strength in a very short time. As opposed to these quick recoveries, most refugees who have had to remain in the camps for a prolonged period have grown progressively more anxious and aggressive, with serious consequences to themselves. This body of refugees, with which the present chapter will attempt to deal, consists mainly of the five hundred thousand residual IRO refugees scattered throughout camps in Germany, Austria, and Italy, many of whom are spending their tenth successive year in a displaced persons camp.

The validity of generalizing from the experience of these IRO residual refugees may be questionable. Yet, many of their symptoms are also characteristic of Arab, Indian, and Pakistani refugees who are ethnically completely different and entered DP camps under quite dissimilar circumstances. This suggests that the element common to all these groups, namely the fact that they spent more than three years in refugee camps, elicits certain typical responses. Since no such symptoms are as yet observable in those refugees who have escaped from the Iron Curtain countries only recently and have spent a comparatively brief period in the camps prepared to receive them, an attempt will be made to evaluate the psychological symptoms typical of refugees who have lived for more than three years in a camp environment. Wherever relevant, comparison will be attempted with the groups that were fortunate enough to be able to leave the camps before a period of approximately three years had elapsed.

The Freudian school of psychoanalysis, believing that man is, in a sense, "a slave of his childhood," adheres to the conviction that all adult reactions to environment are, for better or for worse, conditioned by early reactions to parental authority. A man's capacity to withstand prolonged pressure of extreme situations depends upon his ego strength, that is, upon an ego which through favorable childhood conditions has been enabled to establish defenses which will prevent disintegration.

This approach, while affording some penetrating insights that will be discussed later, seems somewhat incomplete in the light of available evidence. Observations of large heterogeneous groups of displaced persons suggest that situational features of the environment may also play an important role in the selection and utilization of behavior patterns. This view seems justified by the fact that thousands of culturally and ethnically different displaced persons with diverse patterns of parent-child relationships nevertheless exhibit essentially similar reactions after prolonged existence in a displaced persons camp.

Perhaps the primary factor typical of the "old camp refugees" is a state of social disintegration with symptoms surprisingly similar to those which the eminent French sociologist Durkheim found in people who were most prone to commit suicide.[5] This state of "anomie" is characterized by a loosening of all primary relationships, erotic and otherwise, due to an utter apathy founded on a wholesale and deep suppression of anxiety. It seems that these people, many of whom have survived a concentration camp, see themselves abandoned and betrayed a second time. Fearful of awakening their emotions, which had only caused them suffering, the refugees subconsciously stifle and suppress their cultural instinct – the instinct of sociability that binds together all community life with the ties of love and affection – in order to survive.

Some psychiatrists have given the name of *Stacheldrahtkrankheit* (stalag-mentality) to this phenomenon, since it is somewhat reminiscent of the attitude displayed by prisoners of war who have been interned for a considerable period. But the symptoms in the refugees are more advanced, probably because there is little hope for them to go "home"—a hope which prisoners have always nurtured. The shock of dislocation is greater and something of the suspiciousness of primitive man shows up in the "old camp refugees." Unable to find a safe haven in this world and dependent upon the arbitrariness of others, the refugee becomes an unreasonably nervous being. Idleness, boredom, monotony, and sterility of life all contribute to a state of suppressed anxiety. The enslaved workers had at least been forced to work and, however humiliating this might have been, it protected them against the insidious effects of boredom in displaced persons camps.

The displaced person in a camp is never alone and so cannot find the seclusion that cultured man needs from time to time. Consequently he often begins to hate his comrades and frequent violent outbreaks of "camp madness" occur. The loss of privacy and individuality is felt as an extreme form of humiliation and social degradation. The refugee is conscious of his decline without being able to stem it and his irritation and frustration over his helplessness vent themselves on the innocent, not the guilty.

Most of the "old camp refugees," whether in Europe or in the Near East, seem to develop types of behavior which are characteristic of infancy or early youth. The displaced persons live, like children, only in the immediate present. They lose a feeling for the sequence of time and become unable to plan for the future or to give up immediate pleasure satisfactions to gain greater ones in the near future. This regression into childhood is accompanied by a decline of restraint in the display of emotions. They become rude, unreliable, and, finally, completely asocial.

To compensate for their mental distress, the refugees indulge in childlike daydreams about the future. Such escapes only serve to make the refugee lose his remaining sense of perspective and consequently lead to much bitterness and disappointment when re-establishment is finally in sight. When such a refugee finally does succeed in leaving the camp, his expectations of the outside world are often too high because he had romanticized it too much while still in the camp. Nothing then comes up to his expectations and he does not feel at home in this harsh new world in which there is little room for romanticizing. He expects a great amount of warmth and understanding from others though he himself is not able to give either.

Aggression becomes the universal problem-solving device. It is expressed both verbally and physically and is directed against outsiders as well as other displaced persons. Whereas the "new refugees" usually resort to group efforts to remove a given irritation, the "old camp refugees" make no such effort. The behavior of each individual is violently asocial and every person is convinced that his need is greatest. A generalized attitude of helplessness, a loss of initiative and self-confidence begin to prevail. Many of the refugees have the feeling that they can do nothing on their own, that they always need outside help, and more important, that it is unquestionably due them.

The long separation from a normal environment appears to arouse so much anxiety that the refugee loses his sense of reality and continuously makes false evaluations of his surroundings. Frequently, paranoid reactions and other extreme indications of social trauma are exhibited by the camp population. This metamorphosis in the personality structure sometimes goes so far that schizophrenic symptoms of more or less acute character become noticeable.[6] A typical defense mechanism developed by the refugee is to become convinced that the camp experience is somehow happening not to "him" as a subject, but only to "him" as an object. As one observer paraphrased a typical refugee reaction: "What I am doing here or what is happening to me does not count at all. I feel as if I were living in an unreal world and all I want to do is to get away with as much as possible to make my life comfortable." [7]

Psychoanalysts know that the function of the ego is to mediate between the demands of our instincts and the prohibitions of our inculcated conscience. When, as in the "old camp refugees," the conscience — that social department of the ego, or what psychoanalysis calls the superego — is continually overruled and negated, the ego does not grow stronger. All that does grow stronger is the driving force of man's most primitive instinct, that of self-preservation. It begins to dominate the personality of the refugee and finally possesses it at the expense of almost every other drive.

Needless to say, the general anomic apathy of the "old camp refugees" is extended to their political life as well. Whereas many of them, upon entering the camps, were full of hopes and high aspirations for making their contribution to a democratic society, most of these hopes have by now given way to either disillusioned cynicism or complete political indifference. In fact, some observations show that more recent escapees from behind the Iron Curtain who have been lingering in displaced persons camps for prolonged periods are beginning to exhibit similar characteristics.[8] Since many of these refugees once were among the most inveterate enemies of totalitarianism, having risked their lives in order to re-establish themselves in a free society, their possible disintegration is not only a human loss, but a political loss as well.

The hope for migration in the foreseeable future has served as a unique dynamic force in the refugee camps. For example, the symptoms described above were least applicable to the Jewish populations in the European camps since migration to Palestine was always open to them.[9] But those same Jews, when intercepted by the British on their way to Palestine and interned indefinitely on the island of Cyprus, exhibited the disintegrative factors in a very severe form.[10] So long as Zionism as an ideological force offered concrete migration prospects in the future, it prevented serious personality disintegration.[11] This suggests that one part of the refugees' psychological trauma derives from the fact of being unwanted. The lack of hope for a change in status seems to promote psychic malaise among refugees quite as much as the actual circumstances of refugee camp life.

If we generalize from this example it may be stated that the hope for eventual migration which was held out to the refugees by IRO helped to prevent the acute "anomic apathy" which was characteristic of these same refugees once they had become part of the post-IRO "hard-core." In the Near East, similar disintegration has been observed in the Arab refugee population. Suicide rates are far higher among the "free-floating" camp population than among those Arab refugees who have been permanently reintegrated by UNRWA.[12] Many of the *Fedayen* – terrorist "suicide groups" infiltrating Israeli territory – are drawn from the Arab refugee camps. Their incendiary activities help maintain the explosive character of the Near Eastern political picture.[13]

Futher prolonged refugee status in the camps seems to be fraught with dangers not only to the displaced persons but to the international community as a whole. The longer the refugee spends in the camp, the less true to reality become his daydreams and evaluations of the outside world. The discrepancy between the idealized fantasies of the life which is awaiting him and which will compensate him for his suffering, and the difficult and complicated reality which he finds, is bound to lead to disappointment. Furthermore, many of the "old camp refugees" are to a high degree incapable or even afraid of believing again in genuinely good intentions or kindness in spite of their profound craving for signs of such kindness.

Continued camp existence with no hope for re-establishment might well turn the refugees into an unassimilable stratum in the international body politic. Their erstwhile friendliness toward democratic ideals might at best deteriorate into apathy and at worst flare into open hostility against the community which refuses them a haven of refuge. The growing rate of redefection of refugees to Soviet territory seems to support this contention. Men and women, after endangering their lives to escape from Soviet areas, now risk death a second time to return. "I will go home and they will put me in a labor camp," a redefector stated recently; "it will be no worse than what I have here and if I must die, at least it will be among my own people – not in a foreign country where everybody is my enemy." [14]

Particularly the young displaced persons are a source of anxiety. Instead of constant educational exercise in moral and social adaptation, they are subject to the destructive spirit of the camp and the cynicism of the hopeless. Seventy per cent of the adult males in some camps have served time in West German jails for common crimes and misdemeanors.[15] The corrosive influence of the camp is bound to tell particularly heavily upon the refugee children. Many psychiatrists fear that in the future their misery is bound to break through with a delayed shock reaction.[16] In other words, a whole generation of dangerously neurotic people may now be growing up in the displaced persons camps.

It seems that only the efforts of an international refugee organization accompanied by a liberalization of immigration restrictions can achieve a partial solution of this growing problem. The successful collaboration of IRO with over one hundred private voluntary organizations has also shown that in this delicate matter the "personalization" and individual attention of private societies are indispensable. The establishment of such an organization not only might coordinate the many disjointed international efforts prevalent at the present time and thus be a net economic gain for the United States and other member nations as well, but might also avert a progressive deterioration of thousands of human beings. Haste, however, is imperative. If the refugees are allowed to deteriorate further in the camps, the time may soon be reached when these human beings will no longer be assimilable in a normal environment. And, more broadly, as a thorough student of the problem has warned:

> The danger in the existence of such people is twofold: First, and more obviously, their ever-increasing numbers threaten our political life, our human artifice, the world which is the result of our common and coordinated effort in much the same, perhaps even more terrifying, way as the wild elements of nature once threatened the existence of man-made cities and countrysides. Deadly danger to any civilization is no longer likely to come from without. Nature has been mastered and no barbarians threaten to destroy what they cannot understand, as the Mongolians threatened Europe for centuries. Even the emergence of totalitarian governments is a phenomenon within, not outside, our civilization. The danger is that a global, universally interrelated civilization may produce barbarians from its own midst by forcing millions of people into conditions which, despite all appearances, are the conditions of savages.[17]

12

Quo Vadis?

"Every parting is a foretaste of death but every coming together is a glimpse of the resurrection." SCHOPENHAUER [1]

SINCE the inception of the League of Nations, governments have consistently attempted to deal with the refugee problem, though, as a rule, within rather narrowly defined limits of time and space. Parading through the annals of international organization is an uninterrupted procession of temporary agencies, each established to solve what is essentially a long-range problem. Not only have all these agencies been limited in time, but each has had jurisdiction over only specific parts of the world's refugee population. Although very diversified in international apparatus, international organizations dealing with refugees have remained essentially within this pattern and differences among them have been in degree rather than kind.

In addition to the spatial and temporal limitations, there has also been among the refugee agencies a rather clear-cut division of labor regarding the various aspects of refugee work. With one exception, the International Refugee Organization, each agency has exercised responsibility in only one major activity. Thus, the Nansen Office concentrated mainly on matters of legal protection similar to the function of the present United Nations High Commissioner's Office for Refugees. UNRRA's responsibility has been primarily relief and repatriation, while the Inter-Governmental Committee for Refugees has been interested mainly in the exploration of resettlement opportunties. Only the International Refugee Organization, while also limited like the other agencies in time and space, has combined all the above activities under one roof and treated the refugee problem in totality.

In view of such a division of labor, it is not surprising that the problem of coordination has always loomed large in the work of refugee agencies on the international scene. Generally, the relationships of the various organizations to their parent bodies, whether the League of Nations, as in the case of the Nansen Office, or the United Nations, as in the case of the International Refugee Organization, have been rather tenuous and in practice have tended toward even greater decentralization of efforts. Some agencies, like the Inter-Governmental Committee for European Migration, have been dissociated completely from the world organization. Coordination among the diverse international refugee organs has been sporadic and lacking in institutional basis.

Instances of duplication and overlapping resulting from such a decentralized approach have detracted markedly from operational and administrative efficiency. The lack of coordination among the Nansen Office, the Inter-Governmental Committee for Refugees, and the International Labour Office was partly to blame for the failure of international organization to use its resources to the fullest during the League period. Similarly, insufficient coordination among the United Nations High Commissioner's Office, UNRWA, UNKRA, ICEM, and USEP is partially responsible for the present state of confusion in international refugee work. In contrast, the International Refugee Organization which, for a time at least, was the sole agency dealing with the refugee problem internationally by coordinating all intergovernmental activities on behalf of displaced persons attained a remarkable degree of efficiency.

This integrated approach by IRO probably accounts in part for the comparatively greater bargaining power with refugee-receiving states which the Organization possessed, and neither prestige nor funds were dispersed in many different directions. The presently functioning UNHCOR as well as ICEM, both possessing little money and even less prestige, seem to lack almost completely IRO's ability to influence policy decisions of soverign governments.

Intimately connected with the problem of coordinating international refugee agencies is the necessity for international organizations to coordinate their policies with those of national governments. In this connection, the problem of national leadership has recently come into focus. While during the League period no one state occupied the limelight in refugee work, this picture has changed significantly since World War II. International refugee activity under the League was dominated by an individual, Fridtjof Nansen, but in the United Nations this role has accrued to a national state, the United States.

This development has given rise to some weighty implications. While in the League there was no single arbiter of the refugees' fate among the member states, all post-World War II international refugee agencies have, in fact, been the creatures of the United States. The United States, by footing by far the largest part of the bill, has enjoyed a veto power over their life and death. The success of the International Refugee Organization would have been impossible without American leadership and, conversely, the hardships of the United Nations High Commissioner's Office are, in large part, due to American reluctance to grant support.

An important corollary of this development has been the direct influence which domestic political considerations have had upon international refugee work. Thus, the fortuitous circumstance whereby the majority of postwar displaced persons were concentrated in the United States zones of Germany and Austria prompted the American Senate to ratify the IRO Constitution and by this act breathe life into the Organization. Also, in 1947, the Congress was still in favor of a United Nations organ including Communist representatives. On the other hand, by 1950, the mood of the Congress had changed to such an extent that it would not permit the creation of an international refugee organ on whose policy-making body representatives from the Iron Curtain countries would have a voice. The conviction that the Soviet and its satellites should not be included in any refugee organization, coupled with the unexamined yet widely prevalent assumption that a United Nations organ would *ipso facto* be inefficient, prompted the Congress to insist upon ICEM's establishment outside the United Nations framework and persuaded it to withhold all financial support from the United Nations High Commissioner's Office.

The one permanent factor on the scene has been the work of the voluntary agencies. For this reason, coordination among them and the governmental organs has been playing a very important part and is steadily gaining in significance. The most fruitful of such relationships was that during IRO's operation, when more than a hundred voluntary agencies were trained not only to perform complementary functions, but to assume primary responsibilities, as exemplified in the migration movements to Israel and in the securing of assurances basic to the administration of the United States Displaced Persons Act. To a considerable extent, these voluntary agencies are at present shouldering the operational burden of international refugee work.

In sum, it may be said that the unified and integrated approach of IRO resulted in a more efficient and more economical attack upon the refugee problem than the decentralized approaches of both the League and the post-IRO periods. It might be argued that, since the refugee problem today is quantitatively ten times as large as that which confronted IRO, only a unified IRO-type attack offers hope for a solution. In the words of the United Nations High Commissioner: "There remains a continuing need for some central international organization concerned with the problems of refugees." [2] However, what in theory is advisable is not necessarily feasible in practical politics.

In the first place, the United States, which has the deciding voice, is definitely set against the establishment of a United Nations body with operational responsibilities in international refugee work.[3] Secondly, the character of the problem since 1947 has changed to a considerable degree. While, at the time IRO was founded, refugees were geographically confined mainly to the European continent, the present picture is far more decentralized. Besides the European refugees, Arab displaced persons are stranded in the Near East, Hindu and Pakistani refugees are on the Indian subcontinent,[4] and millions of uprooted people wander aimlessly over the Korean peninsula.

This geographical decentralization of the refugee problem has invited a haphazard approach. Specific agencies have been created to deal with specific problems definable in geographic terms, and the valuable experience of the IRO staff in international administration and coordination has largely been dissipated. In fact, the present approach is in essence a regression to that of the League of Nations.

Not only is the establishment of another International Refugee Organization highly problematical, but there also seems to be little hope that the essentially long-range character of the refugee problem will be recognized by the creation of permanent organizations to deal with it. There has always been a reluctance by governments to legislate *in vacuo*, to nip a nascent refugee situation in the bud or to guard against possible future problems by having pre-existing machinery on hand. Also, perhaps the fundamental problem is not the urgent need for another IRO per se, but for national policies of openness toward immigration. Perhaps the international reluctance to establish a new IRO is symptomatic of national states' unwillingness to accept refugees. States could hardly be expected to set up an international organization for the purpose of persuading them to reverse their own immigration policies. It would be difficult to deny that such national policy viewpoints are more important than international gadgetry.

In the last analysis it seems that the present fairly chaotic situation will continue for an indefinite period. But it would be uncharitable not to acknowledge the significant accomplishments that have been made by the post-IRO international agencies. Although all are operating with a minimum of coordination with each other and some, such as ICEM and USEP, are divorced completely from the United Nations, their achievements have nevertheless been considerable. Moreover, the American Refugee Relief Act granting 106,000 refugees admission to the United States might set the stage for further liberalization throughout the Western world. If such a development should occur, the role of international organization in refugee work might be correspondingly enhanced.

Further increasing the complexity of refugee work is the extremely subtle and never constant relationship between "politics" and humanitarianism. The two factors have never played the role of two conflicting forces in the international arena nor would it be correct to maintain that international organizations have at all times defended the cause of humanitarianism against the primarily political motivations of national governments. Rather, the relationship might be seen in terms of a delicate balance. At times, the two factors have coalesced and become identical, on a few occasions they have been in open conflict, but in most instances some kind of compromise has been reached.

Broadly speaking, it is probably true that political considerations caused fundamentally different approaches to the refugee problem by the League and the United Nations. The League, which pursued a policy of universality of membership, regarded every nation as either an actual or a potential member state. Enemies of a given state who became refugees from it thus could not be given wholehearted support by the League because the world organization was reluctant to offend any of its members by offering succor to the refugees. It is significant in this connection that League assistance to Russian refugees declined when the Soviet Union was admitted to the world organization and rose again sharply when she was expelled. Belated efforts to come to the aid of the Jewish refugees were attempted by the League only after Germany had left the organization.

On the other hand, the United Nations, despite an avowed policy of universality, has practiced selective membership and since its inception has been divided by a profound ideological schism between the Eastern and Western ways of life. The United Nations has not felt constrained to display the sensitivity and cautiousness which was so characteristic of the League's work in refugee matters and it has been able to attack the problem in a more decisive manner.

There were further considerations which prompted the United Nations to adopt a more vigorous policy in aid of the postwar refugees. One grew out of the demand of certain countries for the unconditional repatriation of those who disagreed with their modes of government. Never before had the return of civilian dissidents been demanded in so absolute a fashion; rather the practice had been to attempt permanent expulsion of such undesirable elements. The new Soviet position, motivated by a need for reconstruction workers and a punitive policy toward its dissident elements, was met by an increasingly hardening reaction by the Western powers in the United Nations. Western policy in UNRRA had been imbued with the hope of finding a permanent *modus vivendi* with the Soviet Union and thus leaned toward a compromise between political and humanitarian considerations. Although freedom of choice for the individual refugee during the UNRRA period remained unimpaired, UNRRA attempted to "bribe" displaced persons into repatriating by promising extra rations and threatening "cut-off dates" to those refugees who refused to be repatriated. When during the debate before the establishment of the International Refugee Organization, the Soviet position increased in intransigence and it became clear that most remaining refugees were, in fact, refugees from Communism, the Western position became more adamant. The only remaining compromise with the Iron Curtain countries was the provision of three months' food rations to repatriating refugees, a provision which was never fully put into execution. But the Western powers who were to constitute IRO insisted upon freedom of choice for each individual refugee by including in IRO's constitution the proviso that "valid objections" to repatriation could be of a political nature.

In this decision political wisdom and humanitarian necessity became identical. Needless to say, it would have been both inhumane and politically unwise for the Western powers to accede to Soviet demands foi compulsory repatriation of the refugees. All the Western powers in the United Nations were deeply conscious of this fact although it must be stated that the primary motive of the United States Congress, on whose approval IRO's life depended, was neither political nor humanitarian but fiscal in nature.

In evaluating the comparatively short life of IRO, the general observation may be made that the Organization in most instances attempted to strike a balance between political and humanitarian considerations. Thus, in the countries of first asylum, especially Germany and Austria, IRO attempted to place its refugees squarely into a changing political picture. The privileged status of the displaced persons in relation to the native populations was slowly eliminated in order to keep pace with a Germany advancing toward renewed political emancipation. In its agreements with other countries of first asylum, IRO often assumed the role of a sovereign state, albeit dedicated to charitable rather than political aims.

In its overseas resettlement operations, IRO quite unambiguously attempted to safeguard the interests of its refugees against economic exploitation. In this instance, a rather clear policy was apparent. The international organization, through lobbying, publicity, and insistent pressure, attempted to protect the humanitarian interests of the refugees by successfully persuading most recipient governments to liberalize their admission requirements. The "model" agreements with Turkey and Israel as well as the resettlement of many hard-core refugees in the Scandinavian countries are successful cases in point.

The post-IRO pattern is again of greater complexity because political and humanitarian considerations in some instances are hopelessly far apart. The psychological deterioration of most of the IRO residual refugees has by now progressed to a point where the refugees could only with great difficulty become an asset to a country willing to receive them. For this reason, settlement in the area where they are presently living is probably the only feasible solution for the Asian refugees. In the case of the IRO residual displaced persons, the question should be raised, however, whether they might not come to constitute an even greater danger to the civilized community if allowed to continue in their present state.

The United States Escapee Program has already attempted a solution of this dilemma in primarily political terms. By discriminating between the "old camp refugees" and the new escapees in favor of the latter, it has certainly pushed humanitarian considerations into the background. It might well be that the admirable courage and ingenuity displayed by the new escapees have appealed to the American Congress. However, the "old camp refugees" have probably suffered as much and as long, albeit with less publicity.

It seems to be true, at least to some extent, that the absence of a unified International Refugee Organization has sharpened the dichotomy between "politics" and humanitarianism. The American Escapee Program is a case in point. The Inter-Governmental Committee for European Migration, weak and lacking in prestige, is another. It has failed completely in effecting even a few of the immigration liberalizations which had been achieved by IRO. Only the recent American move admitting 106,000 is an exception to this prevailing trend.

If we survey international refugee work since the birth of the League, it seems that IRO, of all the organizations involved, succeeded in striking the healthiest balance between humanitarian and political considerations. IRO's policy at its best was to prove to governments that political expediency and humanitarian wisdom were identical. However, when an irreconcilable conflict did arise the political factor usually triumphed, since IRO was not able to assume the role of a sovereign state. Mr. Kingsley's futile plea to continue the life of IRO is probably the best example. However, IRO's decision to lobby in the United States for the admission of refugees was an instance in which the Organization's staff successfully contravened a national policy in the humanitarian interest of its refugee wards. Thus, although the Organization was not able always to avert a conflict between the two principles, it succeeded in demonstrating to the world that humanitarianism and "politics" were not necessarily competitive values.

Three methods of attack upon the refugee problem have been employed by international organization: repatriation, re-establishment in the countries of first asylum, and resettlement in new environments. As the techniques of international organization have improved, the last of these three alternatives has perhaps attained the greatest significance. However, international organization has only been able to deal with the symptom, namely the refugee, but has not been allowed sufficient access to the cause, largely found in the abuse of fundamental human rights. The League was not able to ameliorate such abuses in Germany, nor has the United Nations been able significantly to influence Soviet policy in this respect. According to our analysis of United Nations documents pertaining to human rights and, indirectly, to refugees, the discrepancies between moral aspirations and political realities are still very great. It is doubtful that the foreseeable future will bring any considerable advance in this field and it is likely, therefore, that so long as we do not yet fully understand the causes of man's inhumanity to man and so long as such inhumanity remains primarily within the domestic jurisdiction of states, international organization will be confronted with a long-range problem.

It may be that the refugee question is one of those international problems that is difficult to solve by direct frontal attack. Perhaps the activities of international organizations not directly related to refugees might end the refugee problem by undercutting the conditions which produce uprootedness. The activities of diverse functional organizations, the codification of international legal procedures, the birth of new regional security arrangements, all may open "back-door" approaches to the refugee problem. However, it seems that the very nations which produce refugees are least inclined to cooperate in those international activities that might make such approaches possible.

Despite many limitations, international refugee work has made great strides forward by meeting the problem frontally. Fridtjof Nansen in his most fervent hopes never dreamed of mass overseas resettlement as a working reality. Yet, two decades after his death, the greatest overseas resettlement scheme for refugees ever to be conceived was nearing completion. IRO, although primarily the instrument of national policies, at times developed a drive of its own which turned its staff into an operational *corpus separatum.* As a result of IRO's work a social consciousness toward the refugee which was completely lacking during the League period emerged in the international body politic. It is highly probable that this consciousness has not now been extinguished, but merely the sense of urgency prevalent during the immediate postwar period. A latent awareness of the refugee problem might result in more energetic efforts by the Western powers should the refugee again become an acute political issue.

Finally, international organization has not succeeded in solving the "means versus end" dilemma with which it has consistently been confronted in its work with refugees. The functionalist dream, hoping for a slow development of habits of collaboration between East and West in refugee work, an experience that might ultimately be transferred to the political sphere as well, has proved to be just a dream. The refugee problem is itself too vitally political to lend itself to such an approach. In fact, by dealing with displaced persons international organization, instead of bringing East and West actively together, has tended to push them further apart.

Thus, international organization has had to choose between universality and paralysis on the one hand and selectivity and effectiveness on the other. By taking the latter course, international organization has salvaged millions of homeless people uprooted through the forces of bigotry and intolerance and has subscribed to the conviction that men should be allowed freedom from fear and liberty of individual decision. In this sense, it has succeeded in cutting through that most pernicious layer of national sovereignty which still claims final jurisdiction over individual action. Having taken this road, international organization has set its future course in its work for refugees: So long as basic human rights continue to be abused, so long will the primary task of international organization in refugee work remain the transfer of human beings from areas where fundamental human liberties are not yet recognized to those parts of our earth where freedom beckons.

NOTES, BIBLIOGRAPHY AND INDEX

Notes

Chapter 1

[1] Quoted in Sir John Hope Simpson, *The Refugee Problem* (Oxford: Oxford University Press, 1939), p. 239.

[2] Cicero, *Laws*, I, 10, pp. 28–29. (Translation by C. W. Keyes.)

[3] Cicero, *Republic*, III, p. 22. (Translation by Sabine and Smith.)

[4] Emphasis mine.

[5] Thomas Paine, *Rights of Man*, edited by M. D. Conway (New York, 1894), II, p. 311. (Emphasis mine.)

[6] H. Lauterpacht, *An International Bill of the Rights of Man* (New York: Columbia University Press, 1945), p. 26.

[7] Edmund Burke, *Reflections on the Revolution in France* (1790), edited by E. J. Payne, Everyman's Library, p. 96.

[8] The "Nansen Passport," an identity document held by most Russian refugees, described its bearer as *personne d'origine russe* at the insistence of the leading refugees themselves.

[9] Hannah Arendt, *The Origins of Totalitarianism* (New York: Harcourt, Brace & Company, 1951), p. 268.

[10] *Ibid.*, p. 294.

[11] Elfan Rees, "The Refugee and the United Nations," *International Conciliation*, June 1953, No. 492, p. 313.

Chapter 2

[1] Sigmund Freud, "The Disillusionment of the War," *Civilization, War and Death*, edited by John Rickman, M.D. (London: The Hogarth Press, 1953), p. 11.

[2] Simpson, *op. cit.*, p. 75.

[3] C. A. Macartney, *Refugees – The Work of the League* (London: League of Nations Union, 1930), p. 19.

[4] *Ibid.*, p. 20.

[5] Simpson, *op. cit.*, p. 199.

[6] Clarence A. Clausen, "Dr. Fridtjof Nansen's Work as High Commissioner of the League of Nations" (abstract of thesis, University of Illinois, 1932), p. 6.

[7] Simpson, *op. cit.*, p. 200.

[8] Article 23 of the Covenant merely provided that "Members of the League will endeavor to secure and maintain fair and humane conditions of labor for men, women, and children, and for that purpose will establish and maintain the necessary international organizations."

[9] Dorothy Thompson, *Refugees* (New York: Random House, 1938), p. 19.

[10] League of Nations Document No. A/L/35, Minutes of the Fourth Committee of the Second Assembly, Annex 23, p. 305.

[11] Simpson, *op. cit.*, p. 194.

[12] Macartney, *op. cit.*, p. 29.

[13] It was estimated by the League Assembly that the annual cost incurred by European governments in supporting their unemployed and helpless refugees was £2,000,000. *Ibid.*, p. 19.

[14] Macartney, *op. cit.*, p. 36.

[15] League of Nations Document No. CRR30/1, 1922.

[16] League of Nations Document No. CL79/B, 1922.

[17] In Germany, the Nansen Certificate was granted only to Russian refugees arriving before 6 May 1921, a date subsequently extended to January 1923.

[18] Macartney, *op. cit.*, p. 31.

[19] Clausen, *op. cit.*, p. 14.

[20] E. E. Reynolds, *Nansen* (London: Penguin Books, 1949), p. 225.

[21] League Council, *Official Journal,* April 1922, p. 349.

[22] Report by Sir Samuel Hoare to the League Council, *Official Journal,* May 1922, p. 401.

[23] Louise W. Holborn, "The League of Nations and the Refugee Problem," *Annals of the American Academy of Political and Social Science*, May 1939, p. 126.

[24] Macartney, *op. cit.*, p. 34.

[25] Holborn, *op. cit.*, p. 126.

[26] Macartney, *op. cit.*, p. 47.

[27] E. J. Phelan, *Yes and Albert Thomas* (New York: Columbia University Press, 1949), p. 196.

[28] Macartney, *op. cit.*, p. 16.

[29] League Council, Minutes of the Fourth Committee, *Official Journal,* Special Supplement. No. 27, 1924, p. 49.

[30] Simpson, *op. cit.*, p. 32.

[31] Macartney, *op. cit.*, p. 50.

[32] League Council, Minutes in *Official Journal,* November 1920, p. 5.

[33] Macartney, *op. cit.*, p. 50.

[34] Holborn, *op. cit.*, p. 127.

[35] Simpson, *op. cit.*, p. 34.

[36] *Ibid.*, p. 240.

[37] *Ibid.*, p. 205.

[38] *Ibid.*, p. 36.

[39] *Ibid.*, p. 37.

[40] League of Nations Document No. A23/12, August 1924, p. 9.

[41] League Council, *Official Journal,* August 1924, p. 206.

[42] Macartney, *op. cit.*, p. 62.

[43] Simpson, *op. cit.*, p. 38.

[44] Thompson, *op. cit.*, pp. 35–36.

[45] Simpson, *op. cit.*, p. 37.

[46] Macartney, *op. cit.*, p. 65. The great bulk of the Armenians in Syria were crowded into three huge camps at Alexandretta, Aleppo, and Beirut.

[47] The affinity of this idea to Fourier's "agricultural phalanxes" is perhaps not coincidental. Both Fourier and Thomas were French socialists.

[48] Simpson, *op. cit.*, p. 18.

[49] Macartney, *op. cit.*, p. 85.

[50] Holborn, *op. cit.*, p. 127.

[51] Simpson, *op. cit.*, p. 22.

[52] *Ibid.*, p. 24.

[53] League Council, *Official Journal,* February 1930, p. 69.

[54] Holborn, *op. cit.*, p. 131.

[55] The Governing Body consisted of the president, chairman, three representatives

of the Inter-Governmental Advisory Committee for Refugees (set up by the Council in 1928), a nominee of the secretary-general, a nominee of the director of the ILO, three members of the Advisory Committee of Private Organizations, and two members of the principal international relief organizations chosen by a majority vote of the other members of the Governing Body. Holborn, *op. cit.*, p. 131.

[56] *Ibid.*, p. 132. The "Arrangement of 1928" refers to a third inter-governmental conference summoned by Dr. Nansen in 1928 at which the benefits of the "Nansen Passport" had been extended to Assyrian, Assyro-Chaldean, Turkish, and various other groups of refugees. The new arrangement had been accepted by thirteen countries. See Simpson, *op. cit.*, p. 240.

[57] Thompson, *op. cit.*, p. 40.

[58] Macartney, *op. cit.*, p. 63.

Chapter 3

[1] Gertrude Kummer, "Is There an Answer?" *Survey Graphic*, August 1944, p. 360.

[2] Heinrich Heine, *Zur Geschichte der Religion und Philosophie in Deutschland* (Berlin: Aufbau-Verlag, 1951), Vol. 5, p. 329.

[3] Thompson, *op. cit.*, p. 64.

[4] Maurice R. Davie, *Refugees in America* (New York: Harper and Brothers, 1947), p. 6.

[5] *Ibid.*, p. 7. Jews constituted approximately 1 per cent of the total German population.

[6] *Ibid.*, p. 7.

[7] Simpson, *op. cit.*, p. 215.

[8] League of Nations Document No. A/14, 1 November 1934, p. 1.

[9] *Ibid.*, p. 2.

[10] League of Nations Document No. CL120/12, 1935.

[11] League of Nations Document No. CM13/12, 1936.

[12] League Council, *Official Journal*, February 1937, p. 202.

[13] League of Nations Document No. A9, 1936, pp. 8–12.

[14] Davie, *op. cit.*, p. 11.

[15] American Jewish Committee, *To the Counsellors of Peace* (New York, 1945), pp. 64–65.

[16] Davie, *op. cit.*, pp. 10–11.

[17] Senator Herbert H. Lehman, "Towards a New Immigration Policy," *Journal of International Affairs*, May 1953, pp. 87–88.

[18] Holborn, *op. cit.*, p. 134.

[19] The following states were represented at the Evian Conference in March 1938: Australia, Argentina, Belgium, Bolivia, Brazil, United Kingdom, Canada, Chile, Colombia, Costa Rica, Cuba, Denmark, Dominican Republic, Ecuador, France, Guatemala, Haiti, Honduras, Ireland, Mexico, Netherlands, New Zealand, Nicaragua, Norway, Panama, Paraguay, Peru, Sweden, Switzerland, United States, and Venezuela.

[20] Proceedings of the Intergovernmental Committee, Evian, 16 July 1938, Part II, Agenda of the Committee, p. 14.

[21] *Ibid.*, p. 16.

[22] Proceedings of the Intergovernmental Committee, *op. cit.*, p. 6.

[23] Eric Eristock, "The Evian Conference and the Intergovernmental Committee," *Annals of the American Academy of Political and Social Science*, May 1939, p. 137.

[24] *Ibid.*, p. 137.

[25] Holborn, *op. cit.*, p. 135.

[26] British Foreign Office Report, "Intergovernmental Committee to Continue and Develop the Work of the Evian Meeting," London, August 3, 1938, p. 2.

[27] Proceedings of the Intergovernmental Committee, *op. cit.*, p. 4.

[28] Jacques Vernant, *The Refugee in the Post-War World, Preliminary Report of a Survey* (Geneva, 1951), p. 27.
[29] *Ibid.*, p. 27.
[30] *Ibid.*, p. 27.
[31] Davie, *op. cit.*, p. 12.
[32] *Ibid.*, p. 13.
[33] United States War Refugee Board, *Final Summary Report* (Washington, D.C.: Government Printing Office, 15 September 1945), p. 1.
[34] *Ibid.*, p. 10.
[35] *Ibid.*, p. 16.

Chapter 4

[1] Chapter 36, verse 24.
[2] Eugene M. Kulischer, *Europe on the Move* (New York: Columbia University Press, 1948), p. 255.
[3] *Ibid.*, p. 257.
[4] *Ibid.*, p. 258.
[5] *Ibid.*, p. 260.
[6] *Ibid.*, p. 261.
[7] *Deutsche Allgemeine Zeitung*, 22 July 1942.
[8] Kulischer, *Europe on the Move*, p. 264.
[9] Arendt, *op. cit.*, p. 417.
[10] Eugene Kogon, *Der SS Staat* (Munich, 1946), p. 58.
[11] Bruno Bettelheim, "On Dachau and Buchenwald," *Journal of Abnormal and Social Psychology*, October 1943, pp. 831–832.
[12] Arendt, *op. cit.*, pp. 417–418.
[13] Eugene M. Kulischer, "Displaced Persons in the Modern World," *Annals of the American Academy of Political and Social Science*, March 1949, p. 169.
[14] *Ibid.*, p. 168.
[15] *Reichsdeutsche* according to the German laws were considered German citizens prior to 1939, regardless of residence.
[16] *Volksdeutsche* were ethnic Germans who lived outside the Reich's 1939 boundaries and were not German citizens.
[17] Kulischer, *Europe on the Move*, p. 266.
[18] *Der Bund* (Bern, Switzerland), 5 February 1945.
[19] Kulischer, "Displaced Persons in the Modern World," p. 169.
[20] George Woodbridge, compiler, *UNRRA: The History of the United Nations Relief and Rehabilitation Administration* (New York: Columbia University Press, 1950), I, 10–11.
[21] The nations participating in UNRRA were Australia, Belgium, Bolivia, Brazil, Canada, Chile, China, Colombia, Costa Rica, Cuba, Czechoslovakia, Dominican Republic, Ecuador, Egypt, El Salvador, Ethiopia, France, Greece, Guatemala, Haiti, Honduras, Iceland, India, Iran, Iraq, Liberia, Luxembourg, Mexico, Netherlands, New Zealand, Nicaragua, Norway, Panama, Paraguay, Peru, Philippines, Poland, South Africa, USSR, United Kingdom, United States, Uruguay, Venezuela, and Yugoslavia.
[22] Woodbridge, *op. cit.*, I, 67.
[23] The General Council was the policy-determining organ of the organization. All forty-four members of UNRRA were represented on it. In practice, however, authority for both policy formulation and execution became centralized in the Executive Committee, comprising the United States, United Kingdom, China, and the USSR.

Regarding the details on the organization structure of UNRRA, see Robert H. Johnson, "The Case of UNRRA," *World Politics*, July 1951.
[24] UNRRA Council Resolutions on Policy, Resolution 40, July 1945, p. 9.

[25] *Ibid.*, p. 10.
[26] U.S. Department of State Publication No. 2783, *Occupation of Germany*, August 1947, p. 151.
[27] The Potsdam expellees called themselves *Heimatvertriebene* (expelled from home), thus attempting to set themselvs apart from native Germans.
[28] According to Germany's first postwar census on 29 October 1946.
[29] UNRRA Council Resolutions on Policy, Resolution 44, July 1945, p. 1.
[30] UNRRA Council Resolutions on Policy, Resolution I—Section II, 1944, p. 9. (Emphasis mine.)
[31] Woodbridge, *op. cit.*, II, 473–474.
[32] *New York Times*, 14 December 1945.
[33] *Ibid.*
[34] The United States with 72 per cent of the budget was the main contributing nation, followed by the United Kingdom with 24 per cent. The USSR, although represented on the Executive Committee, contributed very little to the cost of UNRRA operations.
[35] Woodbridge, *op. cit.*, I, 486, 487. Also UNRRA General Council Resolution No. 99.
[36] Woodbridge, *op. cit.*, I, 487.
[37] UNRRA Executive Committee Resolution No. R-13, 1 October 1946.
[38] UNRRA, *UNRRA in Europe, 1945–1947*, Operational Analysis Paper No. 49 (London, June 1947). A temporary monthly increase of about 10 per cent resulted from the Ration Plan, but after three months, repatriation fell off sharply to about 50 per cent of the previous figure.
[39] *New York Times*, 7 March 1947.
[40] Elliott Schryver, "The International Refugee Organization," *American Institute of International Information* (New York), May 1947, p. 3.
[41] *UNRRA in Europe*, p. 81.
[42] Schryver, *op. cit.*, p. 4.
[43] *Ibid.*, p. 5.
[44] René Ristelhueber, "The International Refugee Organization," *International Conciliation*, April 1951, No. 470, p. 189.
[45] The objection raised in some quarters that German and Austrian Jews were ineligible for UNRRA assistance since they were not United Nations nationals was neatly dismissed when it was pointed out that the Jews had been denaturalized by Hitler and had thus become eligible for international protection.
[46] Ristelhueber, *op. cit.*, p. 173.
[47] The Spanish Republicans, although technically not United Nations nationals, had been made eligible for UNRRA assistance by special dispensation; in fact, most of the burden for their maintenance was borne by the French government and French voluntary agencies.
[48] Ristelhueber, *op. cit.*, p. 173.
[49] Schryver, *op. cit.*, p. 4.
[50] This is the UNRRA figure given for October 1945; it is not very accurate because a considerable number of Yugoslavs were not living in UNRRA camps but preferred to eke out a clandestine existence in various parts of Italy.
[51] Ristelhueber, *op. cit.*, p. 188.
[52] *Ibid.*, p. 188.
[53] Simpson, *op. cit.*, p. 1. (Emphasis mine.)

Chapter 5

[1] UN Doc. E/Ref. 1, 15 February 1946, p. 19.
[2] *Ibid.*, p. 23.
[3] *New York Times*, 13 January 1946.

[4] *London Times*, 14 January 1946.
[5] Preamble, United Nations Charter.
[6] *Ibid.*
[7] David Mitrany, *A Working Peace System* (London: Royal Institute of International Affairs, 1943), p. 7.
[8] The launching of the Food and Agriculture Organization by Franklin D. Roosevelt in June 1943 is a case in point.
[9] The Iranian dispute was formally brought before the Security Council on 19 January 1946.
[10] The member states present during the refugee debates in the Third Committee were Australia, Byelorussia, USSR, Belgium, United Kingdom, United States, Yugoslavia, Ukraine, Netherlands, Canada, Poland, Denmark, Philippines, Czechoslovakia, South Africa, France, Panama, Egypt, Lebanon, Iraq, and New Zealand.
[11] UN Doc. A/45, 15 February 1946.
[12] The member governments were Australia, Byelorussia, Brazil, France, Lebanon, Poland, USSR, Ukraine, Belgium, Canada, China, Colombia, Czechoslovakia, Dominican Republic, New Zealand, United States, Peru, United Kingdom, and Yugoslavia.
[13] Roger Nathan-Chapotot, *Les Nations Unies et les Réfugiés* (Paris: A. Pedone, 1949), p. 98.
[14] Verbatim Records of the Meetings of the Third Committee of the General Assembly, 28 January 1946, p. 9; also UN Doc. E/Ref. 1. The "existing bodies" were UNRRA, IGC, and the military authorities.
[15] Verbatim Records, 28 January 1946, p. 13. Also UN Doc. E/Ref. 1.
[16] Verbatim Records, 8 February 1946, p. 6. Also UN Doc. E/Ref. 1.
[17] Verbatim Records, 28 January 1946, p. 17. Also UN Doc. E/Ref. 1.
[18] Verbatim Records, 29 January 1946, p. 13. Also UN Doc. E/Ref. 1.
[19] *New York Times*, 2 February 1946.
[20] Verbatim Records, 3 February 1946, p. 1. Also UN Doc. E/Ref. 1.
[21] UN Doc. E/Ref. 1, p. 35.
[22] Verbatim Records, 4 February, p. 3. Also UN Doc. E/Ref. 1, 1946.
[23] *Ibid.*, p. 20.
[24] *Ibid.*, p. 21.
[25] UN Doc. E/Ref. 1.
[26] UN Doc. A/C–3/12, p. 5, Annex H.
[27] Verbatim Records, 4 February 1946, p. 24.
[28] *Ibid.*, 5 February 1946, p. 5.
[29] *New York Times*, 5 February 1946.
[30] See Comments by the Rapporteur on Proceedings of the Third Committee, UN Doc. E/Ref. 75, 1 June 1946.
[31] Verbatim Records, 3 February 1946. Also UN Doc. E/Ref. 1.
[32] *Ibid.*, p. 15.
[33] Verbatim Records, 6 February 1946, p. 14. Also UN Doc. E/Ref. 1.
[34] *Ibid.*, p. 21.
[35] UN Doc. E/Ref. 31, 7 February 1946.
[36] Verbatim Records, 7 February 1946, p. 4. Also UN Doc. E/Ref. 1.
[37] UN Docs. E/Ref. 1 and E/Ref. 75.
[38] Verbatim Records, 6 February 1946, p. 10. Also UN Doc. E/Ref. 1.
[39] *Ibid.*, p. 12 Also UN Doc. E/Ref. 1.
[40] *Ibid.*, p. 16.
[41] UN Doc. E/15, Annex A, 14 February 1946.
[42] *Ibid.*
[43] UN Doc. E/Ref. 1.
[44] *Ibid.*
[45] *Ibid.*

[46] *Ibid.*
[47] UN Doc. E/Ref. 75, Addendum 1.
[48] *Ibid.*
[49] *Ibid.*
[50] *Ibid.*
[51] UN Doc. E/87 and E/92, 6 February 1946.
[52] UN Doc. A/C/2/23.
[53] UN Doc. E/Ref. 1.
[54] UN Doc. E/Ref. 75.
[55] UN Doc. E/Ref. 1.
[56] *Ibid.*
[57] Verbatim Records, 9 February 1946.
[58] *Ibid.*
[59] *Ibid.*
[60] *New York Times*, 10 February 1946.
[61] *Christian Science Monitor*, 10 February 1946.
[62] Verbatim Records, 10 February 1946.
[63] *Ibid.*
[64] *Ibid.*
[65] UN Doc. E/15, 14 February 1946.
[66] UN Doc. E/Ref. 75.
[67] Verbatim Records, 10 February 1946.
[68] *Ibid.*
[69] *Ibid.*
[70] *Pro*: Australia, Belgium, United Kingdom, United States, Netherlands, Canada, Denmark, Philippines, South Africa, France, Panama, Egypt, New Zealand. *Con*: USSR, Byelorussia, Ukraine, Poland, Yugoslavia. *Abstaining*: Czechoslovakia, Lebanon, Iraq.
[71] *New York Times*, 13 February 1946.
[72] *Pravda*, 13 February 1946.
[73] UN Doc. A/C 3/23, 1 March 1946.
[74] UN Doc. E/Ref. 1.
[75] *Ibid.*
[76] UN Doc. A/C 3/23, 1 March 1946.
[77] UN Doc. E/Ref. 75.
[78] UN Doc. A/C 3/ 24, 1 March 1946.
[79] UN Doc. E/15.
[80] *New York Times*, 13 February 1946.
[81] *New York Times*, 14 February 1946.
[82] UN Doc. E/Ref. 54, 3 May 1946.
[83] UN Doc. E/Ref. 39, 25 April 1946.
[84] *Ibid.*
[85] UN Doc. E/Ref. 54.
[86] *Ibid.*
[87] *Pro*: Brazil, Byelorussia, China, Colombia, Czechoslovakia, Dominican Republic, Peru, Poland, Ukraine, USSR, United States, Yugoslavia. *Con*: Australia, Canada, Lebanon, Netherlands, New Zealand, United Kingdom. *Abstaining*: Belgium, France. UN Doc. E/Ref. 59.
[88] United Nations Charter, Article 63.
[89] The members were Canada, Colombia, Czechoslovakia, Dominican Republic, France, Lebanon, Netherlands, New Zealand, Poland, Ukraine, United Kingdom, United States, USSR, and Yugoslavia.
[90] UN Doc. E/Ref/Finances/23, 15 July 1946.
[91] *Ibid.*
[92] UN Doc. E/Ref/Fact Finding/25, 18 July 1946.

[93] UN Doc. E/Ref/Finances/23.

[94] UN Doc. E/Ref. 75.

[95] The members were USSR, Yugoslavia, France, United Kingdom, and the United States.

[96] UN Doc. Records, General Assembly, Second Session, p. 1447.

[97] *Ibid.*, p. 1453.

[98] *Pro*: Belgium, Canada, China, Cuba, Denmark, Dominican Republic, Ecuador, France, Greece, Guatemala, Honduras, Iceland, Iran, Lebanon, Liberia, Luxembourg, Mexico, Netherlands, Nicaragua, Norway, Panama, Paraguay, Peru, Philippines, South Africa, United Kingdom, United States, Uruguay, Venezuela. *Con*: USSR, Ukraine, Byelorussia, Yugoslavia, Poland. *Abstaining*: Afghanistan, Argentina, Australia, Bolivia, Brazil, Chile, Colombia, Costa Rica, Czechoslovakia, Egypt, Ethiopia, Haiti, India, Iraq, Saudi Arabia, Sweden, Syria, Turkey.

[99] The technical distinction between a "refugee" and a "displaced person" is explained in Chapter 6.

[100] E. F. Penrose, "Refugees and Displaced Persons," *Negotiating with the Russians*, edited by Raymond Dennett and Joseph E. Johnson (Boston: World Peace Foundation, 1951), p. 166.

[101] *Ibid.*, p. 167.

Chapter 6

[1] L. Michael Hacking, "Draft History of the International Refugee Organization" (unpublished document in mimeographed form), Chapter III, p. 47.

[2] Part II of Annex I to the IRO Constitution.

[3] Journals of the Third Committee of the General Assembly: No. 43, Supplement No. 3 A/C 3/100.

[4] UN Doc. E/Ref. 65, 20 May 1946.

[5] Article 2, IRO Constitution.

[6] Section C, Part I, Annex, IRO Constitution.

[7] "Specialized agency" is the generic term given to organizations established by intergovernmental agreement, having wide international responsibilities in economic, social, cultural, educational, health, and related fields, and brought into formal relationship with the United Nations, which may make recommendations for the coordination of their policies and activities. See Charter of the United Nations, Articles 55, 57, 58.

[8] Article 4, IRO Constitution.

[9] The eighteen members of IRO were Canada, Dominican Republic, France, Guatemala, Netherlands, Norway, United Kingdom, United States, Australia, Belgium, China, Iceland, New Zealand, Denmark, Luxembourg, Italy, Switzerland, and Venezuela.

[10] Article 5, IRO Constitution.

[11] Article 6, IRO Constitution.

[12] *Agreement between the United Nations and the International Refugee Organization*, Article 15, United Nations Publication, Lake Success, 1949.

[13] UN Doc. E/Ref. 1.

[14] UN Doc. E/Ref. 75.

[15] Hacking, *op. cit.*, Chapter IV, p. 14.

[16] *Ibid.*, p. 15.

[17] *Ibid.*

[18] *Ibid.*, p. 16.

[19] IRO Constitution, Article 4.

[20] Hearing before the Committee on Foreign Relations, United States Senate, S.J. Resolution No. 77, 1 March 1947, p. 11.

[21] *Ibid.*, p. 9.

[22] *Ibid.*, pp. 37–38.

[23] *Ibid.*, p. 39.
[24] Hacking, *op. cit.*, Chapter III, p. 15.
[25] Iceland, for example, met its obligation in the form of cod-liver oil.
[26] Report of the Committee on Expenditure in the Executive Departments, United States Relations with International Organizations, United States Congress, 8 June 1949.
[27] See Allied Control Commission for Germany, Proclamation No. 2, *IRO and the Occupation Authorities*, July 1947, paragraphs 9 and 35.
[28] General Council, Report on the 6th Session, 18 November 1950, Doc. GC/194

Chapter 7

[1] C. V. Gheorghiu, *La Vingt-Cinquième Heure* (Paris: Plon, 1951), p. 248.
[2] As authorized by its constitution, cf. Article 2, paragraph 2e.
[3] United Nations Department of Social Affairs, *A Study of Statelessness* (Lake Success, August 1949), p. 50.
[4] René Ristelhueber, *Au Secours des Réfugiés* (Paris: Plon, 1951), p. 151.
[5] *Ibid.*, p. 152.
[6] *Ibid.*, p. 154.
[7] Hacking, *op. cit.*, Chapter X, p. 20.
[8] *Ibid.*, p. 24.
[9] PCIRO Doc. Leg. 12, 15 August 1947.
[10] The El Shatt Camp, housing 3000 refugees, which was taken over by IRO from UNRRA.
[11] Hacking, *op. cit.*, Chapter X, p. 9.
[12] *Ibid.*, p. 10.
[13] A more detailed discussion of the activities of UNRWA will be found in Chapter 10.
[14] PCIRO Doc. Leg. 30, 30 March 1948.
[15] Annual Report of the Executive Committee to the General Council, 30 June 1949.
[16] Hacking, *op. cit.*, Chapter XI, p. 9.
[17] General Council Doc. GC/230, 3 August 1951.
[18] IRO Constitution, Article 2.
[19] Hacking, *op. cit.*, Chapter XI, p. 14.
[20] Ristelhueber, *op. cit.*, p. 274.
[21] Hacking, *op. cit.*, Chapter XI, p. 16.
[22] *Ibid.*, Chapter VII, p. 13.
[23] *Ibid.*, p. 15.
[24] Ristelhueber, *op. cit.*, p. 179.
[25] The *Wiedergutmachungsgesetz*, passed in the U.S. zone of Germany in October 1947.
[26] This sum was also sent to those eligible refugees who had already been either repatriated or resettled by the Organization.
[27] Most of these funds were earmarked for the Jewish refugees under IRO jurisdiction.
[28] *New York Times*, 1 August 1947.
[29] A more detailed discussion of this phenomenon will be found in Chapter 11.
[30] Mostly patterned after the American "strong mayor" type of city government.
[31] General Council Doc. GC/152, 3 September 1943.
[32] Ristelhueber, *op. cit.*, p. 168.
[33] Except in case of extra rations issued to repatriants under the IRO constitution.
[34] General Council Doc. GC/304, 21 March 1950.
[35] Hacking, *op. cit.*, Chapter XIV, p. 24.
[36] IRO Constitution, Article 2.
[37] PCIRO Doc. No. 174, 3 December 1947.

[38] For a more detailed discussion of the work of voluntary agencies with refugees, see Chapter 9.

[39] Report by the Executive Committee to the General Council, Fiscal Year 1947/48.

[40] First Annual Report by IRO to the United Nations, 1949.

[41] Ristelhueber, *op. cit.*, p. 176.

[42] The constitutional provision defining the absolute primacy of repatriation to the contrary notwithstanding.

[43] Ristelhueber, *op. cit.*, p. 176.

[44] General Council Doc. GC/92, 10 November 1943.

[45] The valuable activity of the "Organization for Rehabilitation and Training" (ORT) is deserving of particular emphasis in this regard.

[46] For a further discussion, see Chapter 8.

[47] General Council Doc. GC/96, 12 November 1948.

[48] For a discussion of the work of the voluntary agencies, see Chapter 9.

[49] IRO Constitution, Article 2.

[50] Hacking, *op. cit.*, Chapter XV, p. 11.

[51] IRO Provisional Order 80, 8 July 1948.

[52] PCIRO Statistical Report, Geneva, July 1947.

[53] IRO Statistical Report, Geneva, December 1951.

[54] *Ibid.*, December 1948.

[55] IRO Doc. PREP/93, 11 July 1947, Report of the Executive Secretary on the Status of the Organization.

[56] Hacking, *op. cit.*, Chapter XV, p. 14.

[57] Cf. Section C, Annex I, IRO Constitution.

[58] Hacking, *op. cit.*, Chapter XV, p. 16.

[59] *Ibid.*, p. 17.

[60] *Ibid.*, p. 18.

[61] *Ibid.*, p. 23.

[62] General Council Doc. GC/317, 16 December 1949.

[63] Ristelhueber, *op. cit.*, p. 209.

[64] Monograph, Chief of Mission, IRO Warsaw, 1950, IRO Archives, United Nations, N.Y.

[65] Letter, Yugoslav Ministry of Foreign Affairs to IRO Chief of Mission, Belgrade, 8 July 1948. Quoted by Hacking, *op. cit.*, Chapter XV, p. 29.

[66] Hacking, *op. cit.*, Chapter XV, p. 34.

[67] After the closing of the IRO missions, Poland, Yugoslavia, and Czechoslovakia no longer pressed for repatriation. Particularly in the case of approximately 12,000 "Overseas Chinese" IRO received very little if any encouragement.

[68] Arendt, *op. cit.*, p. 417.

Chapter 8

[1] Ristelhueber, *op. cit.*, p. 217.

[2] The IGCR had sent "exploratory missions" to Great Britain, Belgium, and the Netherlands in 1946.

[3] Ristelhueber, *op. cit.*, p. 230.

[4] Hacking, *op. cit.*, Chapter XVI, p. 85.

[5] PCIRO Doc. PREP/22, 19 July 1947.

[6] PCIRO Dec. Leg. 8, 17 January 1948.

[7] PCIRO Doc. PREP/131, 1 February 1948.

[8] PCIRO Doc. Leg. 9, 8 February 1948.

[9] IRO Statistical Report, Geneva, 31 December 1948.

[10] PCIRO Doc. Leg. 9, 8 February 1948.

[11] General Council Doc. GC/17, 1 August 1948.

[12] *Ibid.*

[13] Statement of Minister of Labour in House of Commons; Hansard No. 105, week ending 11 November 1948, p. 1724.

[14] IRO Doc. HCM/W/18, 7 November 1948.

[15] General Council Doc. GC/SR/130, 20 December 1948.

[16] *Ibid.*, Doc. GS/270, 15 December 1948.

[17] Agreement between the government of Belgium, the occupation authorities of the U.S. zone of Germany, and the IGCR, as quoted by Hacking, *op. cit.*, Chapter XVI, p. 19.

[18] PCIRO Doc. Leg. W.2, 11 June 1948.

[19] *Ibid.*

[20] *Ibid.*

[21] Hacking, *op. cit.*, Chapter XVI, p. 56.

[22] *Ibid.*, p. 58.

[23] General Council Doc. GC/180, 2 November 1948.

[24] For a description of the functions of the Eligibility Review Board, see Chapter 6.

[25] General Council Doc. GC/188, 21 November 1948.

[26] *Ibid.*

[27] *Ibid.*

[28] PCIRO Doc. Leg. 32, 5 August 1948.

[29] IRO Monograph: Paris Office, B/1, *Re-établissement dans les territoires appartenant à la France ou Places sous son Protectorat* (IRO Archives, United Nations, N.Y.).

[30] IRO Statistical Report, Geneva, 31 December 1951.

[31] Agreement between the government of the Turkish Republic and PCIRO relative to the immigration of DP's into Turkey, concluded on 24 June 1948, PCIRO Doc. Leg. 28.

[32] *Ibid.*, p. 7.

[33] IRO Statistical Report, Geneva, 31 December 1951.

[34] IRO Doc. Leg. 28, 24 March 1950.

[35] *New York Times*, 25 February 1948.

[36] PCIRO Doc. PREP/340, 12 March 1948.

[37] PCIRO Doc. Leg. 14, 16 March 1948.

[38] IRO Archives, Letter of 15 September 1948, 42/2 Australia, United Nations, N.Y.

[39] *Ibid.*, Letter of 30 October 1948.

[40] *Ibid.*, Letter of 3 December 1948.

[41] Letter by White Russian refugee to author for forwarding to IRO headquarters, Geneva. Dated 7 May 1950.

[42] IRO Statistical Report, Geneva, 31 December 1951.

[43] Hacking, *op. cit.*, Chapter XVI, p. 61.

[44] IRO Statistical Report, Geneva, 31 December 1951.

[45] IRO Archives, 42/2 New Zealand, Document No. 53, United Nations, N.Y.

[46] General Council Doc. GC/SR/130, 4 March 1949.

[47] PCIRO Doc. PREP/SR/45, 15 July 1948, p. 3.

[48] *Ibid.*, p. 7.

[49] IRO Canada, Monthly Narrative Report, Montreal, December 1949.

[50] Hacking, *op. cit.*, Chapter XV, p. 65.

[51] General Council Doc. GC/SR/13, 25 September 1948.

[52] The Latin American governments who signed the IRO Constitution were Argentina, Bolivia, Brazil, Dominican Republic, Guatemala, Honduras, Panama, Peru, and Venezuela.

[53] The booklet was revised and made more comprehensive by the IRO Resettlement Placement Service in July 1949.

[54] PCIRO Doc. PREP/279, 29 April 1949.

[55] Report from IRO Office, Caracas, 1 December 1948, IRO Archives, 29/2, Venezuela, United Nations, N.Y.

[56] Hacking, *op. cit.*, Chapter XV, p. 92.

[57] *Ibid.*, p. 94.

[58] *Ibid.*

[59] *Ibid.*, p. 95.

[60] IRO Statistical Report, Geneva, 31 December 1951.

[61] IRO Archives, 31/2, Chile, Doc. 17, 17 September 1949, United Nations, N.Y.

[62] IGCR Memorandum to British Foreign Office Refugee Department, London, 14 March 1947.

[63] The IGCR had commissioned a group of experts appointed by the Brookings Institute to report upon possibilities for refugee integration in the Republic. The survey recommended negatively because of the "unsympathetic character of the region and the poor prospects open to most of the refugees."

[64] General Council Doc. GC/318, 4 February 1950.

[65] *New York Times*, 14 July 1953.

[66] IRO Archives, 30/2, Argentina, Doc. 36, 2 October 1948, United Nations, N.Y.

[67] IRO Statistical Report, Geneva, 31 December 1951.

[68] Historical Report on the activities of the IRO Individual Migration Section, Geneva, 25 February 1950, p. 26.

[69] *Ibid.*, p. 32. This agreement included neither religious nor ethnic restrictions.

[70] IRO Statistical Report, Geneva, 31 December 1951.

[71] Hacking, *op. cit.*, Chapter XV, p. 70.

[72] *Ibid.*, p. 71.

[73] Statement by Prime Minister Ben-Gurion to the Israeli Knesseth, 5 June 1948.

[74] Press Release No. 89 of 18 May 1948, IRO Archives, United Nations, N.Y.

[75] *Ibid.*

[76] Press Release No. 177, PCIRO Doc., No. 134, 13 August 1948.

[77] Letter from the chairman of the commission to the IRO director-general. Quoted by Hacking, *op. cit.*, Chapter XV, p. 118.

[78] General Council Doc. GC/SR/247, 26 April 1949.

[79] Annual Report of Director-General to the General Council, Geneva, July 1949.

[80] Exchange of letters, 6 November 1950 and 10 November 1950 between directors of IRO and AJDC. IRO Archives, 42/2 Palestine, United Nations, N.Y.

[81] Ristelhueber, *op. cit.*, p. 251.

[82] IRO Statistical Report, Geneva, 31 December 1951.

[83] Hacking, *op. cit.*, Chapter XV, p. 110.

[84] *New York Times*, 15 December 1945.

[85] Hacking, *op. cit.*, Chapter XV, p. 111.

[86] PCIRO Doc. PREP/SR/19, 2 August 1947.

[87] *Ibid.*

[88] *New York Times*, 1 October 1947.

[89] *New York Herald Tribune*, 27 March 1948.

[90] *Washington Post*, 9 September 1947.

[91] *Christian Science Monitor*, 29 March 1948.

[92] Senator Pat McCarran, as quoted by Senator Lehman in "Towards a New Immigration Policy," *Journal of International Affairs*, May 1953, p. 91.

[93] *Chicago Tribune*, 30 March 1948.

[94] Congressman Wood of Idaho, as quoted by Senator Lehman, *ibid.*, p. 90.

[95] *Ibid.*, p. 91.

[96] Hacking, *op. cit.*, Chapter XV, p. 120.

[97] Quoted in "The DP Story," *Final Report of the United States Displaced Persons Commission* (Washington, D.C., 1952), p. 11.

[98] *New York Times*, 26 June 1948.

[99] *Ibid.*
[100] For example, the Latvian quota, with 236 numbers allowed each year, was mortgaged until the year 2255.
[101] *New York Times*, 26 June 1948.
[102] "The DP Story," *op. cit.*, p. 26.
[103] *Ibid.*, p. 32.
[104] *New York Times*, 3 September 1949.
[105] "The DP Story," *op. cit.*, p. 33.
[106] *New York Times*, 1 July 1950.
[107] *Ibid.*
[108] *Ibid.*
[109] IRO Statistical Report, Geneva, 31 December 1951.
[110] "The DP Story," *op. cit.*, p. 39.
[111] *Ibid.*
[112] *Ibid.*, p. 40.
[113] IRO Statistical Report, Geneva, 31 December 1951.
[114] IRO Department of Public Information, *The Forgotten Elite* (Geneva, July 1949), p. 1.
[115] Final Report of the Resettlement Placement Service to the General Council, Geneva, December 1951.
[116] General Council Doc. GC/SR/507, 15 August 1951.
[117] Ristelhueber, *op. cit.*, p. 266.
[118] *Ibid.*, p. 267.

Chapter 9

[1] Statement by Father Killion, observer to IRO from the Holy See; General Council Doc. GC/SR/25, 21 August 1949.
[2] The title of this chapter is borrowed from Crane Brinton, *From Many One* (Cambridge, Mass.: Harvard University Press, 1948).
[3] Ristelhueber, *op. cit.*, p. 54.
[4] IRO Constitution, Article 6.
[5] Hacking, *op. cit.*, Chapter XIX, p. 4.
[6] Agreement between the United Nations and the International Refugee Organization, United Nations, Lake Success, 1949, Articles 3, 5, 8, 15.
[7] Hacking, *op. cit.*, Chapter XIII, p. 21.
[8] *La Suisse*, Geneva, 8 January 1950.
[9] *Ibid.*
[10] Hacking, *op. cit.*, Chapter XIII, p. 16. The remaining three ships were purchased by IRO from the IGCR.
[11] *Ibid.*, Chapter XII, p. 3.
[12] IRO Doc. GC/72/Leg. 13.
[13] 80th Congress; Hearings before a Special Subcommittee of the Committee of Foreign Affairs on H.J. 207, 15 May 1947, p. 34.
[14] Hacking, *op. cit.*, Chapter XIX, p. 38.
[15] IRO Constitution, Article 7.
[16] IRO Doc. GC/SR/307, 3 September 1950 and IRO Doc. GC/SR/389, 28 December 1950.
[17] Interview with Mr. L. Dawson, adviser on refugees and displaced persons, Department of State.
[18] IRO Constitution, Article 9.
[19] Hacking, *op. cit.*, Chapter XII, p. 4.
[20] Interview with Miss Helen Wilson, former officer of public information, IRO, 7 August 1953, United Nations, N.Y.
[21] *Ibid.*

[22] Ristelhueber, *op. cit.*, p. 6.
[23] *Ibid.*
[24] *Ibid.*, p. 65.
[25] Hacking, *op. cit.*, Chapter XII, p. 11.
[26] Interview with Miss Helen Wilson, former officer of public information, IRO, 7 August 1953, United Nations, N.Y.
[27] United Nations Charter, Article 100.
[28] The fact that not a single IRO refugee was deported from the United States for security reasons is a case in point. See "The DP Story," *op. cit.*, p. 40.
[29] Official United Nations terminology.
[30] Hacking, *op. cit.*, Chapter XVIII, p. 12.
[31] Julius A. Elias, "Relation between Voluntary Agencies and International Organizations," *Journal of International Affairs*, May 1953, p. 30.
[32] Hacking, *op. cit.*, Chapter XVIII, p. 50.
[33] Monograph on the Jewish DP and refugee activities of the AJDC and the JAFP in the framework of agreements with the IRO; quoted by Hacking, *op. cit.*, Chapter XVIII, p. 37.
[34] "The DP Story," *op. cit.*, p. 268.
[35] Elfan Rees, "The Refugee and the United Nations," *International Conciliation*, June 1953, p. 306.
[36] IRO Doc. GC/257/ Rev. 1, 8 November 1951.
[37] *Ibid.*
[38] UN Doc. A/1948, 10 November 1951.
[39] For an analysis of the United States policy to stay aloof of the United Nations in refugee matters, see Chapter 10.

Chapter 10

[1] G. J. Van Heuven Goedhart, "People Adrift," *Journal of International Affairs*, May 1953, p. 10.
[2] William Henderson, "Refugees in India-Pakistan," *Journal of International Affairs*, May 1953, p. 60.
[3] *Ibid.*, p. 64.
[4] Annual Report of Director of UNRWAPRNE, UN Doc. Seventh Session of General Assembly, No. 13 (A/2127), 1952.
[5] For the activities of UNRWAPRNE, see pp. 301–308.
[6] *New York Times*, 13 May 1951.
[7] L. Allen, "History of Supply and Transport," IRO Geneva HQ, p. 47, IRO Archives, United Nations, N.Y.
[8] IRO Statistical Report, Geneva, December 1951.
[9] *Ibid.*
[10] IRO Doc. GC/Leg. 102, 4 November 1951.
[11] *New York Times*, 4 January 1952.
[12] In one single instance were *Volksdeutsche* eligible for IRO assistance: they were able to borrow small amounts of Deutsche Marks from the Expellee Bank, an institution established jointly by the German government and IRO for the benefit of the refugee population.
[13] Charles Sternberg, "The German Refugees and Expellees," *Journal of International Affairs*, May 1953, p. 39.
[14] *New York Times*, 4 March 1952.
[15] George L. Warren, "The Escapee Program," *Journal of International Affairs*, May 1953, p. 83.
[16] *New York Times*, 2 July 1952.
[17] Warren, *op. cit.*, p. 84.

[18] This definition would coincide with the classic one of Sir John Hope Simpson; see *The Refugee Problem*, p. 1.
[19] Elfan Rees in "The Refugee and the United Nations," *International Conciliation*, June 1953, p. 276, places his estimate at 30,000,000. However, the factors of assimilation and local settlement must be taken into account. Thus, my estimate is broken down into 7,500,000 Indian, 6,000,000 Korean, 800,000 Arab refugees and 700,000 IRO residual and new escapees from behind the Iron Curtain.
[20] Rees, *op. cit.*, p. 278.
[21] *United Nations Bulletin*, Vol. XII, No. 3 (1 February 1952), p. 133.
[22] *Ibid.*
[23] The vote was almost identical with that which had established IRO. Again, only the Soviet bloc voted against the High Commissioner's Office.
[24] Statute of the Office of the United Nations High Commissioner for Refugees, Chapter II, Article 6, para. B.
[25] Ristelhueber, *op. cit.*, p. 271.
[26] Vernant, *op. cit.*, p. 39.
[27] *Ibid.*
[28] The High Commissioner had managed to negotiate an agreement to that effect with the Chinese Communist government, cf. Hacking, *op. cit.*, Chapter XIX, p. 30.
[29] Rees, *op. cit.*, p. 281.
[30] Statute of the High Commissioner, Chapter II, Art. 10.
[31] *United Nations Bulletin*, Vol. XII, No. 3 (1 February 1952), p. 139.
[32] *United Nations Bulletin*, Vol. XIII, No. 3 (1 February 1953), p. 135.
[33] *Ibid.*
[34] *Ibid.*, p. 139.
[35] The following countries have contributed to the fund: Australia, Austria, Denmark, Germany, Greece, Luxembourg, the Netherlands, New Zealand, Norway, Sweden, Switzerland, and the United Kingdom.
[36] *New York Times*, 26 October 1952.
[37] UN Doc. FF/14, 15 April 1953, "The Uprooted Strike Root," p. 1.
[38] *New York Times*, 15 April 1954.
[39] *Ibid.*, 24 October 1953.
[40] *Ibid.*, 4 November 1955.
[41] *Ibid.*, 8 September 1949.
[42] The distribution was as follows: Lebanon, 104,000; Syria, 84,000; Jordan, 470,000; Gaza, 204,000; and Iraq, 19,000 refugees. *New York Times*, 8 September 1949.
[43] UN Doc. A/1237, 9 December 1949; UNRWA is identical with UNRWAPRNE.
[44] Annual Report of Director of UNRWAPRNE, UN Doc. Seventh Session of General Assembly, No. 13 (A/2171) 1952, p. 13.
[45] *Ibid.*
[46] Lucille W. Pevsner, "The Arab Refugees," *Journal of International Affairs*, May 1953, p. 46.
[47] UN Doc. A/38/152, 22 December 1950.
[48] The Jewish Agency's Digest of Press and Events, New York, 28 July 1950.
[49] Al-Sayyad, 17 February 1949. Quoted by Schechtman, *The Arab Refugee Problem*, p. 24.
[50] UN Doc. A/A38/152, 22 December 1950.
[51] Annual Report of Director of UNRWAPRNE, *op. cit.*, p. 13.
[52] *Ibid.*, p. 8.
[53] *Ibid.*, pp. 8–9.
[54] *Ibid.*, p. 8.
[55] *Ibid.*

[56] *New York Times*, 16 January 1953.

[57] *Ibid.*

[58] *Ibid.*, 16 January 1955. This is almost the exact number of refugees registered as destitute at the inception of UNRWA in 1950. New refugees and normal population growth have prevented a reduction of the total figure, resettlement in Jordan notwithstanding.

[59] Schechtman, *op. cit.*, p. 122.

[60] Report of the Agent General of UNKRA, UN Doc. General Assembly, Seventh Session, Supplement No. 19 (A/2222), 21 October 1952, p. 1.

[61] *Ibid.*, pp. 38, 39.

[62] *Ibid.*

[63] *New York Times*, 11 May 1953.

[64] *Ibid.*, 14 May 1953.

[65] *Ibid.*, 29 July 1953.

[66] The member nations are Argentina, Australia, Austria, Belgium, Brazil, Canada, Chile, Costa Rica, Denmark, France, Germany, Greece, Israel, Italy, the Netherlands, Norway, Paraguay, Sweden, Switzerland, the United States, and Venezuela.

[67] *United States Department of State Bulletin*, Vol. XXVI, No. 658 (4 February 1952), p. 171.

[68] *Ibid.*

[69] Interview with George Warren, U.S. Department of State adviser on refugees and displaced persons, Washington, 19 June 1953.

[70] Since the United States contributed by far the largest portion (almost 30 per cent), it enjoyed what amounted to a veto power at the conference. The remaining $24 million was borne on an almost equal basis by the other twenty governments.

[71] IRO Doc. GC/SR/530, 28 December 1951.

[72] *New York Times*, 3 May 1955.

[73] *United States Department of State Bulletin*, Vol. XXVIII, No. 723 (4 May 1953), pp. 640, 641.

[74] *New York Times*, 4 June 1953.

[75] Warren, *op. cit.*, p. 84.

[76] *Ibid.*

[77] *New York Times*, 23 July 1955.

[78] Of these 200,000 are escapees from Eastern Germany while the remainder have fled from the other satellites.

[79] Warren, *op. cit.*, p. 85.

[80] Rees, *op. cit.*, p. 295.

[81] The highly restrictive McCarran-Walter Immigration Law passed by the United States Congress in June 1952 was followed by similarly rigid provisions by the Canadian, Australian, and South African governments.

[82] Rees, *op. cit.*, p. 296.

[83] Report No. 12, IRO Liquidation Office, 6 March 1952, IRO Archives 62/2, United Nations, N.Y.

[84] *United States Department of State Bulletin*, Vol. XXVI, No. 658 (4 February 1952), p. 171.

[85] Interview with T. P. Cope, director, Unitarian Service Committee, Boston, 19 September 1953.

[86] Interview with Helen Wilson, UNKRA, United Nations, N.Y., 4 August 1953.

[87] UN Doc. General Assembly, Official Records, Seventh Session, 1952, Supplement No. 16, p. 13.

[88] Oppenheim-Lauterpacht, *International Law* (New York: Longmans Green, 1947), I, 583.

[89] Josef L. Kunz, "The United Nations Declaration of Human Rights," *American Journal of International Law*, April 1949, p. 320.

[90] Inis L. Claude, *National Minorities, An International Problem* (Cambridge, Mass.: Harvard University Press, 1955), pp. 154, 155.
[91] G. A. Res. 96 (I).
[92] Philip E. Jacob, "The United Nations and the Struggle for Human Rights," *Pennsylvania School Journal*, January 1951, p. 200.
[93] A/C3/SR 121, p. 16.
[94] H. Lauterpacht, *International Law and Human Rights* (New York: Praeger, 1950), p. 422.
[95] *Ibid.*, p. 423.
[96] "Magna Carta for Refugees," *United Nations Department of Public Information*, New York, August 1951, p. 6.
[97] "Progress in Achievement of Human Rights," *United Nations Review*, July 1956, p. 7.
[98] Oscar Svarlien, *An Introduction to the Law of Nations* (New York: McGraw-Hill, 1955), p. 429, 430.
[99] G. A. Res. 543 (VI), 5 February 1952.
[100] Svarlien, *op. cit.*, p. 442.
[101] This convention was signed by the governments of Belgium, Denmark, France, the German Federal Republic, Greece, Iceland, Ireland, Italy, Luxembourg, the Netherlands, Norway, the Saar, Sweden, Turkey, and the United Kingdom.
[102] The accession of Austria to the Council of Europe on 20 February 1956 implied ratification of the convention.
[103] Svarlien, *op. cit.*, p. 443.
[104] Lauterpacht, *op. cit.*, p. 438.
[105] *New York Times*, 19 July 1953.
[106] Louise Holborn, *The International Refugee Organization* (Oxford: Oxford University Press, 1956).
[107] *New York Times*, 30 July 1953.
[108] 60,000 *Volksdeutsche*, 25,000 escapees from Iron Curtain countries, 2000 refugees from Shanghai presently in Hong Kong, 2000 Chinese refugees, 15,000 refugees in Europe, and 2000 Arab refugees.
[109] *New York Times*, 29 July 1953.
[110] *Ibid.*, 28 April 1955.
[111] See Maurice R. Davie, *Refugees in America* (New York: Harper, 1947); Donald P. Kent, *The Refugee Intellectual* (New York: Columbia University Press, 1953); Leo W. Schwarz, *The Redeemers* (New York: Farrar, Straus, and Young, 1953).

Chapter 11

[1] David Rousset, *Les Jours de notre Mort*, as quoted by Arendt, *op. cit.*, p. 299.
[2] Sigmund Freud, *Civilization and its Discontents* (London: The International Psycho-Analytical Library, Hogarth Press, 1953).
[3] See H. Fensterheim, "A Case Study of Group Ideology and Individual Adjustment," *Journal of Abnormal and Social Psychology*, October 1950.
[4] Libuse Tyhurst, "Displacement and Migration," *American Journal of Psychiatry*, March 1951.
[5] Emile Durkheim, *Suicide*, American edition (Glencoe, Ill.: The Free Press, 1951), pp. 241ff.
[6] Stefi Pederson, "Psychopathological Reactions to Extreme Social Displacements," *Psychoanalytic Review*, October 1949.
[7] Interview with Professor Sigmund Neumann, 1 August 1953, Harvard University.
[8] *New York Times*, 23 June 1953.
[9] A. Segalman, "The Psychology of the Jewish Displaced Person," *Jewish Sociological Quarterly*, September 1947.

[10] Tyhurst, *op. cit.*, p. 508.

[11] See Vladimir Jabotinsky, *The War and the Jew* (New York: Dial Press, 1942); Max Nordau, *Nordau to His People* (New York: Scopus, 1941); Chaim Weizmann, *Trial and Error* (New York: Harper, 1949).

[12] Paul Frings, *Das Internationale Flüchtlingsproblem* (Frankfurt am Main: Frankfurter Hefte, 1951), p. 177.

[13] *New York Times*, 27 May 1956.

[14] *Ibid.*, 9 May 1956.

[15] *Ibid.*, 10 May 1956.

[16] B. Althoff, "The Psychology of Children in a DP Camp," *Social Casework*, May 1948.

[17] Arendt, *op. cit.*, p. 298.

Chapter 12

[1] Arthur Schopenhauer, *Gesammelte Werke* (Leipzig, 1929), V, 28.

[2] Report of the United Nations High Commissioner for Refugees, General Assembly, Eighth Session, Supplement No. 11 (A/2394), New York, 1953, p. 25.

[3] For a discussion of this, see Chapter 10.

[4] Although these have presumably reached their final destination, about 7.5 million remain unassimilable.

Bibliography

Primary Sources

LEAGUE OF NATIONS DOCUMENTS

Agreement with Regard to the Issue of Certificates of Identity to Russian Refugees, Signed at Geneva, 5 July 1922. (Treaty Series V. 13.)

Agreements Relating to the Issue of Identity Certificates to Russian and Armenian Refugees, Supplementing and Amending the Previous Arrangements. Dated 5 July 1922, and 31 May 1924; Signed at Geneva, 12 May 1926. (Treaty Series V. 89.)

Committee on International Assistance to Refugees. Report Submitted to the Council. (C.2.M.2. 1936–XII.)

Conference Intergouvernmentale Pour le Statut Juridique des Réfugiés, Geneva, 1928, Documents Préparatoires et Procès Verbaux, 28–30 Juin 1928.

Convention Relating to the Status of Refugees, Nansen Office for Refugees, Paris, 1938.

Covenant of the League of Nations.

High Commissioner for Refugees (Jewish and Other) Coming from Germany, Letter of Resignation of J. G. McDonald, London, 1936. (Doc. C.13.M.12. 1936.)

International Conference for the Adoption of a Convention Concerning the Status of Refugees Coming from Germany. Final Act. (C.75 (a). M.30 (a), 1938, XII.)

Nansen, Fridtjof. Russian Refugees, General Report on the Work Accomplished up to 15 March 1922. (C.124.M.74. 1922.)

Nansen International Office for Refugees. Report of the Governing Body. (C.29. 1931, XIII.)

Official Journal, Council of the League of Nations.

Report on the Work of the High Commission for Refugees. (A.30.1923, XIII, i.e. IV.)

Verbatim Records of the Inter-Governmental Conference for Refugees, Geneva, 26 to 28 October 1933. (C.113.M.41.1934.)

UNITED NATIONS DOCUMENTS

Annual Reports of the Director of the United Nations Relief and Works Agency for Palestine Refugees in the Near East to the General Assembly of the United Nations, New York, 1950 to 1952.

Charter of the United Nations Organization.

Documents of the Special Committee for Refugees and Displaced Persons, Economic and Social Council, United Nations, London, 8 April to 1 June 1946. Particularly Documents E/Ref. 1. and E/Ref. 75.

Journal of the Social, Cultural, and Humanitarian Committee (Third Committee) of the General Assembly, United Nations, London, January, 1946.

Office of the United Nations High Commissioner for Refugees, "The Uprooted Strike Root," Geneva, 15 April 1953. (FF/14.)

Official Documents of the Economic and Social Council, United Nations. First, Second, and Third Sessions, and Supplements.

Official Documents of the Second Part of the First Session of the General Assembly of the United Nations (Plenary Session), New York, 1946. Also Journal and Supplements.

United Nations Document A/1948, 10 November 1951; Problems of Assistance to Refugees; Communication from the General Council of the International Refugee Organization.

United Nations Document A/Conf.2/108, August 1951: Convention relating to the Status of Refugees.

United Nations Document ST/SOA/15, 15 January 1953: Handbook of International Measures for Protection of Migrants.

United Nations General Assembly. Official Records, Sixth Session, Supplement No. 19 (A/2011), United Nations High Commissioner for Refugees, First Annual Report, 1951.

United Nations General Assembly. Official Records, Seventh Session, Supplement No. 16 (A/2126 and Addendum), 1952, United Nations High Commissioner for Refugees, Second Annual Report.

United Nations General Assembly. Official Records, Eighth Session, Supplement No. 11 (A/2394), 1953, United Nations High Commissioner for Refugees, Third Annual Report.

United Nations General Assembly Resolution 428 (V) and Annex; 14 December 1950; Statute of the Office of the United Nations High Commissioner for Refugees.

United Nations General Assembly Resolution 538 B (VI); 2 February 1952.

Verbatim Records of the Social, Cultural, and Humanitarian Committee (Third Committee) of the General Assembly, United Nations, London, January 1946.

IRO DOCUMENTS

Agreement between the United Nations and the International Refugee Organization, Lake Success, 1949.

Annual Reports of the General Council of the International Refugee Organization to the United Nations, Geneva, 1947 to 1952.

Constitution of the International Refugee Organization.

Minutes of the Executive Committee of the International Refugee Organization, First through Eighth Sessions, Geneva, August 1948 to February 1952.

Monthly Narrative Reports of the International Refugee Organization, Geneva, 1947 to 1952.

Preparatory Commission of the International Refugee Organization. Official Records, Geneva, June 1947 to July 1948, Documents PCIRO 1 to 232.

Statistical Reports of the International Refugee Organization, Geneva, 1947 to 1952.

Summary Records of the Executive Committee of the International Refugee Organization, First through Eighth Sessions, August 1948 to February 1952, IRO Documents EXEC/SR 1 to 202.

Summary Records of the General Council of the International Refugee Organization, First through Ninth Sessions, Geneva, August 1948 to February 1952, IRO Documents SR1 to 189.

Verbatim Records of the General Council of the International Refugee Organization, First through Ninth Sessions, Geneva, August 1948 to February 1952.

OTHER DOCUMENTS

British Foreign Office Report, "Inter-Governmental Committee to Continue and Develop the Work of the Evian Meeting," London, August 1938.

Council of Europe, Committee of Experts. Final Report on the Problem of Refugees and Surplus Population, Strasbourg, 8 October 1951, CM (51) 69.
Council of Europe, Consultative Assembly. Fifth Ordinary Session, First Part, AS (5) 126, Resolution (53) 23, Appended to the Message addressed by the Committee of Ministers to the Consultative Assembly on the Occasion of the Fifth Ordinary Session, Strasbourg, 7 May 1953.
Final Report of the United States Displaced Persons Commission, *The DP Story.* Washington, D.C.: Government Printing Office, 1952.
Hearings before a Special Subcommittee of the Committee on Foreign Affairs, United States House of Representatives, H.J. No. 207, 15 May 1947, 80th Congress.
Hearings before the Committee on Foreign Relations, United States Senate, S.J. Resolution No. 77, 1 March 1947, 80th Congress.
Minutes of the Fifth Plenary Session of the Inter-Governmental Committee for Refugees, Paris, November 1945.
Proceedings of the Inter-Governmental Committee for Refugees (IGCR), Evian, 5 to 16 July 1938.
Report of a Special Subcommittee of the Committee of Foreign Affairs, United States House of Representatives, "Displaced Persons and the International Refugee Organization," 80th Congress, Washington, D.C., 1947.
Report of the Committee on Expenditures in the Executive Branch, "United States Relations with International Organizations," United States Congress, 8 June 1949.
United States Department of State. Publication No. 2783, "Occupation of Germany," Washington, D.C., May 1946.
United States War Refugee Board. Final Report, Washington, D.C., August 1945.

Secondary Sources

BOOKS

Adamic, Louis. *America and the Refugees.* Public Affairs Pamphlet No. 29. New York: Public Affairs Committee, 1939.
Arendt, Hannah. *The Origins of Totalitarianism.* New York: Harcourt, Brace and Company, 1951.
Bentwich, N. *The International Problem of Refugees.* New York: Foreign Policy Association, 1936.
Burke, Edmund. *Reflections on the Revolution in France,* edited by E. J. Payne. Everyman's Library.
Cicero. *Republic,* translated by Sabine and Smith. Columbus, Ohio: Ohio State University Press, 1929.
———. *Laws,* translated by C. W. Keyes. Cambridge, Mass.: Harvard University Press, 1948.
Claude, Inis L. *National Minorities, An International Problem.* Cambridge, Mass.: Harvard University Press, 1955.
Clausen, Clarence A. "Dr. Fridtjof Nansen's Work as High Commissioner of the League of Nations." Abstract of thesis, University of Illinois, 1932.
Davie, Maurice R. *Refugees in America.* New York: Harper and Brothers, 1947.
———, and S. Koenig. *The Refugees Are Now Americans.* Public Affairs Pamphlet No. 111. New York: Public Affairs Committee, 1945.
———. *World Immigration.* New York: Macmillan, 1949.
Duggan, Stephen, and Betty Drury. *The Rescue of Science and Learning.* New York: Macmillan, 1948.
Durkheim, Emile. *Suicide.* Glencoe, Ill. The Free Press, 1951.
Freud, Sigmund. *Civilization and Its Discontents,* edited by Ernest Jones, M.D. London: International Psychoanalytical Library, Hogarth Press, 1953.

Frings, Paul. *Das Internationale Flüchtlingsproblem.* Frankfurt am Main: Verlag der Frankfurter Hefte, 1951.
Gheorghiu, C. U. *La Vingt-Cinquième Heure.* Paris: Plon, 1951.
Guggenheim, Paul. *Vülkerrechtspolitische Bemerkungen zum Flüchtlingsproblem.* Zurich: Verlag für Recht und Gesellschaft, 1945.
Hacking, L. Michael. "History of the International Refugee Organization." Unpublished document in mimeographed form, IRO Archives, United Nations, New York.
Hansson, Michael. *The Refugee Problem.* London: League of Nations Union, 1936.
Hay, Malcolm. *The Foot of Pride.* Boston: The Beacon Press, 1951.
Heine, Heinrich. *Zur Geschichte der Religion und Philosophie in Deutschland.* Berlin: Aufbau Verlag, 1951.
Holborn, Louise. *The International Refugee Organization.* London: Oxford University Press, 1956.
Jabotinsky, Vladimir. *The War and the Jew.* New York: Dial Press, 1942.
Janowsky, Oscar, and Melvin M. Fagen. *International Aspects of German Racial Policies.* Oxford: Oxford University Press, 1937.
Jessup, Philip C. *A Modern Law of Nations.* New York: Macmillan, 1952.
Johnson, T. F. *International Tramps: From Chaos to Permanent World Peace.* London: Hutchinson, 1938.
Kent, Donald P. *The Refugee Intellectual.* New York: Columbia University Press, 1953.
Koestler, Arthur. *Scum of the Earth.* New York: Macmillan, 1941.
Kogon, Eugen. *Der SS Staat.* Munich: Verlag Karl Alber, 1946.
Kulischer, Eugene. *Europe on the Move.* New York: Columbia University Press, 1948.
———. *The Displacement of Population in Europe.* Montreal: International Labour Office, 1943.
Ladas, Stephen P. *The Exchange of Minorities: Bulgaria, Greece, and Turkey.* New York: Macmillan, 1932.
Lauterpacht, Hersch. *An International Bill of Rights of Man.* New York: Columbia University Press, 1945.
———. *International Law and Human Rights.* New York: Praeger, 1950.
Lessing, Gotthold Ephraim. *Nathan der Weise.* Berlin: Hans Heinrich Tillgner Verlag, 1923.
Macartney, Carlile Aylmer. *Refugees – The Work of the League.* London: League of Nations Union, 1930.
———. *Refugees and the League.* London: League of Nations Union, 1935.
MacDonald, James G. *My Mission in Israel.* New York: Simon and Schuster, 1951.
Mitrany, David. *A Working Peace System.* London: Royal Institute of International Affairs, 1943.
Nansen, Fridtjof. *Armenia and the Near East.* London: G. Allen and Unwin, 1928.
Nathan-Chapotot, Roger. *Les Nations Unies et les Réfugiés.* Paris: A. Pedone, 1949.
Nordau, Max. *Nordau to His People.* New York: Scopus Press, 1941.
Paine, Thomas. *The Rights of Man*, edited by M. D. Conway. New York: Putnam, 1894.
Plato. *The Republic*, translated by B. Jowett. New York: Random House, 1937.
Phelan, E. J. *Yes and Albert Thomas.* New York: Columbia University Press, 1949.
Rappard, William E. *The Quest for Peace since the World War.* Cambridge, Mass.: Harvard University Press, 1940.
Reynolds, E. E. *Nansen.* London: Penguin Books, 1949.
Rickman, J., ed. *Psychological Problems of Displaced Persons.* UNRRA Publication. December 1945.
Ristelhueber, René. *Au Secours des Réfugiés.* Paris: Plon, 1951.
Rousset, David. *Les Jours de Notre Mort.* Paris: Plon, 1946.

Sabine, George H. *A History of Political Theory.* New York: Henry Holt and Company, 1950.
Schechtman, Joseph B. *Population Transfers in Asia.* New York: Hallsby Press, 1949.
———. *European Population Transfers, 1939–1945.* New York: Oxford University Press, 1946.
———. *The Arab Refugee Problem.* New York: Philosophical Library, 1952.
Schwarz, Leo W. *The Redeemers.* New York: Farrar, Straus, and Young, 1953.
Simpson, Sir John Hope. *The Refugee Problem, Report of a Survey.* London: Royal Institute of International Affairs, 1938.
Svarlien, Oscar. *An Introduction to the Law of Nations.* New York: McGraw-Hill, 1955.
Thompson, Dorothy. *Refugees: Anarchy or Organization.* New York: Random House, 1938.
United Nations Department of Social Affairs. *A Study of Statelessness.* Lake Success, August 1949.
Vernant, Jacques. *The Refugee in the Post-War World: Preliminary Report of a Survey.* Geneva, 1951.
Warhaftig, Zorah. *Uprooted Jewish Refugees and Displaced Persons after Liberation.* New York: Institute of Jewish Affairs, 1946.
Weizmann, Chaim. *Trial and Error.* New York: Harper, 1949.
Woodbridge, George. *The History of the United Nations Relief and Rehabilitation Administration.* Vols. I, II, III. New York: Columbia University Press, 1950.
World Jewish Congress. *The Black Book: The Nazi Crime against the Jewish People.* New York: Duell, Sloan, and Pearce, 1946.
Zweig, Stefan. *Die Welt von Gestern.* Stockholm: Bermann-Fischer Verlag, 1946.

NEWSPAPERS AND PERIODICALS

Adams, Walter. "Refugees in Europe," *Annals of the American Academy of Political and Social Science,* May 1939.
———. "The Extent and Nature of the World's Refugee Problem," *Annals of the American Academy of Political and Social Science,* May 1939.
Allport, G. W., J. S. Bruner, and E. M. Jandorf. "Personality under Social Catastrophe," *Character and Personality,* September 1941.
Althoff, B. "The Psychology of Children in a DP Camp," *Social Casework,* January 1948.
Berl, F. "The Adjustment of Displaced Persons," *Jewish Sociological Series,* October 1948.
Bettelheim, Bruno. "Individual and Mass Behavior in Extreme Situations," *Journal of Abnormal and Social Psychology,* October 1943.
Bolles, Blair. "Millions to Rescue," *Survey Graphic,* September 1944.
Brown, F. J., ed. "Refugees," *Annals of the American Academy of Political and Social Science,* May 1939, Special Issue.
Cary, Mary G. "People without a Country," *Survey Graphic,* August 1936.
Christian Science Monitor. Various dates.
Cohen, Morris R. "Minimizing Social Conflicts for Refugees," *Annals of the American Academy of Political and Social Science,* May 1939.
Cohn, Alfred E. "Exiled Physicians in the United States," *American Scholar,* Summer 1943.
Dean, Vera Micheles. "European Power Politics and the Refugee Problem," *Annals of the American Acadamy of Political and Social Science,* May 1939.
Der Bund, Berne, Switzerland. Various dates.
Deutsche Allgemeine Zeitung, Berlin. Various dates.
Elias, Julius A. "Relations between Voluntary Agencies and International Organizations," *Journal of International Affairs,* May 1953.

Estorick, Eric. "The Evian Conference and the Intergovernmental Committee," *Annals of the American Academy of Political and Social Science*, May 1939.
——— and Erika Mann. "Private and Governmental Aid of Refugees," *Annals of the American Academy of Political and Social Science*, May 1939.
Fensterheim, H., and A. G. Birch. "A Case Study of Group Ideology and Individual Adjustment in a Displaced Persons Camp," *Journal of Abnormal and Social Psychology*, October 1950.
Friedman, Paul. "The Road Back for Displaced Persons," *Commentary*, December 1948.
Ginsberg, Marie. "Adjustment of the Professional Refugee," *Annals of the American Academy of Political and Social Science*, May 1939.
Goedhart, G. J. Van Heuven. "People Adrift," *Journal of International Affairs*, May 1953.
Grattan, C. Hartley. "Refugees and an Underdeveloped Economy," *Annals of the American Academy of Political and Social Science*, May 1939.
Henderson, William. "Refugees in India-Pakistan," *Journal of International Affairs*, May 1953.
Holborn, Louise W. "The League of Nations and the Refugee Problem," *Annals of the American Acadamy of Political and Social Science*, May 1939.
Inman, Samuel Guy. "Refugee Settlement in Latin America," *Annals of the American Academy of Political and Social Science*, May 1939.
Jacob, Philip E. "The United Nations and the Struggle for Human Rights," *Pennsylvania School Journal*, January 1951.
Jaszi, Oscar. "Political Refugees," *Annals of the American Academy of Political and Social Science*, May 1939.
Johnson, Robert H. "The Case of UNRRA," *World Politics*, July 1951.
Kage, J. "Ego Supportive Therapy with Displaced Persons," *Social Casework*, February 1950.
Kraus, Hertha. "Starting Life Anew in a Strange Country," *Annals of the American Academy of Political and Social Science*, May 1939.
Kuhn, Ferdinand, Jr. "Refugee Committee Accepts Nazi Emigration Proposal," *Scholastic*, 4 March 1939.
———. "Refugee Settlement," *Commonweal*, 24 February 1939.
Kulischer, Eugene M. "Displaced Persons in the Modern World," *Annals of the American Academy of Political and Social Science*, March 1949.
Kummer, Gertrude. "Is There an Answer?" *Survey Graphic*, August 1944.
Kunz, Josef L. "The United Nations Declaration of Human Rights," *American Journal of International Law*, April 1949.
La Suisse, Geneva, Switzerland. Various dates.
Lasher, L. D. "Test for Civilization," *Survey Graphic*, December 1938.
Lehman, Herbert H. "Towards a New Immigration Policy," *Journal of International Affairs*, May 1953.
London Times. Various dates.
Malin, Patrick M. "The Work of the Intergovernmental Committee on Refugees," *Interpreter Releases*, June 1944.
———. "The Refugee: A Problem for International Organization," *International Organization*, September 1947.
Mann, Thomas. "America and the Refugees," *New Republic*, 8 November 1939.
Meerloo, A. M. "Psychopathic Reactions in Liberated Countries," *Lancet*, April 1945.
New York Herald Tribune. Various dates.
New York Times. Various dates.
Peake, Cyrus H. "Refugees in the Far East," *Annals of the American Academy of Political and Social Science*, May 1939.
Pederson, Stefi. "Psychopathological Reactions to Extreme Social Displacements," *Psychoanalytic Review*, July 1949.

Penrose, E. F. "Refugees and Displaced Persons," *Negotiating with the Russians.* Boston: World Peace Foundation, 1951.
Pevsner, Lucille. "The Arab Refugees," *Journal of International Affairs,* May 1953.
Pfister, M. "Das Problem der Entwurzelung," *Schweizer Medizinische Woche,* October 1950.
Popper, David H. "A Homeland for Refugees," *Annals of the American Academy of Political and Social Science,* May 1939.
Pravda. Various dates.
Rees, Elfan. "The Refugee and the United Nations," *International Conciliation,* June 1953.
Reinhold, Frances L. "Exiles and Refugees in American History," *Annals of the American Academy of Political and Social Science,* May 1939.
Ristelhueber, René. "The International Refugee Organization," *International Conciliation,* April 1951.
Roucek, Joseph S. "Minorities – A Basis of the Refugee Problem," *Annals of the American Academy of Political and Social Science,* May 1939.
Saenger, G. "The Psychology of the Refugee," *Contemporary Jewish Record,* No. 264, 1940.
Schaufuss, Tatiana. "The White Russian Refugees," *Annals of the American Academy of Political and Social Science,* May 1939.
Schisby, Read Lewis and Marian. "Status of the Refugee under American Immigration Laws," *Annals of the American Academy of Political and Social Science,* May 1939.
Schryver, Elliott. "The International Refugee Organization," *American Institute of International Information,* May 1947.
Segelman, A. "The Psychology of the Jewish Displaced Person," *Jewish Sociological Series,* July 1947.
Shapiro, S., and I. Berman. "Psychological Problems Met in Counseling and Placement of Refugees," *Jewish Sociological Series,* January 1949.
Sternberg, Charles. "The German Refugees and the Expellees," *Journal of International Affairs,* May 1953.
Tyhurst, Libuse. "Displacement and Migration," *American Journal of Psychiatry,* July 1951.
United Nations Bulletin. Various dates.
United States Department of State Bulletin. Various dates.
Warren, George L. "The Escapee Program," *Journal of International Affairs,* May 1953.
Washington Post. Various dates.

Index